"In *More with Less,* Jodi shares her philosophy for cooking sim[...] medicine to create recipes full of texture and flavor that we w[...] eyes and our hearty appetites."

—ARAN GOYOAGA, author of *Small Plates & Sweet Treats* and creator of the blog *Cannelle et Vanille*

"*More with Less* is a tour de force in sharing indulgent food that is deliciously healthy. Jodi Moreno is such a clever cook—she has a unique way of turning everyday ingredients into a spectacular, flavor-punching dish. Dishes like Caraway Tomato Baked Eggs, Deviled Brussels Sprout Salad, Piri Piri Broccoli Bites, and Thai Peanut Sweet Potato Skins are stellar examples of how we can all incorporate more smashing vegetables into our busy lives. Jodi is truly the "Condiment Queen"—her comprehensive chapter of homemade sauces, dressings, and condiments is truly exciting and I plan on making all of these soon! *More with Less* is an essential modern guide on how to eat more wholesome food in a tasty way."

—HETTY McKINNON, owner of Arthur Street Kitchen, and author of *Community* and *Neighborhood*

"As Jodi Moreno is a neighbor in Amagansett, I have had the pleasure of cooking with her on many occasions. I can also recall going to her place for the first time—I stood in awe of her beautifully stocked refrigerator, complete with condiments galore. Through these and many other kitchen interactions I have learned a great deal about Jodi's cooking practices and principles and her steadfast belief in simple, quality ingredients and innovative techniques for healthier eating. Now with her beautiful cookbook everyone can gain insight into her kitchen, pantry, and refrigerator. Jodi shares how condiments are the secret weapon for throwing together a delicious meal, and I could not agree more. With *More with Less,* all of our kitchen encounters will be that much more wholesome, natural, and delicious!"

—ATHENA CALDERONE, author of *Cook Beautiful* and creator of the blog *EyeSwoon*

Recipes from the Filipino-American Dream

AMBOY

ALVIN CAILAN

WITH ALEXANDRA CUERDO AND SUSAN CHOUNG

PHOTOGRAPHY BY WYATT CONLON

HOUGHTON MIFFLIN HARCOURT · BOSTON · NEW YORK · 2020

For information about permission to reproduce selections from this book, write to trade.permissions@hmhco.com or to Permissions, Houghton Mifflin Harcourt Publishing Company, 3 Park Avenue, 19th Floor, New York, New York 10016.

hmhbooks.com

Library of Congress Cataloging-in-Publication Data

Names: Cailan, Alvin, author. | Cuerdo, Alexandra, author.

Title: Amboy : recipes from the Filipino-American dream / Alvin Cailan with Alexandra Cuerdo and Susan Choung ; photography by Wyatt Conlon.

Description: Boston : Houghton Mifflin Harcourt, 2020. | Includes index.

Identifiers: LCCN 2019045713 (print) | LCCN 2019045714 (ebook) | ISBN 9781328931733 (hardback) | ISBN 9781328931740 (ebook)

Subjects: LCSH: Cooking, Philippine. | LCGFT: Cookbooks.

Classification: LCC TX724.5.P5 C35 2020 (print) | LCC TX724.5.P5 (ebook) | DDC 641.59599—dc23

LC record available at https://lccn.loc.gov/2019045713

LC ebook record available at https://lccn.loc.gov/2019045714

Book design by Allison Chi

Printed in China

Tatay Peps,

You always knew I was going to do something great, even though everyone else told you I was trouble. You taught me how to love unconditionally and to follow my dreams. You left this world before I could make something of myself, and every time I accomplished something major in my career, I was alone, but I know you were there with me.

Contents

Acknowledgments

More like SHOUT-OUTS. This crazy life, the machine of failures and victories, could not have been bearable without my incredible support system made up of family, friends, and colleagues. You'll learn about most of them in this book. This is really tough for me because I'm a pretty private dude. My social media and my show only display my professional side, so here's my chance to shout out to everyone who helped make this all happen.

First, I'd like to thank Angela. You're my rock, and without you I'd be nothing.

Shout-out to Justin Schwartz, Allie Cuerdo, Susan Choung, Wyatt Conlon, and Danielle Svetcov, the incredible team that put this book together.

Shout-out to my family! Mom, Dad, Brother, Auntie Cita, Nanay Grace, Kuya KC, Ate Nyrie, Ate Careen, Ate Lorie, and JR. Thank you!

Shout-out to my brothers from another mother, Arjun and Nakul Mahendro. I love y'all and thank you for being there for me when no one else was.

Shout-out to Christian Natividad, Dave Kocab, Johanna Merida, Ted Montoya, Lung Ly, Justin Carleton, Bryan Sudjati, Jeremy Mitra, Christian Cruz, Xavier Fermin, and Javier Flores. These are the people I've shared the trenches with, my Band of Brothers and Sisters.

Shout-out to David Shein and Antonio Reyes for helping me build my business and for working with me day in and day out to keep this dream alive.

Shout-out to Mark Tagnipez, Cyrus Mirabueno, Michael Prieto, Gail Vales, Max Nocete, Norman Mirabueno, Vivian Mirabueno, Leo Mirabueno, Andrew Osorio, Hoogie Osorio, and Oliver Osorio, my homies from day one. I grew up with these guys and, ultimately, they're the reason why I've got tough skin. They've seen me at my worst and pushed me to be the best.

Shout-out to Ken Concepcion, Michelle Mungcal, Chad Valencia, Chase Valencia, Nico de Leon, Stephanie Valencia, Charles Olalia, Ria Barbosa, Maynard Llera, Johneric Concordia, Christine Concordia, Andre Guerrero, Amy Besa, Romy Dorotan, and Christian Alquiza, my Pinoy brothers and sisters, the Filipino chefs who shape the Filipino cuisine in America. They all inspire me and through the years have become like family.

Shout-out to George Yu, Michael Sudjati, and Colin Stafford. I consider you gentlemen my mentors. I've learned so much from you, and I thank you for molding me into the professional that I am today.

Shout-out to EVERYONE at the Oregon Culinary Institute, the best culinary school in the world!

Shout-out to all my fans, young cooks, and haters! Y'all keep my blood pumping.

9

Preface

"EGGSLUT CHEF WRITES FIRST COOKBOOK!" If you're looking for one hundred food-porny egg sandwich recipes, then you're going to be extremely disappointed in this book. I'm the creator of Eggslut. I created the recipes that millions of people from all over the world have taken pictures of. I worked my ass off for two and half years, sacrificing friendships and leveraging all my credit cards for the brand to become what it is today.

But this is not a story about a shiny, subway-tiled egg restaurant and its campaign to be America's next major food chain. This is a story about a brown kid, from a brown family, whose roots are in Southeast Asia. More specifically, the Philippines. That makes me American-born Filipino, or, as my grandma used to call us: Amboy.

Amboy describes my cuisine, my lifestyle. It's how I cook. It's how I talk. This cookbook is the story of Amboy. It's the story of not being Filipino enough to be Filipino, and not being American enough to be American. It's about a Filipino-American kid trying to make it work in a world where everyone says *no*. About making it happen and being true to who I am. About just owning it.

My family migrated to America to escape a government that literally had no idea how to govern. In the 1980s, we landed in Los Angeles. Back then, we were just a shadow in a bright and shiny world. My mom was a bookkeeper, and my dad was a locksmith. We lived in a suburb five minutes from downtown LA called Pico Rivera. It was an unassuming place where unassuming people lived, where everyone was God-fearing and blue-collared, no one left for greener pastures, and everyone kept to themselves.

Except for me, baby! I got the hell out of there. It took me 24 years to leave, but I did, and I didn't look back. I focused on me. I was selfish. And then I birthed Eggslut. It started as a food truck in 2011 and opened as my first brick-and-mortar restaurant in Los Angeles, at Grand Central Market, in 2013. MSNBC declared it the Most Instagrammed Restaurant in the World, and *Bon Appétit* named it one of the Top 50 Best Restaurants in the United States. A year later, I won a StarChefs Rising Stars Award, opened a controversial ramen restaurant, Ramen Champ, and created the 2016 *Los Angeles* magazine Restaurant of the Year, Unit 120.

Amboy is the story behind the headlines, my struggle, the greatest highs and the lowest of lows. It's about achieving success—and, every day, dealing with the threat that it can be taken away in a heartbeat.

I started out thinking my life's purpose was to make money. Then I decided it was to make delicious food. Later, I realized I represented so much more. This book is that *more*. It's for the dreamer. It's for El Mágico—the person who has been dealt nothing but shit his entire life but continues to work his ass off and make dreams happen, by any means necessary.

I spent half my life making the mistake of trying to please everyone around me—my parents, my family, and my lovers. If there is something I've mastered, it's failure! I've failed at everything, and I've failed everyone who's meant anything to me. But I took that experience and disappointment and used it as fuel to do better—and to ultimately become the best I can be at what I do.

This isn't a self-help book. It's just my story and the recipes that were inspired by my life's journey. Take it for what it is, use it as a cookbook, read it, and compare it to your life. Hate it or love it, but know that the book was made to show the world that a child of immigrants who didn't follow a traditional path to success can still keep the American dream alive during a time when our president doesn't even believe that we deserve to dream, let alone be in America.

My can-do ego gave me faith that I could write an entire book on my own, but I quickly got straight with myself: *Writing is not your strength, Amboy.* Talking, yeah. Writing, nah. It hasn't helped that I'm semi-fobby, live in a slang world, and got used to no one correcting me for the last ten years. So I reached out to my good friend Alexandra Cuerdo.

Alexandra (aka Allie) is the writer and director of *ULAM: Main Dish*, the first documentary about the rise of Filipino food in America. We met in 2015 at a Filipino food conference, which became a movement that both of us helped shape. As much as it's my story, it's hers as well.

Alexandra got the story out of my heart and into this book. The pages ahead reflect our conversations about being Filipino-American and the recipes that go with them. You'll also get a lot of me talking shit, making mountains out of molehills. Alexandra tried to rein me in, make sense of it all. I think it worked. Thank you, Alexandra. Let's do this.

—ALVIN CAILAN

Meeting Alvin

Our meet-cute was less cinematic and more pure chance. I was working on a Sundance film and simultaneously double-dipping as a production manager for Walt Disney Imagineering. One early weekday, I stumbled half-dead into a coffee shop called Crème Caramel. It was an unassuming little place sandwiched between a laundromat and a freeway sign. The place had caught my eye on Yelp with the promise of sugary treats and ube lattes. Were there Filipinos here?

Inside, the kind and bespectacled owner, Kristine de la Cruz, offered me her take on the classic Filipino dessert leche flan. It was an explosion of flavor: caramelly, melty, ultra-creamy, and perfect. I ate it so fast I needed another one right away. As she was packing up the rest of the pastry case, I mentioned I was a filmmaker.

She asked what I was working on, and instead of mentioning either of my jobs, I told her my secret: I wanted to direct a Filipino food documentary. I had started on a pitch for *ULAM: Main Dish*, and I was scheming about my dream cast. She was delighted. Turns out, there was a Filipino conference coming up, where I might be able to meet a few of the chefs I had mentioned. It was called Next Day Better. I got tickets for it that night.

I remember the minute Alvin Cailan walked onstage. He opened his mouth and immediately made the audience laugh. During his 45-minute speech, I remember looking around, watching the audience fully loving the experience. He was clearly not a practiced public speaker—he would cuss and apologize, then forget and cuss again. But the audience wasn't just engaged—Alvin had them. They were enthralled.

His story is a fairy tale: brown kid from Pico Rivera grows up to rule the City of Angels as the "King of LA." How is that real? A child of Filipino immigrants creates the most Instagram-famous, all-American breakfast sandwich. How is that possible?

He ended his set—because that's what it felt like, with the audience laughing and crying and *living* for it—to raucous applause. I was stunned. I looked down at my *ULAM* pitch, printed on the nicest, glossiest paper from the Copymat. My hands were shaking. Five pages. Five pages would end up detailing the next four years of my life.

I still don't know how I managed to walk up to Alvin that day. I hung around, looking at my shoes and squaring my shoulders, till the line of well-wishers dwindled.

It was my turn. I handed him my pitch. Then, I held out my hand, and he shook it.

I had no idea that moment would change my life forever. I know it sounds overly dramatic to say it like that, but it's true. This big brown guy in a beanie would end up being the star of my first movie, and the hero of my first book.

As a young child, I had read hundreds of books, and I never once met a character like him. As a young filmmaker, I had watched hundreds of films, and I never once saw a hero like him. In my favorite stories, there was never room for Alvin Cailan.

But here he was, saying things like "You should never listen to your family, because as much as they love you, they hold you back" and "I spent all my life making money for a white man. I eventually asked, when do I make money for myself?"

What most sets Alvin apart isn't any of that, though. What sets Alvin apart is his awareness. He knows himself and his place in the world. He takes setting an example—for all Filipinos and all Americans—to heart.

When I met Alvin five years ago, I had no idea who he was. In the following pages, I'll endeavor to show you—with recipes, conversations, essays, and, ultimately, stories—who this man is, how he was made, and why he matters. And I hope you can also see a bit of who Filipino-Americans are, how we're made, why we matter, and what our stories hold.

Maraming salamat for your time and consideration. Thank you all very much.

—ALEXANDRA "ALLIE" CUERDO

Mom and Dad

NORALYN AND ANTONIO Cailan—they're the ones to blame for this mess that I call a life. My parents weren't the conventional mom and pop you would see on TV. Hugs and kisses were rare. I didn't celebrate my birthdays with extravagant parties. I didn't get expensive gifts. My parents didn't care about any of that. All they cared about was that I was smart, so they could brag about me after church on Sunday.

My parents came from the Philippines, and they had no idea how to raise a child in the 1980s and '90s. They definitely didn't know how to raise a young dude who would end up loving gangster rap and hip-hop. They didn't know how to raise a knucklehead kid who wanted to be Gordon Gekko, either. How could they know? They were from the Philippines, where people beat the crap out of their kids so they're well behaved and don't embarrass the family name.

On paper, I was a kid with halfway decent grades. I went to four high schools, bounced around colleges, and ultimately finished school as a cook. Some would say my mom and dad failed at parenting.

But did they? You're reading about how I made it happen. So, shout-out to my parents! I know you meant well. I know you thought that I would fail you, but I did my best. I hope you're proud.

This bit is the story of my parents. If it weren't for them, I wouldn't be here.

Love Under Martial Law

Imagine you're me. In 1969, in the Philippines, your mom was 13 and went to Western High School in Cavite. She was a local girl. She would grow up to be an accountant, but she didn't know that yet. Your dad was 16, a local guy, no education beyond high school. He would grow up to be a locksmith, a businessman, but he didn't know that yet, either.

Back then, they were just friends, two kids from the same hometown who spoke the same language, Tagalog, in a country full of dialects.

In July 1972, President Ferdinand Marcos declared martial law in the Philippines, and the world changed forever. College protesters were deemed radical revolutionaries, then terrorists, then prisoners of the state. Families divided between those who supported the government and those who didn't. The country became known for Imelda's shoes and spending, and Marcos's extrajudicial killings and tyranny. The Philippines, formerly the jewel of the Orient, became the sick man of Asia.

History was forever divided into before and after martial law—before and after Marcos. But for my parents, it was the period in between that defined them. During that in-between time, my mom and dad fell in love. They were high school friends, then sweethearts, and then hitched. When student activists were being taken in for questioning, my mom decided to go to Far East University. Dad went to work on merchant ships as a deckhand. His brothers had all joined the military, and his mom's father was a captain. Imagine your dad at 22, like so many Filipinos before him, traveling the world, sending money back home, remembering those he loved.

Filipinos are the ship workers of the world. Officially, they're called OFWs—Overseas Foreign Workers. Unofficially, they're the hardest-working people on Earth. Their love moves around the country via balikbayan, the cardboard care packages carrying supplies from overseas: second-hand clothes, new toys, cans of Spam, books of all kinds. Every time you receive one of these boxes, you know you're about to experience something special. It's the repayment of *utang na loob,* what is owed from within. It's love from thousands of miles away. It's a gift without words.

But after eight years under martial law, eight years of separation, my parents decided enough was enough. Like so many others, they looked to America for a fresh start.

MOM AND DAD

Red, White, and Blue?

ALEXANDRA: When did your parents come over to America?

ALVIN: My mom got petitioned by her uncle Corny in 1979. He was a US Navy guy. He brought most of my mom's family over. My dad came here illegally, but found a job immediately at Caesars Palace in Lake Tahoe. The casino paid for employees' room and board, so it made sense. He worked there as a housekeeper for three years. Then, I was born.

ALEXANDRA: Where were you born?

ALVIN: Sunset Kaiser in Hollywood, January 10, 1983. My family lived in East Hollywood on New Hampshire Avenue on the cusp of Filipinotown till I was three years old. My first memories are all about food: going to the doughnut shop next door, or getting hot pan de sal from Betsy's Bakery. Back then, my dad was a locksmith and my mom was a bookkeeper in Beverly Hills. She worked right next to Spago.

Kitchen Daddy

Growing up, my dad was the cook for his seven brothers and sisters. Mom was one of five, and luckily she never had to cook. So Dad was the chef in the house when I was growing up, and he loved the classics. Imagine: From birth till five years old, all you know is Filipino food. You grow up with champorado in the mornings, the dessert-for-breakfast dish of nutty chocolate rice with evaporated milk. For lunch, you have Mom's favorite sinigang, the tamarind-soured, vegetable-packed soup made with or without the well-loved Knorr seasoning packets. For breakfast on the weekends, you eat a heap of white rice, sunny-side-up eggs, and a piece of tangy, citrus-marinated bistek, well-done. When you're sick, Dad makes arroz caldo, a soul-warming chicken, ginger, and rice stew. Later, when your brother is sick you learn to make lugaw, the little sister of arroz caldo, a simple congee topped with scallions and eaten by the bowlful.

You grow up watching Dad make adobo, braising chicken in vinegar and soy sauce. You hate munggo, the mung bean stew that looks like a brown gruel. Now, you crave it—its earthiness, its simplicity. Almost every day, Dad makes his favorite dish, nilaga, a humble braised beef soup with potatoes, carrots, and other vegetables.

To you, food is comfort, because your dad always seems to be making hella comfort food—hearty stews, piles of white rice, meat-and-potatoes fare with emphasis on the meat. It's workers' food, and Mom and Dad work hard.

You always smell like Filipino food, heavy onion and heavy garlic, but you don't care. This food and these people nourish you and care for you. They form the very building blocks of what you know, and who you are.

The recipes that follow are the ones that I was raised on—and the ones that raised me.

Steamed Jasmine Rice

SERVES 12

If you're Filipino, you're probably saying, "Dude, I have a rice cooker, and I don't need to learn how to make rice on the stove." Trust me, there's satisfaction in cooking your rice the old-school style. This is how I cook rice all the time, and I wouldn't have it any other way.

Make sure you wash your rice thoroughly. This is so important: Unwashed rice is the worst thing you can ever serve to a Filipino person. I remember serving half-assed washed rice to my dad, and the look of disappointment on his face scarred me for life. And don't forget the finger method—if you know, you know. Touch your hand to the bottom of the inside of the pot and use the first line on your middle finger to measure the water (see photo on page 25). Every Filipino swears it's the perfect way to cook rice.

---

4 cups white jasmine rice

Put the rice in a medium pot. Rinse the rice under running water and rub the grains in your palm until the starch and impurities cloud the water. Pour out the water and do it over and over again until the water stays clear. Drain off the water one last time.

Add 6 cups fresh water to the pot. Cover and bring to a boil over medium-high heat. Tilt the lid on the pot so a little bit of the steam pressure can escape and continue to cook until all the water has cooked off, 3 to 5 minutes. You'll see the steam reduce to just a thin wisp when this happens. Remove from the heat, cover the pot completely, and let the rice steam for 10 to 15 minutes. Fluff the rice with a fork and serve.

Talking Rice

ALEXANDRA: Who made the best rice growing up?

ALVIN: My dad. Till this day, he makes the best rice on the planet. It's his best dish. The texture has this perfect wetness and perfect fluffiness. You can tell the dude's been making rice right his whole life.

ALEXANDRA: Does he use a rice cooker or does he make rice on a stovetop?

ALVIN: He uses a rice cooker. But I don't own a rice cooker. My recipe is on the stovetop, cooked in a pot. To me, it's more satisfying, knowing you did that, not a machine! And there's a trick.

ALEXANDRA: What's the trick?

ALVIN: You have to play with your fire. You tilt the lid so that a little bit of the steam pressure is released. If you don't, the water bounces back down into the rice, and the rice becomes soggy.

You have to use your senses. Once the water evaporates, you put the lid back on securely and turn off the heat so the rice doesn't burn. You just let it steam for 10 to 15 minutes, and then it's perfect, every single time. It's a craft. In Pico, me and my Filipino boys all make rice this way. It's a type of swag that we developed. We're proud of it. We can be in the forest and make rice perfectly. We don't need a rice cooker.

ALEXANDRA: Have you ever done that? Have you ever gone camping and made rice?

ALVIN: No, no . . . I don't camp. I went on a date with a girl, she took me on a hike, we got lost for 13 miles, and I broke up with her.

ALEXANDRA: That's hilarious.

ALVIN: We just know how to survive, right? Give me a backpack full of rice and I will make you happy, anywhere in the world.

Beef Nilaga

SERVES 6

Nilaga is the one dish that represents growing up as a Cailan. My dad would make it all the time, so we ate it at least two or three times a week. Cuz I'm such a fat boy, I thought, hey, at least I'm gonna have a hot dinner. My parents worked a lot, so sometimes hot dinner wasn't an option. We'd eat leftovers, or we'd get takeout that would be cold by the time we got home. The worst was 29-cent cheeseburger day. Think of a platter of McDonald's cheeseburgers that's been sitting out for the whole day.

Back then, nilaga was sustenance, the foundation of my love of beef. Growing up, I remember the kitchen smelling like nilaga. I remember doing my homework at the dinner table and seeing that beefy steam wafting up from the pot. Every time I have nilaga it brings me back to that image.

My dad made his with carrots, but I skip them in my version. Instead I put garlic chips on it, or I eat it with fish sauce. I talk about it with my friends, because it's nostalgic for all of us.

One night, I made nilaga for Chinatown After Dark, a "First Thursday" event in LA. Every single Filipino who ate it that night was like, "Bro. This shit is so good." Nilaga is our version of chicken noodle soup. It's a hug in a bowl.

---

1 tablespoon canola oil

2 pounds boneless beef short ribs, cut into 2-inch cubes

4 quarts Homemade Beef Stock (page 45)

2 tablespoons Rufina patis (Filipino fish sauce; available at Asian markets and on Amazon)

10 black peppercorns

2 russet potatoes (about 1 pound), peeled and cut into 1-inch cubes

1 large yellow onion, cut into ½-inch-wide strips

Heat a medium stockpot over high heat for 2 minutes. Add the oil and let that heat until you see it ripple, about 1 minute. Working in batches to avoid crowding the pot, add the short ribs and sear until caramelized all around, about 2 minutes on each side. Use a slotted spoon or tongs to transfer to a plate, reserving all the fat in the pot. When all the short ribs are seared, return them to the pot, along with any accumulated juices. Add the beef stock, fish sauce, and peppercorns and bring to a boil. Then, reduce the heat to a nice simmer and let the beef braise until fork-tender, about 4 hours. Skim the fat from the surface occasionally.

Add the potatoes and onion and simmer for 15 minutes. Add the cabbage and simmer until the cabbage is tender and soft, about 10 minutes. Season to your liking with salt. Ladle the soup into bowls, garnish with the scallions, and serve piping hot with rice.

(ingredients and recipe continue)

½ small head napa cabbage (about 1 pound), cored and cut into ½-inch-wide strips to yield about 3 cups

Kosher salt

3 scallions, thinly sliced, for garnish

Steamed Jasmine Rice (page 20), for serving

Homemade Stock

It's worth your time to make stock from scratch (see pages 44 to 46). If you can't for some reason, get yourself some high-quality stock from a butcher shop or specialty market. That stuff's going to be so much better than the salty, flavorless kind you find in a box or can.

Sinigang

SERVES 6

As often as we had it, sinigang was always celebrated in my house. It was my mom's favorite dish, and my dad knew it. She loved sinigang so much, she had a bread box in our pantry that held only sinigang flavoring packets.

I vividly remember the colander of vegetables piled high next to the sinigang pot. I think my dad subconsciously stacked the vegetables like a bounty to say: "This is gonna be the feast tonight." Bok choy, tomatoes, turnips, green beans, banana peppers—I remember my dad placing all of it on top of the pot and letting the residual heat from the soup suck in all the vegetables. I loved those banana peppers. I would use my fork and spoon to crack open the chiles, and the spiciness would go straight into the sabao (broth/braising liquid). Heaven.

Growing up, I remember my mom would always eat the sourest fruit, like mangos before they were sweet and ripe. So, of course, her sinigang had to be tangy. If it wasn't, she would have a lot to say. Like, if we would eat sinigang at other people's houses, she would say, "Huh, it's not sour. It's not sour enough." And I would say, "Mom, chill! They probably didn't use a packet."

The most iconic sinigang seasoning packet is probably the Knorr brand. You'll see those green packets in many Filipino households in America. It usually has beef bouillon and tamarind powder in it, and it cuts the cooking time in half. Knorr's brand is what most people think sinigang tastes like. But it's all artificial flavoring. Compared to made-from-scratch sinigang, it's super sour.

When you cook things with heart, without packets, it takes time. Beef stock takes about eight hours. Braising beef or pork the right way takes at least four hours. Making the tamarind base takes two hours. When you mix that together—when you create the love—it'll never ever be the same. And it's always going to be worth it. Making sinigang from scratch results in a rich and bold broth, almost like a pho. It's unctuous and delicious—you can taste the beef flavor coating your tongue.

---

1 tablespoon canola oil

2 pounds boneless beef chuck steak (preferably center cut), cut into 2-inch cubes

2½ quarts Homemade Beef Stock (page 45), plus more as necessary

2 tablespoons Rufina patis (Filipino fish sauce; available at Asian markets and on Amazon)

Heat a stockpot over medium-high heat until hot. Add the oil and heat until you see the oil ripple, about 1 minute. Working in batches, add the beef in a single layer and sear until it's browned and releases easily, about 1 minute per side. Transfer to a plate. Add the beef stock, scraping up the browned bits (fond) from the bottom of the pot. Return the beef, along with any accumulated juices, to the pot.

(ingredients and recipe continue)

1 cup Tamarind Base (recipe
    follows), plus more as desired

½ pound taro root, peeled and
    cut into 1-inch cubes

1 large yellow onion, diced

4 banana peppers or jalapeños

½ pound long beans, cut into
    2-inch long lengths

1 bunch bok choy (about
    ½ pound), quartered
    lengthwise with the stems
    kept intact

Kosher salt

Bring to a boil, then cut the heat to low. Add the patis and tamarind base and simmer, stirring and skimming off the fat occasionally, until the beef is fork-tender, about 4 hours.

Add the taro root, onion, and peppers. Add more stock, if necessary, to cover the taro and simmer until the taro is almost tender, 10 to 15 minutes. Add the long beans and cook for about 5 minutes. Taste and add more tamarind base, if desired.

Add the bok choy, submerging just the stems so they get a head start cooking, and cook for 3 minutes. Then, push the leaves into the broth and simmer until the bok choy is crisp-tender, about 2 minutes. Season with salt, if necessary. Ladle the sinigang into bowls and serve piping hot.

Tamarind Base

MAKES 4 QUARTS

4 quarts water

20 sour tamarind pods, shelled
    and long fibers removed

In a medium stockpot, combine the water and tamarind pods. Bring to a rolling boil over high heat, then cut the heat to a simmer and cook until the water is cloudy and brown, about 2 hours.

Using a spider, pull out the pods and let cool on a plate. Let the tamarind liquid in the pot cool to room temperature.

When the tamarind pods are cool enough to handle, remove the seeds and discard. Transfer the pulp (you should have about 1 cup) to a blender and add 2 cups of the tamarind liquid. Blend until smooth. Add the puree to the remaining tamarind liquid in the pot and stir. Use right away or store in an airtight container in the refrigerator for up to 2 weeks or in the freezer for up to 3 months.

Dad's Tortang Giniling

SERVES 8

When I was growing up, we always had ground beef in the fridge. My mom would buy it for her sweet spaghetti, and there were always leftovers. To me, the smell of ground beef sautéing is heaven. There's something about the fat content hitting the hot pan and the exhaust that it creates—it just smells so good. This is the ground beef dish that made my dad happiest: an omelet that he cooked with pageantry, like he was conducting an orchestra.

With tortang giniling, you cook the meat first. After you drain the fat from the meat, you pop it in the refrigerator so the meat can cool. That way, when you scramble the eggs into the meat, the meat doesn't cook the eggs with its residual heat. My dad would take that eggy-meat mix and use the sinigang ladle to scoop it up and fry it in a pan. The result was awesome: beef omelets for the whole family. This was his after-work meal, his go-to.

My dad would top his omelet with patis, a Filipino fish sauce. As a kid, I would douse it in ketchup. As trashy as it sounds, I loved it. My dad used to plate the omelets like flapjacks. As a chef, I started layering the omelets in stacks of ten. I'd cut the stack like a cake and serve a wedge of it with hot rice.

Canola oil

½ large yellow onion, finely
  chopped

4 garlic cloves, minced

1½ pounds ground beef

1 teaspoon kosher salt

½ teaspoon freshly ground
  black pepper

12 large eggs, beaten

1 tablespoon Rufina patis
  (Filipino fish sauce; available
  at Asian markets and on
  Amazon)

5 scallions, thinly sliced

Sriracha or ketchup, for serving

Steamed Jasmine Rice
  (page 20), for serving

Heat 2 teaspoons oil in a large, deep skillet over medium heat until hot. Add the onion and garlic and cook, stirring often, until the onion is translucent, 5 to 7 minutes. Add the beef and cook, stirring often, until evenly browned, about 8 minutes. Season with the salt and pepper. Drain off and discard any juices and fat from the pan, then transfer the beef mixture to a medium bowl and let cool in the refrigerator for 10 to 15 minutes.

Add the eggs and patis to the bowl and stir to combine.

Heat 1 teaspoon oil in a 10-inch nonstick skillet over medium-low heat until you see the oil ripple, about 1 minute. Using a medium ladle, add ½ cup of the egg-beef mixture to the skillet. Let the omelet set for 3 minutes, then sprinkle with 2 teaspoons of the scallions. Flip the omelet and cook for 2 minutes. Transfer to a plate and repeat with the remaining egg-beef mixture and scallions, adding another 1 teaspoon oil to the pan for each omelet.

To serve, stack the omelets on top of each other and cut into 8 layered wedges. Serve with Sriracha or ketchup and rice.

Lugaw (Rice Porridge)

SERVES 4

Filipino food is generally comforting, and lugaw (a porridgey rice similar to Chinese congee) is probably the most comforting. We eat this unctuous rice porridge when we're sick, hungover, and even when it's gloomy out. It's a bowl of happiness, a hug, and, best of all, it's super easy to make. This is my matzo ball soup; the first slurp always takes me back, and that's truly the best experience when eating.

3 tablespoons canola oil

2 cups minced shallots
   (about 3 large shallots)

2 tablespoons minced fresh
   ginger

2 tablespoons minced garlic

1 cup white jasmine rice

1 cup glutinous rice

8 cups Homemade Vegetable
   Stock (page 46)

1 teaspoon kosher salt

1 teaspoon freshly ground white
   pepper

MANDATORY TOPPINGS
Crispy Garlic Chips
   (page 40)

2 to 3 scallions, thinly sliced

OPTIONAL TOPPING
Dilis (page 122)

Heat a large, heavy-bottomed pot over medium-high heat until hot. Add the oil and heat until you see the oil ripple, about 30 seconds. Add the shallots, ginger, and garlic. Cut the heat to medium-low and cook, stirring, until the shallots are translucent, 3 to 5 minutes.

Turn up the heat to medium. Add both rices and cook, stirring, until the flavors marry, about 3 minutes. Add the vegetable stock and stir constantly so that the rice releases its starch and begins to thicken the stock, 8 to 10 minutes. Bring to a simmer, reduce the heat, and cook, stirring often, until the rice is at your desired texture—I prefer an oatmeal-like texture, not too mushy—another 8 to 10 minutes. Remove the pot from the heat, cover, and let stand for 20 minutes and the magic will start to happen.

Season the lugaw to your liking with salt and white pepper and sprinkle on the garlic chips, scallions, and dilis. Divvy up the lugaw into bowls and serve piping hot.

Filipino Food Is Soul Food: Lugaw

ALVIN: I didn't grow up eating Gerber baby food. I grew up eating lugaw, which is basically congee, which is basically rice porridge. It's so perfect and simple—rice, shallots, garlic, and ginger. You can be one year old or you can be 100, and this dish is still something you can eat. It's nourishing. I think I learned the term *lugaw* before I knew *arroz caldo*.

ALEXANDRA: It's kind of like the prequel. Rice becomes lugaw, which becomes arroz caldo.

ALVIN: Yes! It's all in the rice family.

ALEXANDRA: What's your favorite memory of lugaw?

ALVIN: Eating it when I was sick. Growing up, I remember my grandma saying, "You have to eat this, and it will make you feel better, I promise." I would just look at her like, "How? How is this good for you? It's just rice." But then, I got older. I was 21 years old, sick as a dog, and I hadn't had lugaw in years. Someone made it for me, and I understood. It was so good and comforting.

ALEXANDRA: Grandma was right. Filipino food is soul food.

ALVIN: Exactly! You're eating a brick of carbs. And the sensation is its own memory—I remember the feeling of burning your tongue, and the richness of thick rice porridge. I don't get that sensation when I eat oatmeal, and lugaw is almost the same thing.

ALEXANDRA: To me, lugaw is how you take care of someone.

ALVIN: When my brother was a kid, I would always feed him. Mind you, I'm nine years older than my brother, so I thought I was going to be an only child for a lot of my life. I was so happy to have him. But as a kid, he was sick a lot. He was skinny, and I was big. So I was like, "Dude, you gotta gain weight." I would feed him lugaw all the time. It's our matzo ball soup. I'll probably make it for my kids.

Arroz Caldo (Rice Porridge)

WITH CHICKEN CHICHARON

SERVES 6

Maybe you know the saying "all parts of the buffalo." Well, this is a dish that uses all parts of the chicken to make, essentially, chicken and rice porridge. What makes it Filipino is the customizability of the flavors and the texture of the toppings—it's the savory crunch of chicken chicharon and garlic chips; the pungent, salty fish sauce; the zing of calamansi or toyomansi; and the garlicky, oniony base. (I replace the onions with shallots, which give the dish a milder, sweeter flavor.) The allium foundation is essential: It's one of the building blocks for Filipino food.

When making arroz caldo, some people cook the chicken and the rice together. As a chef, I realized that chicken and rice don't cook in the same amount of time—one will either be undercooked or overcooked. So I like to cook my chicken separately. Plus, using a whole chicken allows you to poach the chicken, shred the meat, save the skin for chicharon, and pile all the goodness into one bowl. You should be able to eat your arroz caldo with just a spoon and a bowl. It's a simple, perfect dining experience.

3 tablespoons canola oil

2 cups minced shallots
(about 3 large shallots)

2 tablespoons minced ginger

2 tablespoons minced garlic

1 cup white jasmine rice

1 cup glutinous rice

8 cups Homemade Chicken
Stock (page 44)

Kosher salt and freshly ground
white pepper

Poached Chicken
(recipe follows)

Chicken Chicharon
(recipe follows)

Heat a large, heavy-bottomed pot over medium-high heat until hot. Add the oil and heat until you see the oil ripple, about 30 seconds. Add the shallots, ginger, and garlic. They should sizzle when they hit the pot, releasing their flavor. Cut the heat to medium-low and cook, stirring, until the garlic and shallots are translucent, 10 to 15 minutes. Carefully, rub a piece of shallot lightly with your finger (or with a fork if it's too hot): If it falls apart, you're good.

Turn up the heat to medium. Add both rices and cook, stirring, to let the flavors marry, about 3 minutes. Add the chicken stock and stir constantly until the rice releases its starch and begins to thicken the stock, 8 to 10 minutes. Bring to a simmer, reduce the heat, and stir the rice every few minutes until the rice is at your desired texture—some like it mushy, some like it al dente—8 to 10 minutes. Remove the pot from the heat, cover, and let stand for 20 minutes. That's when the magic will start to happen. Arroz caldo is more like a risotto than loose-grain rice, so a porridgy texture is perfect.

(ingredients and recipe continue)

MANDATORY TOPPINGS

3 Hard-Cooked Eggs (page 125), halved

Crispy Garlic Chips (recipe follows)

3 scallions, thinly sliced

OPTIONAL TOPPINGS

Rufina patis (Filipino fish sauce; available at Asian markets and on Amazon)

Fresh calamansi juice (see Note, page 68)

Uncover, season with salt and white pepper, and stir out any clumps with a fork. Scoop the arroz caldo into bowls. To each bowl, add some poached chicken and chicharon, half a hard-cooked egg, a sprinkle of garlic chips and scallions, a dash of fish sauce and calamansi, and you're set!

Poached Chicken

MAKES 1 CHICKEN

1 (5-pound) whole chicken

1 cup kosher salt, plus more for seasoning

Remove any giblets from the chicken and reserve for Goto (page 41). Rinse the chicken under very cold water, salt the entire chicken liberally inside and out, and let it rest at room temperature for 1 hour.

Fill a large stockpot with water and add the 1 cup salt. Bring the water to a boil, then cut the heat until the water is slowly simmering. Add the room-temperature chicken and let the chicken bathe in the slow-simmering water until the internal temperature of the breast reaches 155°F, 25 to 35 minutes.

Fill a large bowl with ice and water. Slide your spider under the bottom of the chicken, hook your tongs into the cavity, and airlift it out of the pot and into your ice bath. Submerge the chicken fully to stop the cooking, and leave it in the ice bath until cool enough to handle, 15 to 20 minutes.

Drain the chicken. Carefully peel off the skin with a sharp knife or your hands, and save it to make Chicharon (recipe follows), the perfect garnish for arroz caldo. Shred the meat into even pieces. Discard the bones.

(recipe continues)

Chicken Chicharon

Chicken skin peeled from
  1 (5-pound) raw chicken or
  Poached Chicken (page 39)

Canola oil, for frying

Kosher salt

Slice your chicken skin into 2-inch-wide strips. You should have 15 to 20 strips.

If using raw chicken skin, fill a medium pot with water and bring to a boil over high heat. Add the chicken skin. Cut the heat to medium and poach the skin for 30 minutes, rendering the fat away from the skin. Drain the chicken skin.

Pat each piece of poached chicken skin dry with paper towels. You want them to be very dry, so the skins will crisp up when you fry them. Place them on a wire rack set over a rimmed baking sheet and let them air-dry, uncovered, in your refrigerator for 24 hours.

In a countertop fryer or medium Dutch oven, heat 4 inches of oil to 350°F over medium heat (test this with your fryer thermometer). Working in batches, add the chicken skins and deep-fry till golden brown and crispy, 2 to 5 minutes, depending on the size. Using a spider, transfer the chicharon to paper towels to wick away the excess oil. (Save the chicken-flavored oil to use anytime you want to cook something extra delicious.)

Sprinkle the hot chicharon pieces with salt. Serve immediately as a topping for arroz caldo, or just eat them on their own.

Crispy Garlic Chips

Canola oil, for frying

8 garlic cloves, thinly sliced
  lengthwise (preferably with
  a mandoline)

In a countertop fryer or medium Dutch oven, heat 4 inches of oil to 350°F over medium heat (test with your fryer thermometer). Working in small batches, add the garlic and deep-fry, stirring constantly, till crispy and lightly golden brown, 1½ to 2 minutes. Using a spider, transfer the garlic chips to paper towels to wick away the extra oil.

Serve immediately or store in an airtight container at room temperature for up to 2 weeks.

Goto (Rice Porridge with Offal)

This is the offal version of arroz caldo—aka arroz caldo on crack. Goto is for when you're drunk, or when you're hungover. Not all goto has blood, but adding it gives you a ridiculously savory finish. If Anthony Bourdain had eaten it on his show, I think he would have freaked out. It's his type of shit. Was.

We went to the Philippines last year and had gotong Batangas, which is basically goto in soup form. It was one of the best dishes we ate in the Philippines. Kim, who I work with at The Usual, ate it with hot sauce and nearly died. The guy who made this particular goto was trained in Burma, so he made a Burmese hot sauce that was basically pureed Thai chiles. Fire. I barely put a drop in mine, and it changed my entire dish. Stupid Kim put like three tablespoons in his soup. He ate it—and loved it. He ate the whole thing. But because of how hot it was, it immediately turned his stomach. We had a three-hour ride back to Manila, so for three hours this guy had to hold it in. Poor Angela, my partner, was sitting between us the whole time. Kim turned into Casper. White. Pale. Fucking goto. But great fucking goto. Done right, as soup or thicker, with the right amount of heat, it's brilliant.

3 tablespoons canola oil

2 cups minced shallots (about 3 large shallots)

2 tablespoons minced ginger

2 tablespoons minced garlic

½ cup chicken livers, cleaned and deveined

½ cup chicken gizzards, cleaned and deveined

½ pound beef tripe, cleaned and cut into 1-inch-wide strips

1 cup white jasmine rice

1 cup glutinous rice

9 cups Homemade Chicken Stock (page 44)

6 ounces precooked pork blood (available at Asian markets), cubed

Kosher salt

Heat a large, heavy-bottomed stockpot over medium-high heat until hot. Add the oil and heat until you see the oil ripple, about 30 seconds. Add the shallots, ginger, and garlic. They should sizzle when they hit the pot, releasing their flavor. Cut the heat to medium-low and cook, stirring, until the garlic and shallots are translucent, 10 to 15 minutes. Carefully, rub a piece of shallot lightly with your fingers (or with a fork if it's too hot): If it falls apart, you're good.

Turn up the heat to medium. Toss in your chicken livers, gizzards, and tripe. Cook, stirring, until bouncy but not firm, 7 to 10 minutes.

Add both rices and cook, stirring, to let the flavors marry, about 3 minutes. Add the chicken stock and stir constantly until the rice releases its starch and begins to thicken the stock, 8 to 10 minutes. Fold in the cubes of pork blood and reduce the heat to let the mixture simmer, stirring every few minutes until the rice is at your desired texture—some like it mushy, some like it al dente—8 to 10 minutes. Remove the

(recipe and ingredients continue)

MANDATORY TOPPINGS

Poached Chicken (page 39)

3 Hard-Cooked Eggs (page 125), halved

Crispy Garlic Chips (page 40)

3 scallions, thinly sliced

OPTIONAL TOPPINGS

Rufina patis (Filipino fish sauce; available at Asian markets and on Amazon)

Fresh calamansi juice (see Note, page 68)

pot from the heat, cover, and let stand for 20 minutes. Remember that the texture should resemble a risotto more than loose-grain rice, so porridgy is perfect.

Uncover, season with salt, and stir out any clumps with a fork. Scoop the goto into bowls. To each bowl, add some poached chicken, half a hard-cooked egg, a sprinkle of garlic chips and scallions, a dash of fish sauce and calamansi, and serve.

Homemade Chicken Stock

MAKES ABOUT 6 QUARTS

Having stocks on hand at all times is a pure Amboy move. It's a mandatory pantry ingredient. Homemade or store-bought, fresh or frozen—stock makes all of your food taste better. As a culinary school chef once told me, stock just tastes so much better than water.

5 pounds chicken bones

1 pound yellow onions, halved

½ pound carrots, halved crosswise

½ pound leek tops (green parts), halved crosswise

3 gallons water

Preheat the oven to 450°F.

Arrange the bones on one or two rimmed baking sheets and roast until caramelized, about 30 minutes. Transfer the bones to a large stockpot. Add a little water to the baking sheet, scrape up all the browned bits (fond), and add that to the pot as well.

Arrange the onions, carrots, and leek tops on the baking sheet and roast for 20 minutes. Transfer the veggies to the stockpot. Add a little water to the baking sheet, scrape up the fond, and add that to the pot.

Add the 3 gallons water and bring to a boil over high heat. Then, cut the heat to low and let it simmer, skimming occasionally, until the stock is golden brown and deeply flavorful, 6 to 8 hours. Strain the stock and discard the solids. Refrigerate overnight and skim off the fat from the top. Use within the week or transfer to airtight containers and freeze for up to 3 months.

Homemade Beef Stock

MAKES ABOUT 9½ QUARTS

5 pounds beef bones

1 pound yellow onions, halved

½ pound carrots, halved crosswise

½ pound leek tops (green parts), halved crosswise

3 gallons water

Preheat the oven to 450°F.

Arrange the bones on one or two rimmed baking sheets and roast until caramelized, about 30 minutes. Transfer the bones to a large stockpot. Drain off and discard the fat on the baking sheet. Add a little water to the baking sheet, scrape up all the browned bits (fond), and add that to the pot as well.

Arrange the onions, carrots, and leek tops on the baking sheet and roast for 20 minutes. Transfer the veggies to the stockpot. Add a little water to the baking sheet, scrape up the fond, and add that to the pot.

Add the 3 gallons water and bring to a boil over high heat. Then, cut the heat to low and let it simmer, skimming occasionally, until the stock is a rich brown color and tastes like beefy goodness, 8 to 10 hours. Strain the stock and discard the solids. Refrigerate overnight and skim off the fat from the top. Use within the week or transfer to airtight containers and freeze for up to 3 months.

Homemade Vegetable Stock

MAKES ABOUT 2½ QUARTS

2 yellow onions, quartered

4 celery stalks, quartered crosswise

4 leek tops (green parts), quartered crosswise

2 large carrots, quartered crosswise

2 tablespoons fresh thyme leaves

4 quarts water

Combine all the ingredients in a stockpot and bring to a boil over high heat. Cut the heat to a simmer and cook, skimming occasionally, until the stock tastes like vegetables, not water, about 2 hours.

Strain the stock and discard the solids. Use right away or transfer to airtight containers and refrigerate for up to 1 week or freeze for up to 3 months.

Champorado
(Chocolatey Rice)

SERVES 8

When it rains outside, or if it's a cold and gloomy day, there's only one thing I want, and it's champorado, a chocolate rice porridge that my dad used to make us for breakfast or whenever my mother would crave it. When I was younger, it was made with Hershey's chocolate syrup. When my mom's mom came from the Philippines, she brought these pure cocoa balls from some province in the hills, and that champorado changed my life. Naturally, as my life progressed and I became a cook, I would ask my pastry chefs for baller Belgian chocolate so I could make the ultimate version.

6 cups water

2 cups white jasmine rice, rinsed

2 cups glutinous rice

2 cups Chocolate Ganache (recipe follows), plus more if desired

2 cups evaporated milk, for serving

Cool Ranch Doritos, for serving

In a medium, heavy-bottomed pot, bring the water to a boil over medium-high heat. Cut the heat to a simmer and add both of the rices. Continue to simmer, stirring often, until the rice is soft, 8 to 10 minutes. When the rice is at your desired texture—I like it at an oatmeal texture, not too mushy but still porridgy—remove the pot from the heat, cover, and let stand for 20 minutes. (This is a good time to make your ganache.)

Slowly stir the chocolate ganache into the porridge until you no longer see any white from the rice. Scoop the champorado into bowls. Serve with evaporated milk, kind of like coffee creamer. Mix in as much as you want. Dip Cool Ranch Doritos in it for extra cool points, and enjoy your breakfast dessert.

AMBOY

Chocolate Ganache

MAKES 3½ CUPS

1 pound semisweet
  chocolate chips

1½ cups heavy cream

Put the chocolate chips in a large heatproof bowl and set aside.

Heat your cream in a small pot over medium heat until just starting to simmer, about 5 minutes. Pour over the chocolate chips and whisk until the ganache is silky smooth. Use right away or refrigerate in an airtight container for up to 1 week. Reheat gently in a microwave or double boiler before using.

Sweet Dirt and Stinky Fish

ALVIN: Growing up in a Mexican neighborhood, this dish is what set me apart. Their champurrado was completely different from ours. Mexican champurrado is more of a thick drink, like a really thick horchata. I had a lot of pride in our champorado because I thought it tasted so much better.

ALEXANDRA: I remember my mom used to make it in the mornings a lot. It's one of her favorite dishes. When would you eat it?

ALVIN: A rainy Saturday morning, or in the wintertime when it was cold. It was an after-church brunch merienda (snack). Say you go to church Sunday morning, 9:30 a.m., front and center.

ALEXANDRA: Your parents, too?

ALVIN: Yeah! Then, at 11 a.m., you go to Salo-Salo Grill for Filipino brunch. After that, you take a nap. It's a casual Sunday. You wake up, and your grandma's making champorado in the kitchen. I remember she used these Filipino chocolate balls that you would get from the *palengke*, the open-air mart in the Philippines. They're real chocolate balls. I used to pop them in my mouth, and they were nothing like Hershey's. They tasted like sweet dirt.

ALEXANDRA: That's so funny. I remember my parents had something similar—a very dense Spanish hot chocolate that tasted powdery and super rich.

ALVIN: Exactly, because it's real cocoa! Real cocoa doesn't taste like milk chocolate. My grandma would start the dish by making a lugaw-style rice porridge with water. She would throw the chocolate balls in there. And then she would cheat. Because she knew Filipino chocolate balls were so indigenous to us, she would squeeze some Hershey's syrup into the dish. Her grandchildren would love it. I remember she would put the champorado in a bowl, and put evaporated milk on top. She would say, "Evap! You put the evap on there!"

ALEXANDRA: That's awesome. I love evap! Did you eat champorado with anything else?

ALVIN: My mom would eat it with dilis (fried anchovies), and I would eat it with Cool Ranch Doritos. Back then, I hated dilis. I was a rebellious kid. Now, I eat dilis like it's nothing. But at the time, I would say, "Mom, why are you eating this stinky fish with this beautiful chocolate rice concoction?"

My mom would try to explain it to me. She would say, "Because it's salty and sweet." I would counter, and say, "Oh, so you don't mind me eating this with salty Doritos?" My mom welcomed it, and it turned out to be really fantastic.

Pico Rivera, 1986

OH BOY, I'M proud to be from Pico, but it really isn't a place that people brag about. It's a predominantly Chicano neighborhood, mostly populated by Mexican Americans. Growing up, we were the workforce for all of LA County. We were a proud immigrant community. To quote *Hamilton*: "Immigrants? We get the job done."

I moved to Pico Rivera in 1986, when I was three years old. I grew up in a gated tract community where the gates were always broken. The neighbors had well-manicured lawns but also sold meth out of their garages. I saw my first dead body in an alley on my walk to school in the fourth grade.

As kids, we played basketball on the streets, baseball at the park, and football in the empty lots. The teachers tried to teach us, but we didn't listen. Rap music was our life—so was Nirvana and System of a Down. We survived the riots in the '90s, and we enlisted after 9/11.

Gangs were big back in the day, and I was a big-time hip-hop kid. I wanted to be a break-dancer and would dance for fun on the street: the cabbage patch, the running man, whatever moved. After a basketball win, my friends and I would make up choreographed dances. That's just what we did back then.

My family ate at a few restaurants, but never fast food. For me, McDonald's was a reward. If I was good at the dentist, I would get that Mickey D. More often, we would go to chain restaurants as a family. We'd eat

at Black Angus–type steakhouses, or Charley Brown's to celebrate the little victories. At home, the food was a different story. We ate chicken, fish, and bistek. It was food that my parents made because they missed the Philippines. It was food that reminded them of home.

My mom and dad wanted me to be a disciplined student, so I went to Catholic school from sixth to eleventh grade. I ended up getting kicked out of school. I started working as a part-time dishwasher and part-time car-part thief. I was a stoner. I wanted to be like Jay-Z. I ate lots of burgers and burritos. My crew would hang out at El Atacor Taqueria or In-N-Out Burger. We would show off our cars, and I would try to holler at ladies.

That was my childhood, and this is the story of Pico Rivera, the neighborhood I love.

Lost in the Sauce

ALEXANDRA: What's your favorite spot in the kitchen?

ALVIN: Saucier, hands down. Sauce is a magnifying glass for food. It amplifies and takes it to the next level. Even a bad dish can be saved by sauce. Think about it: The reason In-N-Out burgers are so good is because of the spread.

ALEXANDRA: When did you make your first sauces?

ALVIN: In '89, I met this Filipino kid named Mark Tagnipez, who now works as a chef in Australia. We bonded over chocolate milk and became best friends. He ended up working as a chef at E.P. & L.P. and Red Medicine in LA. From kindergarten till fifth grade, Mark's family had this restaurant in Downey called Japan West. They made these incredible teriyaki bowls with homemade teriyaki sauce.

Everyone has their first foray in the kitchen. Some people fail miserably and never go back. My first attempt was in the second grade, making sauce after school with Mark at Japan West. It was like my first bump: It got me hooked. We'd watch how Mark's dad made teriyaki sauce, and then we'd try to do that. We'd put together mayo and ketchup and dip our French fries in it.

When my "Grandma" Emma would visit, she would teach us how to make French sauces. She was really my great-aunt, and she lived in Quebec. She married a French chef. I remember the first time she showed me how to combine yellow mustard and mayo. She used it as a savory dipping sauce for carrots, and it blew my mind. It was so delicious.

AMBOY

Bring Out the Best Mayo

MAKES 1 CUP

Mayo is incredible. My favorite thing to put mayo on is French fries. My aunt was married to a Navy guy, and she traveled the world. One day she held out a French fry and said, "Try it with mayonnaise, it's how the French do it." I did, and I loved it. To this day, it's still how I eat fries.

When I was a kid, I was fascinated by those infomercials for hand blenders. They would throw eggs and oil in a beaker, turn it on, and make mayo. It was like magic: You took two liquids and turned them into a sauce. I begged and begged my mom for that, and I didn't get it until I was in college. Now, I make mayo and other emulsified fat and oil sauces every day. It's the base for the Tartar Sauce (page 103) for my homemade Tilapia Fish Sticks (page 101) and for my White Adobo Sauce (page 338).

2 large egg yolks, at room temperature

2 teaspoons fresh lemon juice

1 teaspoon white vinegar

1 teaspoon kosher salt

1 teaspoon sugar

¾ cup canola oil

In the cup that came with your immersion blender, combine the egg yolks, lemon juice, vinegar, salt, and sugar.

Place the blade of the immersion blender over the egg yolks. Turn the blender on high speed and blend for about 5 seconds just to break up the yolks. Slowly add a couple tablespoons of the oil and blend, moving the blender up and down, until the mixture begins to emulsify and there's no longer a slick of oil in the cup. Repeat until the mixture thickens and turns white. You'll know you're done when there is no more oil left and the emulsion pulls away from the sides of the cup. Use immediately or refrigerate in an airtight container for up to 1 week.

Teriyaki Sauce

MAKES ABOUT 2 QUARTS

Japan West, an LA restaurant in the '80s, made a huge impression on my sauces. The chef was the father of my grade-school best friend, Mark Tagnipez. We'd watch him make teriyaki from scratch and then go home and try to make it in my kitchen. We fucked it up a lot of times, but we kept at it. That's the kind of relationship I had with Mark. We would make grilled cheese sandwiches and quesadillas and put teriyaki sauce on them. I was addicted.

¼ **cup cornstarch**

5 cups water

1 cup Datu Puti or Silver Swan soy sauce (see sidebar; available at Asian markets and on Amazon)

2 cups loosely packed dark brown sugar

3 tablespoons honey

1½ teaspoons ground ginger

1½ teaspoons garlic powder

In a liquid measuring cup, whisk the cornstarch into 1 cup of the water to make a slurry. Set aside.

In a medium saucepan, stir together the remaining 4 cups water, the soy sauce, brown sugar, honey, ground ginger, and garlic powder. Bring to a simmer over medium-high heat. Make sure the mixture is simmering so that the heat will activate the cornstarch properly and thicken the sauce.

Whisk the cornstarch slurry into the saucepan until the sauce thickens enough to coat the back of a spoon. Remove from the heat. Serve the teriyaki sauce right away or transfer it to an airtight container and refrigerate for up to 2 weeks.

Filipino Soy Sauce

Filipino soy sauce is not Kikkoman; rather than a sweet brewed flavor, it has a saltier soy flavor. It's what gives Filipino food its unmistakable savoriness. Go into any Filipino household and I guarantee you'll see a huge jug of Datu Puti or Silver Swan, Filipino soy sauce brands. If you want these recipes to turn out right, get yourself the right soy.

Japan West's Ketchup and Mayo Sauce

MAKES 1¼ CUPS

The burger at LA's Japan West was a beef patty with teriyaki sauce, lettuce, tomato, and this amazing ketchup-mayo sauce. It was the best burger ever. Once I learned how to make the ketchup-mayo sauce, I started to put it on not only burgers but anything else I wanted to make extra delicious, like French fries, fried chicken, and egg rolls. Try it on Cheeseburger Lumpia (page 98) or Lola's Lumpia Shanghai with Pork and Shrimp (page 90).

1 cup mayonnaise

¼ cup Heinz ketchup

1 teaspoon sugar

In a small bowl, stir together the mayo, ketchup, and sugar until the sauce is a uniform color, without any lumps or streaks. Serve right away or refrigerate in an airtight container for up to 1 month.

'90s Pantry BBQ Sauce

I'm the king of this recipe. In the 1990s, the Food Network taught me to mix ketchup, honey, and brown sugar to make a basic BBQ sauce, and I learned you can just improvise from there. If you put chili powder in it, it becomes a little bit smoky and a little bit spicy. If you put chipotles in it, you get more heat. (I was a latchkey kid, so I had the run of the kitchen and made shit up because who was going to stop me.) Serve with Chicken Patty Sandwiches (page 106), ribs, an Amboy Burger (page 118), or anything else you'd have with BBQ sauce.

2 cups Heinz ketchup

½ cup loosely packed dark brown sugar

1 tablespoon apple cider vinegar

1 teaspoon garlic powder

1 teaspoon onion powder

1 teaspoon Worcestershire sauce

1 teaspoon Datu Puti or Silver Swan soy sauce (see page 60; available at Asian markets and on Amazon)

¼ teaspoon French's yellow mustard

Combine all the ingredients in a small saucepan. Whisk together and bring to a boil over medium heat, whisking constantly. Cut the heat to super low and cover the pan so your sauce doesn't splatter. Simmer, whisking occasionally, until you have a nice, smooth texture, about 1 hour. At this point the sugar is fully dissolved, and the onion and garlic powder are fully married into the sauce.

Remove the pan from the heat and let your sauce cool to room temp before using. This will keep in an airtight container in the fridge for 2 weeks, if it lasts that long.

PICO RIVERA, 1986

Grandma Emma's Dijonnaise

MAKES 1⅓ CUPS

My great-aunt "Grandma" Emma introduced me to crudités—radishes, carrots, celery, and lettuce—dipped in a mixture of Dijon mustard and mayo. This was her Quebec influence. It was fantastic. I remember watching *Wheel of Fortune* with her and eating carrots with mustard and mayo. That's probably the healthiest I've ever been in my life. In addition to crudités, it's also good on Egg Whites on Brick Toast (page 100).

1 cup Best Foods or Hellmann's mayonnaise

⅓ cup French's yellow mustard

In a small bowl, whisk together the mayo and mustard until the sauce is a uniform color, without any lumps or streaks. Serve right away or refrigerate in an airtight container for up to 1 month.

Calamansi Beurre Manié

In my early chef years, before Eggslut, I worked as a saucier in French restaurants. There, we'd use a simple roux to thicken sauces. It's so easy, it's almost like cheating. You melt butter, add flour, cook it till it smells like popcorn, and you're done.

A beurre manié is an uncooked version of a roux. It's more butter than flour, and we used it to add richness to a dish. My spin on it is a calamansi beurre manié: butter, a little bit of flour, and calamansi juice. It has a bright flavor and is great for thickening pan sauces made from chicken, pork chops, or even vegetables.

---

1 tablespoon unsalted butter, softened

1 tablespoon all-purpose flour

½ teaspoon fresh calamansi juice (see Note)

Combine all the ingredients in a small bowl. Using a fork, mash the ingredients together until fully incorporated to form a paste.

Take the mixture in your palms and roll it into a ball. You can make a bunch of this stuff ahead of time, throw it into an airtight container, and refrigerate it for up to 2 weeks. Use it anytime you want to make a tasty pan sauce.

> **NOTE:**
>
> Calamansi, the super-lime of the Philippines, is a tart citrus that you can buy at some Asian markets. If you can't find the fresh fruit, use bottled calamansi juice, preferably Sun Tropics. It's available on Amazon.

House Toyomansi
(Calamansi Soy Sauce)

In a Filipino household, toyomansi is universal. It's like our extra-virgin olive oil. We finish lots of dishes with a drizzle of toyomansi.

To make a big vat of mother toyomansi, start with an empty jug and fill it with garlic. You could also add the whites of a scallion, red onion, and, if you want some spice, a few Thai chiles. At the restaurant, I even toss in other vegetable trimmings and let them macerate in soy sauce and calamansi juice for at least a week. The longer the flavors marry, the better the toyomansi tastes. Make a big batch and watch your toyomansi get more delicious every day.

2 cups Datu Puti or Silver Swan soy sauce (see page 60; available at Asian markets and on Amazon)

1 cup fresh calamansi juice (see Note, page 68)

6 large garlic cloves, peeled and lightly smashed

Combine the soy sauce, calamansi juice, and garlic cloves in a quart-size glass jar. Screw on the lid and shake it up for 30 seconds. Refrigerate the sauce overnight to let the flavors marry. Wake up, and bam! You've got toyomansi. Use right away or refrigerate for up to 1 month.

Pickled Chile Fish Sauce

MAKES 2¼ CUPS

I hate wasting food. Say you're working as a chef and you need a half pound of Thai chiles, but you can only order them in one-pound packages. What do you do with the extra half pound? I started pickling the leftovers with salt, sugar, vinegar, and water. Then, I had the idea to add peppercorns and patis, our fish sauce. We put chiles in our vinegar, why not put chiles in our patis? It just made sense to me.

This recipe has such a distinct flavor—it's got the umami wow of a fish sauce, with a nice heat. Put these pickled chiles on Sinigang (page 29), fried rice (pages 109, 186, and 333), pancit (pages 93 and 177), or any pork or chicken dish.

¼ cup Pickled Chiles (about 8 serranos and 4 cayennes; recipe follows)

2 cups Rufina patis (Filipino fish sauce; available at Asian markets and on Amazon)

In a 1-quart mason jar, combine the pickled chiles and fish sauce. Cover and let sit at room temperature for at least 24 hours or up to 5 days before using, then refrigerate for up to 3 weeks.

Pickled Chiles

MAKES ABOUT 1 QUART

4 ounces serrano chiles

4 ounces cayenne chiles

3 cups white vinegar

1 cup cold water

2 cups sugar

¼ cup kosher salt

2 teaspoons whole black peppercorns

Put the chiles in a 2-quart mason jar and set aside.

Combine the vinegar, water, sugar, salt, and peppercorns in a medium saucepan and bring to a boil over high heat, stirring constantly, until the sugar is fully dissolved, about 2 minutes.

Remove the pan from the heat and pour the hot pickling liquid over the chiles in the jar. Let the mixture cool, uncovered, to room temperature.

Stuff the top of the jar with parchment paper crumpled up into a ball, using it to fully submerge the chiles in the pickling liquid. Cover and let the chiles pickle for 3 days in the refrigerator before using. Store in the refrigerator for up to 3 months.

CHAPTER 3

Lola

I CAN STILL smell the Shower to Shower baby powder Lola Pacing used to rub on the back of her neck and chest. I remember Lola yelling the answers to *Wheel of Fortune*. I remember all of the crossword puzzles on her nightstand that were never completely filled out.

Lola, greatest of great-grandmas, I'm a fatty because of you. Remember when you would give me pan de sal slathered in margarine, and let me dunk it in your morning coffee? It's no wonder I accidentally locked myself in the bathroom throwing baby powder everywhere, screaming the bathroom was on fire. I was hopped up on sugar and caffeine.

Every time I eat Filipino food, I think about you. You left this crazy world before I was able to make anything of myself. You taught me more about our culture than anyone else, and my deep-rooted love for dinuguan and pancit is all because of you.

This is the story of Lola Pacing, one of my first kitchen heroes.

Lola's Cooking

In the late 1980s, my parents worked a lot. Like any other immigrant family, they worked to survive. Like any other latchkey kid, I was shipped to my great-grandmother's house to hang out after school.

To a five-year-old like me, Lola Pacing—nicknamed Lola Pacita—was very white. She was hella light-skinned, her maiden name was Martinez, and she was a direct descendant of Spanish lineage. Her hair was always 1920s-style, done up, and super long. She lived till she was 90. She was uneducated. She was a heavy smoker, lighting up cigs every day.

My Lola came from a poor family in the Philippines. At a young age, she was sent to work at a palengke, an open-air market to sell fish. There, she met my great-grandfather. He was one of the wealthier men in the town, owned a bunch of land, and was in the army. She was 13, he was 20, and back then, I guess that made sense. He was like, "Yo, I'm gonna get you out of this, bitch. You don't have to be a fish girl no more."

So she married this rich guy and had three kids with him—Nanay Grace, my grandma; Lola Emma, my great-aunt; and Grandpa Corny, my great-uncle. Grandpa Corny, or Cornelius, was famous in our family for his roast beef, fried chicken, and Stouffer's lasagna. He put American food and Filipino food on the same table all the time. All three of them were great cooks.

Then, World War II came around. Lola Pacita's husband fought in the Philippine army and died.

Soon she remarried and had ten more babies, for a grand total of thirteen. When her new husband squandered all her money and land, she moved to the States.

You'd think that Lola would have suffered more, but she got along just fine. She was a survivor. My Lola's saving grace was her heritage. She was born and raised in Cavite. She was from the province, of the province. It never really escaped her. Money never changed her—not when she had it, not when she lost it. She was who she was. She was Lola Pacita from the block.

She moved in with her gay son, Danny, in America. Danny had married a white dude. She didn't care. She just started making American food for her son and son-in-law, as well as Filipino food. She made the best fried chicken. She would marinate it in patis, our salty, fermented fish sauce. Instead of longanisa, she would make hot dogs and sinangag, our garlic fried rice, for breakfast. One of her best dishes was pancit bihon, a rice noodle staple. She lived in the kitchen and loved it.

As a kid, I remember our mornings. Breakfast with Lola was always hot pan de sal with margarine and instant Maxwell House International Coffee. She was a rebel. "Don't tell your mom," she'd say, handing me that pan de sal for dipping in coffee. I rebelled with her, riding my bike around the neighborhood for hours till the caffeine wore off. Then, I'd come home and fall asleep, exhausted.

Going to the supermarket with her was my favorite thing. "Anak," she would say—*anak* is "son" in Tagalog—"look at the fish. Anak, these are the bones." She would teach me how to recognize products and ask me about them later, testing my memory. Looking back, it was my first product identification test. She was so smart. She taught me everything without me even knowing it.

The recipes that follow are the epitome of my Lola's cooking—decidedly unfancy, from the heart, and for the soul.

Lola's Ginataang Bilo-Bilo (Rice Balls in Coconut Milk)

SERVES 4

My favorite Lola dish was ginataang bilo-bilo. It was a sweet coconut stew, chock-full of Filipino mochi, ripe plantains, jackfruit, sweet potatoes, and boba (tapioca pearls). She taught me that if you have guests over, it's customary to give them bilo-bilo for good luck.

This dish is fairly simple. The base is coconut milk, reduced and thickened with the starch from the bilo-bilo, or glutinous rice balls. In my version, I add white tapioca pearls and jackfruit. I don't use sweet potatoes, bananas, or plantains. I keep it simple.

Ginataang bilo-bilo is a great example of how Filipinos are very textural eaters. The rice balls are wet and soft, and have this chew to them. They're almost like a broken mochi. This dish is usually served hot, but I could eat that shit cold any day.

---

1 cup white tapioca pearls

5 cups boiling water

1 cup coconut milk

⅓ cup sugar

1 recipe Bilo-Bilo (recipe follows)

1 (12-ounce) can jackfruit, drained and julienned

Put the tapioca pearls in a large heatproof bowl and pour in the boiling water. Let soak overnight at room temperature. Drain and set aside.

Heat a medium saucepan over medium-high heat until hot. Add coconut milk, 1 cup of fresh water, and the sugar and bring to a boil. Cook, stirring constantly, until the sugar is fully dissolved, 3 minutes.

Add the drained tapioca to the boiling liquid. Cook, stirring constantly and breaking up any clumps, until the sauce has thickened slightly, about 5 minutes.

Cut the heat to low and add your bilo-bilo. Cook, stirring occasionally, until the stew tastes sweet and has a texture like mochi, with no graininess whatsoever, 15 to 20 minutes.

Remove the ginataang bilo-bilo from the heat and fold in the jackfruit. Ladle into bowls and serve immediately.

Bilo-Bilo (Rice Balls)

1 cup glutinous rice flour, plus more for dusting

½ cup water

In a medium bowl, combine the flour and water. Using a handheld mixer, beat at medium speed until a soft dough forms, 1 to 2 minutes.

Flour the cutting board. Take out your dough and roll it out with your hands into a long rope. Place the rope on the floured cutting board and cut it into 16 equal pieces. Use your hands to roll each piece into a ball. Set aside on the floured cutting board until ready to use.

Patis Fried Chicken

Lola Pacing loved patis, our funky fermented fish sauce. In the Philippines she used to sell fish in the palengke, or open-air market. When she came to America, she would make fried chicken for her American-born grandson, who craved KFC's version. But she would marinate hers in patis—the fish sauce acting almost like a brine, infusing the whole chicken with its salty, intense flavor.

4 quarts cold water

1 cup fresh lemon juice

1 cup Rufina patis (Filipino fish sauce; available at Asian markets and on Amazon)

1 (6-pound) whole chicken, broken down into 10 pieces

Canola oil, for frying

4 cups rice flour

Kosher salt

Gravy, ketchup, or White Adobo Sauce (page 338), for serving

In a large bowl or pot, whisk together the water, lemon juice, and fish sauce until thoroughly mixed. Add the chicken and let it brine for 45 minutes to 1 hour at room temperature.

Drain the chicken and pat it dry with paper towels. Let it stand at room temperature for about 45 minutes.

In a large, heavy pot, heat 4 inches of oil to 350°F over medium-high heat. Make sure to leave 3 to 4 inches of headroom at the top of the pot to prevent the oil from overflowing. Set a wire rack over a rimmed baking sheet and set aside.

Put the rice flour in a pie plate or shallow bowl. Dredge the chicken in the rice flour and shake off the excess. You want to lightly coat the chicken; too much coating will make it clumpy and less crispy.

Starting with the drumsticks and thighs, fry the chicken in batches, flipping as necessary, until the internal temperature reaches 165°F for the dark meat and 155°F for the white meat, 17 to 25 minutes. The legs and thighs will take longer to cook than the breast and wings. Using a spider, lift up each piece and test for doneness with an instant-read thermometer. Remember, the goal is golden brown and delicious.

When each chicken piece is done, pull it out and transfer to the wire rack. Season the chicken lightly with salt and let rest for 5 minutes. Plate the fried chicken and serve with gravy, ketchup, or white adobo sauce.

Pan de Sal (Sweet Rolls)

MAKES ABOUT 1 DOZEN

Dear Pan de Sal,

Thank you for existing. Because of you, I'm deeply in love with all things bread. I can remember when I was a child, walking into the Filipino bakery and smelling your fresh baked scent. I would immediately crave you. To this day, when I smell fresh baked pan de sal, my knees buckle, and no matter what kind of crazy diet program I'm on, I will always cheat on it with you. Your rough bread crumb exterior and your super fluffy interior serve as great vessels for peanut butter and jelly. In the mornings, I want to dip you in coffee, and when I'm home drunk from the club, I want to lather you with mayo and stuff you with Spam. I pray every night that God takes care of me and doesn't curse me with a disease that will take you away from me.

I LOVE YOU!

Alvin

STARTER

1¼ cups whole milk, warmed to 104°F

2 tablespoons active dry yeast

1 tablespoon all-purpose flour

1 teaspoon sugar

DOUGH

4 cups all-purpose flour, plus more for dusting

½ cup sugar

1 teaspoon baking powder

1 teaspoon fine salt

5 tablespoons unsalted butter, melted, plus softened butter for serving

2 tablespoons canola oil

1 large egg

¼ cup plain bread crumbs

MAKE THE STARTER: In a small bowl, stir together the milk, yeast, flour, and sugar. Let this mixture stand until the yeast is bloomed, 7 to 15 minutes. This step is to ensure that your yeast is alive to make bread magic. If the yeast doesn't bloom, go out and buy a new package of yeast, so your pan de sal doesn't fall flat. Literally.

MAKE THE DOUGH: Sift together the flour, sugar, baking powder, and salt into a large bowl. In the bowl of a stand mixer fitted with the paddle attachment, mix the melted butter, 1 tablespoon of the oil, and the egg at low speed for 15 seconds. Then, add your dry ingredients in thirds, mixing at medium-low speed for about 30 seconds with every addition.

When everything is evenly combined, add the starter and mix at medium speed until it's fully incorporated, or until the dough pulls away from the side of the bowl, 5 to 7 minutes. Change the paddle to the dough hook and knead at medium speed for 7 to 10 minutes. To see if you've achieved dough status, form a ball with the dough and press your finger into the center. If the dough bounces back, you're ready.

(recipe continues)

Pull the dough out onto a lightly floured work surface and knead until the dough forms a nice, smooth surface, about 7 minutes.

Lube the sides of a large bowl with the remaining 1 tablespoon oil so the dough won't stick when it proofs. Add the dough and cover with a damp towel. Let the dough rise somewhere warm until doubled in size, about 2 hours.

Line three baking sheets with parchment paper. On a lightly floured work surface, cut the dough in half. Using a rolling pin, roll each half into a rectangle about ½ inch thick. Using your hands, roll the long edge of each rectangle away from you into a tight log like you're rolling a cinnamon roll. Make sure the seam side is at the bottom of the log. Using a sharp knife, cut the log into 1-inch-thick medallions (see Note).

Lay the medallions on the prepared baking sheets, leaving 2 inches of space in between. Sprinkle the tops with bread crumbs, cover with a damp towel, and let proof until the rolls are doubled in size, 30 minutes to 1 hour.

Meanwhile, preheat the oven to 350°F. Bake the pan de sal until golden brown, rotating and switching the baking sheets halfway through baking, 15 to 20 minutes. Remove from the oven and serve hot, with butter.

NOTE:

Personally, I don't think it matters how you shape pan de sal. I've had arguments about how it has to be cut a certain way, rolled, and then sliced. In the Philippines, I've seen pan de sal that looks like Parker House rolls, or pan de sal stuck together like Hawaiian rolls. So I think it can look different.

Pan de Sal Is
the Ultimate
Sandwich Bread

ALVIN: If I couldn't eat pan de sal ever again, I'd probably get depressed and die. It's one of my favorite things to eat. In New York, I have to substitute it with Hawaiian bread. That's fine, but when I go home, I get pan de sal every week. There's something about it. It's a very basic dough. Making a French baguette requires flour, water, salt, and yeast. Making pan de sal requires flour, water, salt, yeast, and sugar. Some renditions use milk. Ultimately, pan de sal has to have bread crumbs as a topping. If it isn't coated in bread crumbs, to me, it's not pan de sal.

ALEXANDRA: It's a feel-good bread. What would you put on top of it?

ALVIN: Have you ever had pan de sal with peanut butter? Where the peanut butter melts and it's kind of gooey? It's so delicious. Sometimes, I'll top pan de sal with butter, or butter and sugar. You could also use coconut jam.

ALEXANDRA: What are your favorite memories of pan de sal as a kid?

ALVIN: Besides when Lola got me jacked off caffeine and pan de sal? Well, my grandfather on my mom's side, Lolo Pepeng, was a pan de sal freak. If we didn't have pan de sal at the house, he would say, "Okay, I'm going to go, I'm leaving now. I'm going to go to my son or daughter who has pan de sal." Love that. We had a freezer in our garage just stuffed to the gills with pan de sal. When I was a young stoner, I remember sneaking my buddies into my house while my parents were asleep. We would eat pan de sal with Costco hot wings, Tyson chicken patties, Spam, corned beef—you name it, we tried it. We would put my dad's tortang giniling in pan de sal, and it was amazing.

ALEXANDRA: Pan de sal is the ultimate sandwich bread.

ALVIN: It is! I would make pan de sal sandwiches out of anything. You go down the list of what's in your refrigerator, put it in a pan de sal, and it becomes a sandwich. It's a big part of being Amboy: Sandwiches are so American, and pan de sal is so Filipino.

ALEXANDRA: You can put anything in it because the flavor is so good—it's so neutral and also sweet.

ALVIN: One hundred percent. In my house, pan de sal is just as important as rice. This sandwich came from my family's love of pan de sal, and my latchkey-kid Costco life. It's less of a recipe, and more of a philosophy. Throw anything tasty in a pan de sal, and you have the best sandwich of all time.

The Ultimate Pan de Sal Sandwich

- Tyson chicken patty + American cheese + mayo + pan de sal = done

- canned corned beef + any kind of cheese you want (*for me, it has to be Kraft from the can from the Philippines*) + a little bit of mayo + pan de sal = done

- bacon + egg + cheese + pan de sal = done

- fish sticks + tartar sauce + pan de sal = done

- microwaved Vienna sausage + pan de sal = done

- leftover bistek or leftover adobo + pan de sal = done

- Sunday Gravy, sloppy Joe–style + cheese + pan de sal = done

Lola's Lumpia Shanghai
WITH PORK AND SHRIMP

MAKES 24 LUMPIA

As a kid, I remember making lumpia Shanghai, seeing the orange flecks of carrots in a bowl of ground meat. My great-grandma Lola, my grandma, my aunt, and I would gather around the dining room table and roll them together. Today, lumpia Shanghai is often served with sweet chile sauce. But when I was growing up, my family served it with La Choy, a classic sweet and sour sauce. Later on, someone brought this other big bottle of sweet chile sauce to the house. It had Vietnamese writing all over it, and we all switched to that. When we were kids, my cousins and I would pick up the lumpia and pretend we were smoking cigars. Lumpia was the first thing to go at family parties, because it is so addictive and so easy to eat.

FILLING
1 pound ground pork

½ pound peeled, deveined shrimp, minced

¼ cup finely minced garlic (about 10 large cloves)

⅓ cup finely minced onion (1 small onion)

⅓ cup finely minced carrot (1 small carrot)

⅓ cup finely minced celery (1 stalk)

1 large egg

½ teaspoon kosher salt

½ teaspoon freshly ground white pepper

LUMPIA
1 tablespoon canola oil, plus more for frying

1 (1-pound) package Menlo lumpia wrappers, thawed if frozen

MAKE THE FILLING: Put all the ingredients in a large bowl and mix by hand until thoroughly combined. Set aside.

MAKE THE LUMPIA: Heat a small frying pan over medium-high heat until hot, then add the 1 tablespoon oil. Heat until you see the oil ripple, about 30 seconds. Add ½ teaspoon of the filling and fry it for 1 minute. Flatten it with your spatula to make a patty. Flip your mini lumpia patty and fry it for 1 minute on the other side. Pull it off the heat and taste it. Adjust your seasonings, if necessary, for the rest of the filling.

Pull apart the lumpia wrappers so they're not stuck together. This is easier if your wrappers are still cold but not frozen.

In a large stockpot or Dutch oven, heat 4 inches of oil over high heat to 350°F.

Meanwhile, it's time to roll your lumpia! Place 1 lumpia wrapper in front of you so it's diamond shaped. On the bottom half of the wrapper, spread 1 heaping tablespoon of your filling into a 5-inch log.

Fold up the bottom point of the wrapper toward the center of the wrapper, covering the filling tightly. Using a pastry brush, dab some

(recipe and ingredients continue)

1 large egg beaten with 1 tablespoon water

Sweet Chile Sauce (page 156), Japan West's Ketchup and Mayo Sauce (page 63), or just plain old rice vinegar, for serving

of the beaten egg mixture on the left and right corners of the diamond, then fold those corners over toward the center. Tightly roll the lumpia upward until it's completely folded, then dab the last corner with beaten egg to seal it.

Repeat with the remaining wrappers and filling. Working in batches, fry the lumpia, flipping as necessary, until crispy, golden brown, and delicious, 7 to 10 minutes. Drain on paper towels. Plate and serve while hot with your choice of dipping sauces.

Lola's Pancit Bihon (Noodles with Vegetables)

SERVES 4

For this stir-fried noodle dish, my Lola would sit at the kitchen table cutting vegetables in her hand, mounds of snap peas, carrots, cabbage, and onions overflowing the bowl. It was a bounty, and it was about to feed 20 people all day long. These noodles are super thin, similar in texture to rice sticks.

1 pound dried thin rice noodles (the package will say "rice sticks" or "bihon")

1 tablespoon canola oil

⅓ cup thinly sliced onion (½ small onion)

¼ cup minced garlic (about 10 large cloves)

⅓ cup thinly sliced celery (½ stalk)

⅓ cup thinly sliced carrot (1 small carrot)

4 cups Homemade Chicken Stock (page 44)

1 cup Datu Puti or Silver Swan soy sauce (see page 60; available at Asian markets and on Amazon)

½ medium green cabbage, cored and thinly sliced

1 pound shredded meat from Poached Chicken (page 39)

¼ to ½ cup fresh lemon juice, plus lemon wedges for serving

¼ cup thinly sliced scallions (2 to 3 scallions)

Hard-Cooked Eggs (page 125), sliced, for garnish (optional)

Soak the noodles in a large bowl of cold water for 5 minutes, or until the noodles are softened. Drain thoroughly and set aside.

Heat a large wok over high heat until blistering hot. Add your oil, then cut the heat to medium and heat until you see the oil ripple, about 30 seconds. Add the onion and garlic and stir-fry until the onion is translucent, about 2 minutes. Add the celery and carrot and stir-fry until softened, 2 to 4 minutes.

Add the chicken stock and soy sauce and stir to combine. This will essentially deglaze the wok; make sure to scrape the fond (browned bits) from the bottom of the wok so nothing's stuck there. Cook until the liquid is simmering, then gently fold in the drained noodles. Add your cabbage and toss with tongs to combine. Cook, stirring constantly, until the noodles have absorbed the liquid, about 7 minutes. Add the chicken and cook, stirring, until the chicken is heated through, about 2 minutes. Reduce the heat if the noodles start to stick to the wok.

Plate the noodles, sprinkle the lemon juice and scallions over the top, garnish with hard-cooked eggs, and serve immediately with lemon wedges.

Pancit Brings People Together

ALVIN: Lola Pacing was known for her pancit, so she would make it a lot. The wok on the stove would always be filled with pancit. I'd spoon it into a bowl and eat it all day long. I'd even put it in pan de sal. Pancit is basically rice noodles with soy sauce, lemon juice, carrots, onions, celery, and chicken. So simple and so tasty.

ALEXANDRA: Pancit always feeds a lot of people, too. It brings people together.

ALVIN: Absolutely. We would sit at this round table in the kitchen. One person would be cutting celery, another person would be cutting carrots, another person would be cutting scallions, and then my great-grandma would be rinsing the vermicelli under water.

ALEXANDRA: It was literally kitchen stations!

ALVIN: Exactly. It was my first time experiencing that. My old-ass great-grandma would be at the wok sautéing meat, vegetables, noodles, and soy sauce. She would put it in this big foil tray and decorate it with hard-boiled eggs, crushed chicharon, and lemon wedges. That was Saturday. It was all hands on deck. Everyone would help out, and everyone would do their part.

ALEXANDRA: It has to be community-based, because it's too much work for just one person.

ALVIN: That's right. It's a part of the DNA of Filipino food. When you make it, you're with family making *tsismis*, or gossip. You're talking about so-and-so's boyfriend while you're chopping vegetables. Everyone does their part, because everyone has to work for their food. Pancit was great because it was fairly cheap to make, and there were a lot of people to feed. Back then, it was me, my cousins JR, Lorie, Lester, and Nikolai, my uncle and his husband, and my auntie Nene. So there were nine of us, all in the same house. How do you feed nine people every day? Pancit.

ALEXANDRA: Growing up, my parents would always have relatives visiting the house. All my non-Filipino friends would come over, and they just didn't understand it. Why is your aunt living with you for like nine months? Then, it would be someone else. There would be this rotating shift of family members, so there were always so many people in the house. I thought that was a uniquely Filipino experience.

ALVIN: Same! Summer vacations, my parents worked and all my cousins' parents worked. They would leave us kids in one house for three months. Luckily, Lola's son lived in a three-story townhome with a communal pool. So we spent our summers living in Baldwin Park.

We would wake up and eat pan de sal and coffee with Lola. Then, we would jump in the pool and get dark as fuck. My Lola never cared about that "Oh, you're gonna get dark" mentality. But my grandma and my mom would always care, and say, "Put baby powder on your skin, so you look lighter." Lola let us do whatever we wanted. It came at a cost, though. We had to watch her soaps, like *All My Children* and *Days of Our Lives,* all day long. I hated it.

ALEXANDRA: Lola Pacing seems like a badass.

ALVIN: She was legit dope. She was the matriarch of the family. No one messed with her. Thirty years later, our family is so different. No one stepped up and became the leader after she passed. So now, we're not as close as a family. My kids will never be as close as me and my cousins were growing up, because we don't have a matriarch like that in our family anymore. Luckily, I still have a really close-knit group of cousins. Money, power, popularity, none of that ever hindered their love for me. We're still really tight. I still have that unique Filipino family unit; it's just not as big as it used it be.

Cheeseburger Lumpia

MAKES 24 LUMPIA

I was eight or nine and I asked my Lola, "Can we put cheese in the lumpia?" She let me. Lola was cool like that. As long as we weren't causing trouble, she was happy with us. It was so legit, and it worked. It was the first time I did something creative in the kitchen, and I was so proud of it. I would eat all my cheeseburger lumpia with ketchup, or ketchup-and-mayo sauce. It was special, because it was the only time I ate ketchup with lumpia.

Today, a lot of people talk shit on this dish. The critics say, "It's very on the nose, it's too easy, it's not complex." But my American friends say, "Yo, this is funny. I like it. It's relatable." This dish is about being a kid and learning how to be creative. If there's a kid later on who reads this recipe and tries it, and if it ignites a little spark of motivation and creativity, mission accomplished. That's what this recipe was for me: thinking outside the box.

---

2 tablespoons canola oil, plus more for frying

2 large yellow onions, diced

½ teaspoon kosher salt, plus more to taste

1 (1-pound) package Menlo lumpia wrappers, thawed if frozen

20 slices American cheese

2 pounds 80% lean ground beef

Freshly ground black pepper

1 large egg beaten with 1 tablespoon water

Sweet Chile Sauce (page 156) or Japan West's Ketchup and Mayo Sauce (page 63), for serving

Heat a medium frying pan over medium-high heat until hot. Add your 2 tablespoons oil and heat until you see it ripple, about 1 minute. Add the onions and salt and cook, stirring, until translucent, about 3 minutes. Cut the heat to medium-low and cook, stirring occasionally, until caramelized, about 20 minutes. Season with more salt, if necessary. Transfer to a bowl and let cool.

Meanwhile, pull apart the lumpia wrappers so they're not stuck together. This is easier if your wrappers are still cold, but not frozen. Stack your cheese slices into 4 even piles, then cut each stack into 6 logs.

In a large stockpot or Dutch oven, heat 4 inches of oil over high heat to 350°F.

Meanwhile, place 1 lumpia wrapper in front of you so it's diamond shaped. On the bottom half of the wrapper, spread some of the ground beef into a 1 x 5-inch rectangle. Season the beef with salt and pepper. Spread 1 teaspoon of the caramelized onions on top of the beef rectangle, then top that with 1 cheese log.

Fold up the bottom point of the wrapper toward the center of the wrapper, covering the filling tightly. Using a pastry brush, dab some of the beaten egg mixture on the left and right corners, then fold

those corners over toward the center. Tightly roll the lumpia upward until it's completely folded, then dab the last corner with beaten egg to seal it.

Repeat with the remaining wrappers and fillings. Working in batches, fry the lumpia, flipping as necessary, until crispy, golden brown, and delicious, 7 to 10 minutes. Drain on paper towels. Plate and serve while hot, alongside sweet chile sauce or ketchup-and-mayo sauce.

Egg Whites on Brick Toast

MAKES 4 TOASTS

Growing up, I was infatuated with egg whites, Wonder Bread, and mayonnaise. I'd eat it just like a personal pizza, as an after-school snack. Even now, whenever I have leftover egg whites, I make this dish to feel nostalgic, although these days I cut the mayo with some Dijon mustard to give it a sharper bite.

2 teaspoons unsalted butter, softened

1 loaf pain de mie or other square white bread, cut into 4 (1½-inch-thick) slices

1 teaspoon canola oil

1 cup egg whites (from about 12 large eggs; reserve the yolks to make Hollandaise Sauce, page 205)

¼ teaspoon kosher salt

4 teaspoons Grandma Emma's Dijonnaise (page 67)

Heat a large cast-iron frying pan over low heat for 5 minutes. Meanwhile, butter both sides of each slice of bread. Increase the heat to medium-low and heat the pan for 30 seconds. Add your buttered bread in a single layer—work in batches if necessary—and toast until golden brown, about 2 minutes on each side. Transfer the toast to a plate and set aside.

In a medium nonstick frying pan, heat the oil over medium heat until you see the oil ripple, about 1 minute. Add the egg whites to the pan and season with the salt. Turn up the heat to medium-high and cook until set, about 2 minutes. Flip your egg white omelet and cook to set the other side, about 2 minutes. Remove from the heat and cut into 4 wedges.

Smear each slice of toast with 1 teaspoon Dijonnaise and top with 1 omelet wedge. Plate and serve immediately.

Tilapia Fish Sticks

When I was a kid, we pretty much always had a freezer full of fish sticks from Costco, but sometimes my parents would forget to re-up accordingly. When we ran out, I had to learn how to make my own. I remember watching how to make deep-fried catfish on the Food Network. I'd have my dad cut me tilapia fillets, and I would slice those into sticks. I would dip them in Progresso Italian bread crumbs and fry them up.

I served my fish sticks with tartar sauce. When I learned that tartar sauce was just mayonnaise, lemon juice, and relish, I started to make that from scratch, too.

---

2 cups all-purpose flour

2 large eggs

1 (12-ounce) can plain seltzer

4 cups panko bread crumbs

Canola oil, for frying

1 pound skinless tilapia fillets, cut into 1-inch-wide strips

1 teaspoon kosher salt

Tartar Sauce (recipe follows), for serving

In a medium bowl, combine 1 cup of the flour, the eggs, and seltzer. Whisk together until fully incorporated. Set the batter aside.

Put the remaining 1 cup flour in a medium bowl. Put the bread crumbs in a large bowl. Set the bowls aside.

Heat 4 inches of oil in a large, heavy-bottomed pot or deep-fryer over high heat to 350°F. Then cut the heat to low.

Meanwhile, set a wire rack over a rimmed baking sheet and set aside. Place a silicone mat on another rimmed baking sheet and set aside. Working in batches, dredge your fish strips in the flour, tapping off any excess. Dip them in the batter, letting any excess drip back into the bowl. Then dredge them in the bread crumbs. Transfer to the silicone mat, making sure the fish strips don't overlap.

Fry 4 to 6 fish strips at a time, flipping as necessary, until golden brown, 3 to 5 minutes. Make sure to check the temperature of the oil as you fry and adjust the heat as necessary to hit 350°F.

Pull the fish sticks out of the oil and transfer to the wire rack. Season immediately with the salt, plate, and serve right away with tartar sauce.

(recipe continues)

Tartar Sauce

MAKES 1¼ CUPS

1 cup Bring Out the Best Mayo
(page 59)

1 tablespoon sweet relish

1 tablespoon minced onion

2 tablespoons fresh lemon juice

¼ teaspoon celery salt

Kosher salt and freshly ground
black pepper

In a medium bowl, whisk together the mayo, relish, onion, lemon juice, and celery salt for 1 minute, or until fully incorporated. Season with salt and pepper. Serve right away or refrigerate in an airtight container for up to 1 week.

Bobby Flay Showed Me a Cool Quesadilla

Back in the day, Bobby Flay was on this show called *Grillin' & Chillin'*. It was my favorite show ever. One day, Bobby made this crazy quesadilla. He got a flour tortilla, brushed it with oil, and seasoned it with chipotle powder. Then, he fried the tortilla and put cheese on it. Then, he put another tortilla on it and fried that. He basically made a grilled cheese quesadilla, and it looked amazing.

That dish exposed me to a new technique. Bobby got me into a different way of thinking—not just how do you usually make a quesadilla, but how can you remake a quesadilla? That recipe was bomb then, and it's bomb now. Thanks, Bobby Flay, for showing me the way!

---

2 (8-inch) flour tortillas

2 teaspoons extra-virgin olive oil

2 small pinches smoked paprika

¼ cup shredded cheddar cheese

¼ cup shredded Monterey Jack cheese

Cholula or other hot sauce, for serving

Heat a large nonstick frying pan over high heat until hot. Cut the heat to medium.

Meanwhile, brush one side of your first tortilla with 1 teaspoon of the oil. Sprinkle a pinch of smoked paprika over the oil.

Place the tortilla oil-side down in the pan and cook until lightly toasted, about 30 seconds. Sprinkle both cheeses on top of the tortilla and cook until the cheese starts to melt, about 30 seconds.

Cover the cheesy tortilla with your second tortilla. Brush the top of that tortilla with the remaining 1 teaspoon oil and sprinkle on a pinch of smoked paprika. Flip the whole thing and cook until lightly toasted, about 1 minute.

Cut the heat to low and flip the quesadilla again. Cook until the inside is melty goodness. Plate the quesadilla and serve immediately with your favorite hot sauce.

Chicken Patty Sandwiches

MAKES 4 SANDWICHES

This is my classic chicken patty sandwich. My whole life, I've always had some type of chicken—wing, nugget, or patty from Costco—in my freezer. Those are old habits you can't break. I'll always have chicken patties in my pantry, till the day I die. My grandfather always had chicken patties in his refrigerator. I'm sure my mom fell in love with a chicken patty sandwich when she lived with him. That's how this recipe started.

Today, I'll make a real chicken sandwich. It's not Nashville-style. It's just fried, crispy—bad for the body, hella good for the soul.

2 cups all-purpose flour

2 large eggs

1 (12-ounce) can plain seltzer

4 cups panko bread crumbs

Canola oil, for frying

4 boneless, skinless chicken thighs (about 1 pound)

1 teaspoon kosher salt

4 tablespoons Japan West's Ketchup and Mayo sauce (page 63)

4 store-bought or homemade Pan de Sal (page 83), split like hamburger buns and toasted

4 slices American cheese

In a medium bowl, combine 1 cup of the flour, the eggs, and seltzer. Whisk together until fully incorporated. Set the batter aside.

Put the remaining 1 cup flour in a medium bowl. Put the bread crumbs in a large bowl. Set the bowls aside.

Heat 4 inches of oil in a large, heavy-bottomed pot or deep-fryer over high heat to 350°F. Then cut the heat to low.

Meanwhile, set a wire rack over a rimmed baking sheet and set aside. Dredge each chicken thigh in the flour, tapping off the excess. Dip in the batter, letting the excess drip back into the bowl. Dredge in the bread crumbs. Transfer the chicken to a plate.

Fry 1 chicken thigh at a time, flipping the chicken every 30 seconds, until golden brown, about 7 minutes. Make sure to check the temperature of the oil as you fry and adjust the heat as necessary to hit 350°F.

Pull your chicken out of the oil and transfer to the wire rack. Season immediately with ¼ teaspoon of the salt. Repeat with the remaining chicken.

Spread the ketchup-and-mayo sauce on the split sides of the toasted pan de sal. Place 1 chicken patty on each of the bottom buns, top with a slice of cheese, close the sandwiches, and serve immediately.

Hot-Silog!
(Hot Dogs with Garlic Fried Rice)

SERVES 2

The US Navy introduced hot dogs to the Philippines, and they've been Amboy ever since. In my house, sometimes we couldn't buy longanisa—our favorite sausage—because it wasn't available at Asian markets. So, we'd use hot dogs, Spam, or canned corn beef instead.

We were a Costco family, so we bought Hebrew Nationals by the 48-pack. My dad would cut hash marks in them so they'd cook faster. The way the hot dog would plump up would really fascinate me. My uncle's husband taught me how to cut hot dogs in cool ways. He would cut them in thirds, then he'd cut those thirds into pieces—then turn the hot dog, cut a slice, turn it, and cut a slice, so it almost looked like it had tentacles. I ate these decorative hot dogs with garlic fried rice and eggs for breakfast. In Filipino food, anything plus garlic fried rice and egg is called a "silog." Enjoy this recipe for hot-silog!

---

4 hot dogs

1 tablespoon salted butter

Garlic Fried Rice (recipe follows), for serving

2 large eggs, cooked sunny-side up, for serving (optional)

Take the hot dogs and cut them in any decorative way you want.

Heat a medium frying pan over medium-high heat until hot. Add your butter and wait for it to melt while swirling it to coat the pan.

Add your hot dogs to the pan and cook, stirring constantly, until heated through, 4 to 6 minutes. If you want a bit more texture, continue to cook, stirring constantly, until crispy, 3 to 5 more minutes.

Divvy up the hot dogs between 2 plates and serve hot with the fried rice. Top each plate with 1 egg, if desired, for classic breakfast vibes.

(recipe continues)

Garlic Fried Rice (Sinangag)

SERVES 4 TO 6

4 cups cold Steamed Jasmine Rice (page 20)

2 tablespoons Datu Puti or Silver Swan soy sauce (see page 60; available at Asian markets and on Amazon)

2 large eggs

2 tablespoons canola oil

8 garlic cloves, minced (see page 110)

Kosher salt and freshly ground black pepper

¼ cup sliced fresh chives (see page 110)

Put the rice in a large mixing bowl. Run the rice through your fingers to separate the grains from one another. You don't want clusters of rice in this dish—it's not a good look. Once you feel the rice is loose and separate, throw in the soy sauce and toss until the rice looks uniformly brown. Set that bowl aside.

Next, beat the eggs in another bowl and set aside. (I like using a Vitamix blender for this step so the eggs don't get runny.)

Heat a straight-sided sauté pan over medium heat until hot. Add all but 1 teaspoon of the oil and swirl to coat the pan evenly. When you see the oil ripple, add the garlic. Cook, stirring, until the garlic begins to brown evenly and the oil is fragrant, 2 to 3 minutes.

Cut the heat to medium-low. Add the rice and cook, stirring, until the rice and garlic are uniformly mixed and the rice is piping hot, 4 to 6 minutes. There shouldn't be any large clumps of garlic. Make sure that the rice is super hot or else the rice will absorb the egg, and it will take forever to cook and your arm will fall off from stirring too much.

Make a well in the center of the rice, exposing the bottom of the pan. Add the remaining 1 teaspoon oil to the well, add the beaten eggs, and stir vigorously with a silicone spatula and begin incorporating them into the rice. Don't wait until all the eggs are cooked in the well—you want the wet eggs to work their way thoroughly into the hot rice. Continue stirring with your spatula until the eggs are cooked and the

(recipe continues)

rice grains are separated from the eggs. At this point, taste the rice and season with salt and pepper to your liking. Cut the heat to low and stir in the chives until everything is harmonious.

Divvy up the fried rice into bowls and serve.

How to Mince Garlic

The garlic here needs to be minced with a knife, not by food processor or purchased preminced. It tastes better this way, so sharpen those knives! Peel each garlic clove, then cut the garlic into thin slices and mince into uniform 1/16-inch morsels. Why so detailed? It's important that the garlic is all the same size so it can cook in the exact same amount of time. This eliminates the risk of overcooking some pieces and making them bitter. When you have perfect, uniform pieces of garlic, set them aside in a small bowl.

How to Slice Chives

Chives are one of my favorite ingredients. They are so awesome, and when they're prepared properly, the pungent aroma of chives can rival that of truffles! It's vital that you have a sharp knife for slicing. In bunches of 12 to 15 chives, slice them into rings—as thin as possible, using the full length of the knife blade. Aim for uniform slices that are 1/16 inch thick. Transfer them to a bowl and set aside.

LOLA

Ten Summers in a Row in the Philippines

WHEN WE VISITED the Philippines, my body was always covered in baby powder. It was preventative, so I didn't smell like sweat, but sweating was inevitable in the extreme humidity. Sweat would run down my back like a waterfall in a TLC music video.

On visits, we'd spend a lot of time at church. My grandma lived at church. I would hide behind the big statue of Mary so she couldn't find me.

Because I was the son of the great Antonio Cailan, no one much minded. All my other cousins from the Philippines would put me first. They gave me everything I wanted.

This has much to do with my grandfather Jose Vales, who, before he died, was a captain for a successful cargo company; he'd made a small fortune shipping containers all over the world. So in the Philippines, my mother's family was ballin'. They left Cavite in the late '60s and moved into the tract-home community, the suburbs of Manila in Parañaque. Like Pico Rivera, it was a gated community full of sketchy, middle-class people. They had maids, so I got to eat all kinds of home-cooked delicacies. Every day, I would wake up to a breakfast spread. I remember stuffing my face with fresh-cooked longanisa and adobo.

If I wasn't in Manila, I was shipped to my aunt's house in Naic, Cavite, about an hour away. Her home was in a subdivision in the middle of nowhere. She was a widow and stayed with my cousins Apple and Dimple. Their house was next to a bar. I remember being nine years old and falling asleep on their front porch, and when I woke up the next day, I looked over to the bar, and there was a couple having sex by the trees. I remember pointing at them and laughing. I loved Cavite. All kinds of crazy things happened there.

Staying with my dad's family in Naic was awesome, too. We ate lots of suman (sticky rice sweets) and drank lots of soda. We would stay up late, watch Filipino movies, and walk around town like we owned the place.

Do you know who my father is? I can't even say that without feeling like a douchebag. But in Naic, that's how I felt. I was a somebody because my dad was a somebody. In Cavite, my dad was called Brother Tony Cailan. He used to be the leader of the Lips to Lips gang, the group of playboys that would protect the streets of Naic. When he left for America, he never forgot where he came from. In the span of 20 years, my dad was a housekeeper turned locksmith turned successful general contractor. It made him like the Jeff Bezos of his province. He made a ton of money and funneled it all to Naic. In his childhood home, he turned a shack into a massive townhome, towering over its neighbors. He funded a new Catholic church, as well as an elementary school in the neighborhood. In Naic, Tony Cailan is the man!

So it's only natural that his sons were treated like royalty. I remember sitting in the living room of a relative, and families would come over just to introduce me to their daughters. It was like, WTF, dude, I'm nine years old!

As I got older and my love for hip-hop grew, I started to feel weird going to Cavite. I'd hang out in my uncle's car for hours, blasting hip-hop through the speakers. My aunt would fight with my uncle because she thought I was going to steal the car and drive it through town. That fear was straight out of an American movie: ridiculously spoiled, entitled kid runs off with the car for a joyride through the streets. It was crazy. I would never do that, because I was scared of my dad. There was no way I would defy him, especially in his kingdom in Cavite.

By then I wasn't a prince, I was a liability. There were still 15 cousins protecting me at all times, but it wasn't fun anymore. I didn't want to play outside. I'd rather listen to Wu-Tang Clan and draw in my notebook. I missed my friends in Pico Rivera. I missed the block in East LA.

My attitude got me sent back to my mom's side of the family, and then I stopped going back to the Philippines altogether.

I'd gone from good boy to Amboy.

Cavite Heat

ALEXANDRA: When was the first time you went home to the Philippines?

ALVIN: I was three years old. It was summer in Cavite: hot, humid, and super rainy. My great-grandmother Lola Pacing had to go back every year to visit her kids and grandkids. So every time she went home, I went with her. I spent my summer breaks in Cavite every year for ten years. Lola's 13 kids meant tons of cousins, so I was always surrounded by this overprotective family. Every time I'd need a ride, my uncle would pick me up in his tricycle. Every time I'd go to the bathroom, 15 people would go with me. So, in the bathroom, I'd be trying to pee, and all my cousins would be peeing, too. It was hella awkward.

ALEXANDRA: When was the last time you went home?

ALVIN: The last time I went back, I was 14 and fresh off the basketball team in high school. I had hit my growth spurt, so I was already 5 feet 8. I was playing basketball in the Cavite neighborhood spot, and because I was the tallest one of my age group, I just dominated. After the game, I was exhausted and sitting on the bench. Out of nowhere, a slipper flew through the air and hit me across the face. Like, someone threw a slipper at me? WTF? Then, my cousins stood up in formation. They chased down the kid, found him, and beat him up. No questions asked.

ALEXANDRA: That's intense. What else do you remember about your family in the Philippines?

ALVIN: I would wake up every morning to a breakfast spread made by my family's maids. When I was ten, I would hop on a tricycle with my cousin and head to the palengke. We'd run through the market, getting fresh pan de sal and hot chocolate. Then we'd take it home, wait for my dad to wake up, and all eat pan de sal together.

Amboy Burger

When my parents were in church in Cavite, my favorite place to sneak off to was a joint called Elvie's. Elvie's made these amazing hamburgers with pan de sal and this weird tartar-mayonnaise sauce, and it was heaven. Today, Elvie's burger is the inspiration for the Amboy burger.

A lot of chefs feel like burgers are low-brow or low-hanging fruit and they don't want them on their menus. But I don't give a fuck about that. If a burger exposes people to Filipino flavors, then I think it's great.

Plus, I'm in love with lumpia Shanghai meat. Typically, lumpia meat is beef or pork with shrimp. This burger takes lumpia meat and adds onion and fish sauce instead. It's more of a stuffed burger than anything.

Another key element of the Elvie's burger: Kraft pasteurized cheddar. It's basically the cheese of the Philippines. You could argue that queso de bola (Edam cheese) is more well-known, but that's mostly for rich people. Kraft pasteurized cheddar is the cheese of the people; it's similar in concept to American cheese. Growing up, I had it at every breakfast in the Philippines, and it tasted great. If it comes in a block in a cardboard box, is it any less good? Nah! In the Philippines, raising cows is less common. Often, we have powdered milk. So processed cheese makes sense.

In this recipe, you can sub in queso de bola for pasteurized Kraft cheddar, but OG Kraft will always have my heart.

2⅔ pounds 75% lean ground beef

1 tablespoon Rufina patis (Filipino fish sauce; available at Asian markets and on Amazon)

Kosher salt and freshly ground black pepper

6 teaspoons canola oil

6 store-bought or homemade Pan de Sal (page 83), split like hamburger buns

1 small white onion, cut into 6 (¼-inch-thick) rings

Preheat the oven to 375°F.

In a large bowl, mix your ground beef with the fish sauce. Divide the beef into 6 patties. Season with salt and pepper and let stand for 30 minutes, or until they come to room temperature. (If you start off with a cold patty, the exterior will get cooked while the center remains raw and mushy, and we don't want that.)

Heat a medium frying pan over high heat until hot. Add 2 teaspoons of the oil and heat until it sizzles. Cook 2 patties until a nice crust forms, about 2 minutes on each side. Transfer to a rimmed baking sheet. Repeat with the remaining oil and patties. Let the patties rest for 5 minutes.

3 ounces queso de bola
(Edam cheese), rind
discarded and cheese cut into
6 (⅛-inch-thick) slices

6 teaspoons Japan West's
Ketchup and Mayo Sauce
(page 63)

1 ripe tomato, cut into 6 slices
(in season only)

Meanwhile, place your pan de sal, cut sides down, on another rimmed baking sheet. Pop them in the oven and toast until light golden brown, 3 to 4 minutes. Remove from the oven and set aside.

Top each patty with 1 onion slice and 1 cheese slice. Heat the patties in the oven until the cheese is melted, about 2 minutes. Remove from the oven.

Spread ½ teaspoon of the sauce on the cut sides of the buns. Fill each bun with 1 patty. When it's tomato season, please make sure to add a juicy-ripe slice of tomato. Plate the burgers and serve.

Jamonado (Pineapple Pork Loin)

SERVES 4

I had my first jamonado in the Philippines. It's a dish my grandmother's cooks would make, and it was fantastic. Their recipe is a riff on the American ham topped with pineapples and cherries. As a kid with an American palate, it was so relatable. Jamonado is doused in pineapple sauce, with diced pineapples scattered over the top. Sweet, savory, and totally fantastic. With rice and eggs? Double fantastic. Inside pan de sal? I mean, come on. Yes!

The glaze—then and now—is basically pineapple, soy, onions, and brown sugar. It's so simple. We use it on everything from jamonado to embutido. It's perfect for all things pork!

4 cups water

2 cups loosely packed dark brown sugar

½ cup kosher salt

1 (2-pound) boneless pork loin

16 bacon slices

2 cups Pineapple Glaze (recipe follows)

Steamed Jasmine Rice (page 20), Lola's Pancit Bihon (page 93), or Danilo's Pancit Canton (page 177), for serving

In a large saucepan, stir together the water, brown sugar, and salt and bring to a boil over medium-high heat. Remove from the heat and let the brine cool to room temperature, then refrigerate in an airtight container until well chilled.

Pour the brine into a large bowl or airtight plastic container and add the pork loin. Cover and refrigerate for at least 4 hours or preferably up to 8 hours. Remove the pork loin and pat dry with paper towels.

Preheat the oven to 375°F.

Line a rimmed baking sheet with parchment paper. Shingle the bacon over the parchment, with each slice slightly overlapping the last, to form a bacon blanket large enough to wrap around the pork loin.

Place the pork loin horizontally along one long edge of the bacon blanket. Using the parchment paper, roll the bacon blanket tightly around the pork loin. Carefully peel away the parchment so the blanket stays intact. Return the parchment to the baking sheet.

Place the bacon-wrapped loin seam-side down on the baking sheet and bake for 5 minutes. Using a pastry brush, brush pineapple glaze over the entire surface of the jamonado. Continue to bake, brushing the glaze on every 5 minutes, until the internal temperature of the pork loin hits 130°F, about 45 minutes total.

Let the jamonado rest on a cutting board until it coasts to medium-well in temperature, 140°F to 145°F, 8 to 15 minutes.

Slice the jamonado thinly, plate, and enjoy alongside rice or pancit.

Pineapple Glaze

MAKES ABOUT 2 QUARTS

4 cups canned pineapple juice

2 cups diced pineapple

3 large sweet onions, diced

⅔ cup Datu Puti or Silver Swan soy sauce (see page 60; available at Asian markets and on Amazon)

½ cup loosely packed dark brown sugar

3 tablespoons toasted sesame oil

Kosher salt

In a large saucepan, combine the pineapple juice, pineapple, onion, soy sauce, and brown sugar. Bring to a boil over medium-high heat, stirring occasionally, about 12 minutes.

Cut the heat to a simmer and cook, stirring occasionally, until the onions are soft, 20 to 25 minutes.

Transfer the mixture to a blender and blend until smooth. Add the sesame oil and blend until completely incorporated.

Taste the glaze and season with salt if necessary. Use right away or refrigerate in an airtight container for up to 1 week.

Dilis (Fried Anchovies)

MAKES 2 QUARTS, ENOUGH TO SERVE 20 AS A SNACK

These crispy anchovies are my favorite snack. I can remember eating dilis as a kid, running up and down in my diapers and having dilis on my fingertips. In elementary school, I started to get grossed out by them. My American friends would make fun of me, saying, "You're eating small tiny fish? Ewww!" That was a dark time when I stopped liking dilis. My parents would eat Champorado (page 47) with dilis, but I started eating mine with Cool Ranch Doritos.

As I got older, my friend group got more diverse. My Korean and Chinese friends all ate dried anchovies, so I started eating them again. When I started drinking, dilis became a drinking snack. Now, it's just a part of my cuisine. I think of it as our Parmigiano-Reggiano: It's the salt we top our food with. It's a classic.

Canola oil, for frying

1 pound dried anchovies (available at Asian markets)

¼ cup sugar

Heat 4 inches of oil in a medium Dutch oven or heavy-bottomed pot over medium-high heat to 375°F. Line a rimmed baking sheet with paper towels and set aside.

Working in 3 batches, add the dried anchovies to the oil and deep-fry, stirring occasionally, until crispy, evenly cooked, and golden brown, about 2 minutes per batch. Using a spider or slotted spoon, transfer the anchovies to the paper towels and sprinkle with sugar while the anchovies are still hot.

Let the dilis cool, then serve as a snack or as a garnish for your Lugaw (page 34).

Beet-Cured Hard-Cooked Eggs

SERVES 12

Salted duck eggs are a huge thing in the Philippines. When I was a kid, I remember my dad selling salted duck eggs, balut (duck embryo), and five-for-$10 T-shirts to the local Filipino community. To this day, I credit my entrepreneurial spirit to my dad.

At home, we always had salted duck eggs, tomatoes, and patis, mixed like a relish. In the Philippines, if you're poor, that's what you eat with rice. It's an everyday food. When I realized that I wanted to open a Filipino restaurant, that was a must for my menu.

In the Philippines, eggs are colored differently to distinguish what kind they are. When you go to the palengke, there are quail eggs, chicken eggs, balut, duck eggs, and salted duck eggs. The cured salted duck eggs are red. I wanted to mimic that color, plus the flavoring in the salt. My hands were red for a week trying to figure out how to do it. Last year, I finally realized a quick cure in a beet solution created that red look on the inside of the egg, not on the shell. Every day in the restaurant, we cook fresh eggs and cure them right before service.

This recipe has an earthy saltiness to it. The egg whites are springy and chewy, and the yolks are perfectly cooked, with no gray. It's visually appealing, so you want to dive in and eat. It's perfect with any rice dish or a cucumber-tomato salad.

---

3 large beets, peeled

1 cup kosher salt

12 Hard-Cooked Eggs, peeled (recipe follows)

Fill a medium stockpot with water and bring to a boil over medium-high heat. Add the beets and let simmer until fork-tender, about 45 minutes.

Meanwhile, set a wire rack over a rimmed baking sheet. When the beets are cooked, pull them out and let them drain and cool to room temperature on the wire rack. Reserve 1 cup of the beet cooking liquid.

Quarter the beets, transfer them to a blender, and blend until smooth. If necessary, add ¼ cup of the reserved cooking liquid at a time to help blend. Pour the beet puree into a large bowl and stir in the salt. Submerge the eggs in the beet puree and let them marinate at room temperature until all the egg whites are dyed dark purple, about 45 minutes.

Rinse the marinade off the eggs, cut them in half, and serve right away or refrigerate whole in an airtight container for up to 3 days.

(recipe continues)

Hard-Cooked Eggs

MAKES 12 EGGS

12 large eggs

Fill a large stockpot with water and bring to a boil over medium-high heat. When the water is at a rolling boil, add the eggs and let them boil for 7 minutes. Remove the pot from the heat, cover, and let stand for 10 minutes.

Meanwhile, fill a large bowl with ice and water. Pull the eggs out of the pot and dunk them in the ice bath for 15 minutes to stop the cooking. Run the eggs under cold water, peel, and I promise, you will have perfect hard-cooked eggs every time.

Mechado (Spanish-Style Beef Stew)

This dish comes from Spain, but it's also uniquely Cavite. As Caviteños, we're very proud of our mechado, because Cavite was the main port during the Spanish occupation of the Philippines. Honestly, I think we're the only people in the Philippines who take mechado that seriously. It's similar to Batangas, which takes goto seriously, because that's where it's from. Or it's like Malabon, where they take pancit seriously, because that's where pancit Malabon is from. Cavite's mechado has crazy umami. Roasted bell peppers, tomatoes, and potatoes are very prevalent in the dish, but there's also a deeper complexity to the stew.

Growing up, everyone had their secret to making mechado. My dad used pickled relish, and I loved that. It added a sweetness and sourness to the dish. My Auntie Cita added pasteurized cheddar to thicken the sauce. It's similar to how Italians put Parmesan rinds in stews. You can't quite put your finger on the flavor, but you just know it when you taste it. That's what's dope about being a chef and making your own cuisine. That nuance is a game-changer.

When I was younger, I used pot roast for this recipe. It was great, until I realized it was just a piece of chuck. When I moved to Portland, I had this boeuf bourguignon at Le Pigeon. That dish used beef cheeks, and it was so good. But then I realized a cow has only two beef cheeks. Maybe if you're trying to be fancy and serve mechado to two people, you'll be okay. But for a big Filipino family, it just isn't going to work.

At the end of the day, I felt like boneless short rib was the best way to go. It's so tender and comforting to eat. It has a great balance and richness of beef flavor and beef fat. I don't think I would use any other kind of beef because of how important the dish is for my people. If mechado is our thing, we might as well go all out!

---

3 tablespoons canola oil

2 pounds boneless beef short ribs, cut into 2-inch cubes

1 large onion, diced

6 garlic cloves, chopped

1 quart Homemade Beef Stock (page 45), plus more as necessary

1½ cups canned whole peeled tomatoes, with their juices

Set a wire rack over a rimmed baking sheet and set aside.

Heat a large Dutch oven or heavy-bottomed pot over medium-high heat until hot. Add the oil and heat until you see the oil ripple, about 1 minute.

Working in batches to avoid crowding the pot, add the short ribs and sear until caramelized all over, about 2 minutes on each side. Transfer to the wire rack. Reserve all the fat in the pot.

¼ cup Datu Puti or Silver Swan soy sauce (see page 60; available at Asian markets and on Amazon)

1 bay leaf

Grated zest and juice of ½ lemon

1 large russet potato, peeled and diced

Kosher salt and freshly ground black pepper

Steamed Jasmine Rice (page 20) or Pan de Sal (page 83), for serving

Cut the heat to medium-low and add the onion and garlic. Cook, stirring, until the onion is translucent, 5 to 7 minutes. Turn up the heat to medium-high and add the beef stock, scraping up all the browned bits from the bottom of the pot.

Add the tomatoes and their juices and break up the tomatoes with a wooden spoon. Add the soy sauce, bay leaf, and lemon zest. Return the short ribs to the pot and make sure they're submerged in the liquid. Add more stock, if necessary, to cover the beef.

Bring to a boil, then cut the heat to low, cover, and let the beef braise, stirring occasionally, until fork-tender, about 3 hours.

Add the potato to the pot, turn the heat up to medium, and cook, stirring occasionally, until the potato is tender, about 45 minutes. Skim off any fat with a mesh strainer during this time. Remove and discard the bay leaf. Season the mechado with lemon juice, salt, and pepper.

Ladle the mechado over bowls of rice or make sandwiches with pan de sal.

Putahe (Spanish-Style Chicken Stew)

SERVES 4 TO 6

My first experience with putahe, or chicken afritada, was in my family's hometown, Cavite. It's a town that takes food seriously, though it's not given that credit anymore. Today, it's the Pampanga region that gets all the culinary attention.

Let me explain: Pampanga was where the US settled during World War II, so many consider it the Emilia-Romagna of the Philippines purely because of that. It's true that Pampanga is known for sisig, because of the creative way the region uses pork face. It is very innovative and makes a truly Filipino dish post-Spanish colonialism.

On the other hand, long before there was American influence, there was Spanish, and the Spanish landed in Cavite. If you read a provincial Spanish cookbook, you'll find many parallels to pre-American Filipino recipes. Cavite stews lean very Basque Spanish. So do dishes like mechado or putahe, which are taken very seriously in our part of the Philippines. They're standards at any Filipino party in Cavite.

Putahe is a cacciatore-like chicken stew made with tomatoes, bell peppers, and potatoes. The richness of the sauce makes yours lips stick together. Some people use olives in putahe, but I don't. To me, the shot of saltiness and brininess is unnecessary. It adds to the stereotype that "Filipino food is just so salty," and it's a cleaner, more delicious dish without olives.

---

2 pounds bone-in, skin-on chicken pieces

Kosher salt

¼ cup canola oil

1 large onion, diced

4 garlic cloves, chopped

1½ cups canned whole peeled tomatoes, with their juices

2 red bell peppers, roasted (see sidebar), seeded, and chopped

½ cup Datu Puti or Silver Swan soy sauce (see page 60; available at Asian markets and on Amazon)

4 cups Homemade Chicken Stock (page 44)

Arrange the chicken pieces on a platter, season with salt, and let come to room temp, about 45 minutes.

Place a wire rack over a rimmed baking sheet and set aside. Heat a large Dutch oven over high heat until hot. Add the oil and heat until you see the oil ripple, about 30 seconds.

Cut the heat to medium and, working in batches, add the chicken, skin-side down, in a single layer. Sear until browned all over, about 2 minutes on each side. Transfer to the wire rack. Reserve all the fat in the pot.

Add the onion and garlic to the Dutch oven and cook, stirring, until the onion is soft and translucent, 5 to 7 minutes. Add the tomatoes and their juices and break up the tomatoes with a wooden spoon. Add the roasted bell peppers, soy sauce, chicken stock, and bay leaf, scraping up all the browned bits from the bottom of the pot. Return

1 bay leaf

2 cups frozen peas

2 large russet potatoes, peeled
and cut into 1-inch cubes

Freshly ground black pepper

Steamed Jasmine Rice
(page 20), for serving

the chicken to the pot and simmer over low heat for 30 minutes, stirring and skimming off the fat occasionally. Add the frozen peas and potatoes and simmer, stirring occasionally, until the potatoes are tender, 15 to 20 minutes. Remove and discard the bay leaf.

Give the stew a taste and season with salt and pepper. Ladle the putahe over bowls of rice and enjoy.

How to Roast Bell Peppers

Preheat your backyard grill to 400°F. If you're not using an internal thermometer, just let the grill heat for 30 minutes.

Grill your whole red bell peppers until the skins are blistered and charred, about 10 minutes on each side. There are four sides to the bell pepper, so it should take about 40 minutes. Don't worry about overcooking, because the shape of a bell pepper is odd—the main goal is to char the skin.

(Alternatively, place each bell pepper directly over a medium flame on a gas burner. Let the peppers char on one side. Using metal tongs, turn the peppers and let char. Repeat until the peppers are charred and blackened all over.)

Pull your peppers off the heat and put them in a large stainless steel bowl. Cover the bowl with plastic wrap and let them steam for 20 minutes.

Using latex gloves, scrape off the char and peel your peppers, removing all the black soot and exposing the ruby-red flesh.

Lechon (Roast Pork)

To me, lechon is one of the top five Filipino foods of all time. It's a staple. You go to a party, and there's the pig's head with the apple in its mouth. It's one of the first things you remember as a kid that's so truly Filipino.

I love the crispy pork skin. You know a good lechon as soon as you crack into the skin. The sound of the knife hitting the skin is so fucking epic. It sounds like you're breaking thin glass. You hear that, and you just know it's going to be good. Then, there's lechon that falls flat. The knife goes straight in, no noise, nothing. You know it's going to be bad. Bad lechon is bland and dry and you need to put hella sauce on it to make it taste like anything.

I like when the lechon skin is stiff. It feels like the chef predried the carcass before roasting it. I also love when the lechon is slow-roasted. The pork fat melts into the meat, so when you eat it, it almost has its own sauce. Growing up, it was the best when my cousins made lechon. They would talk shit all day to each other. I remember my aunt yelling at them to pay attention, to make sure they didn't burn one side of the pig.

In my family and a lot of families, lechon symbolizes success. It means we have enough money to have a lechon. It's a financial flex. My aunt and my cousins raised pigs in the Philippines because lechon was that important to my family. The downside is that showing off one's success doesn't always translate to showing off one's cooking skill. Sometimes all lechon is doing is symbolizing, just being there, showing off, and that fucks it up, because no one is really thinking about how it tastes.

There's an art to making lechon: It's the whole-hog barbecue obsession in America applied Filipino-style. This is why I love being Amboy. But be warned: This recipe is for real lechon lovers only. You're looking at seven days of sweating it. Don't attempt this if you don't have the space or time to construct a big firepit in your backyard. You can't half-ass this one. But, if you make this and commit 100 percent, you'll never regret it. And guaranteed, you'll be the biggest badass of all time.

NOTE:

For the build, you can get all the materials at any major hardware store, like Home Depot or Lowe's. Or check Craigslist or any Mexican grocery store for a great deal.

(recipe continues)

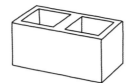

BUILD

Several large buckets

4 (50-pound) bags cement, preferably fine-ground Quikrete cement

70 to 75 hollow block bricks

1 trowel

BRINE

6 gallons cold water

6 cups kosher salt

6 cups dark brown sugar

3 cups fresh calamansi juice (see Note, page 68)

1 (30- to 50-pound) whole pig, gutted and cleaned (reserve the innards for another use, such as Goto, page 41, or Lechon Sauce, page 158)

PREP

3 cups kosher salt

1 cup freshly ground black pepper

1½ pounds lemongrass stalks, left whole

1 pound garlic cloves, peeled

2 pounds onions, halved

1 pound bay leaves

2 pounds lemons, halved

3½ feet butcher twine

1 butcher needle

ROAST

Spit with claws

3 charcoal chimney lighters

4 (50-pound) bags hickory charcoal lump coal

3 pounds scrap paper

1 stick lighter

15 mesquite wood logs

1 (5-foot) fireproof rake

8 quarts coconut water (such as Vita Coco, or Harmless Harvest if you're a baller)

2 quarts liquid aminos (preferably Bragg, available at Whole Foods or on Amazon)

1 large barbecue basting brush

30 banana leaves

Several cups Sarsa (page 136), for serving

DAY 1: BUILD

The good news is, you'll only have to build this once. Map out a 5 x 5-foot space in your backyard. Start with fairly flat ground, manually flattened if necessary. Make sure it's not surrounded by anything flammable—trees, your house, etc.

Using large buckets, follow the package instructions and mix your cement with water. Start off building your back wall—5 hollow blocks long and 5 hollow blocks high. Place each block, then use the trowel to spread cement evenly on it. Use a standard level at each step of the way to check the horizontal and vertical straightness. Place the next block on top, staggering the arrangement for more stability, then press down. Repeat until finished.

Then, build your first layer of the long wall. Line up your first block, perpendicular with the inside edge of your back wall. Then, right on top of that layer, build another layer 4 hollow blocks across, then another layer 3 hollow blocks across, then 2. Repeat this for the second long wall.

Then, let the whole thing sit for 7 days. The concrete will harden, and you will have a firepit that you can use for anything!

DAYS 2–3: BRINE

Combine the water, salt, brown sugar, and calamansi juice in a large stockpot and bring to a rolling boil over high heat. Remove the pot from the heat. Let the brine cool to room temperature, then refrigerate overnight.

Rinse your pig inside and out with cold water. Then, place it in a large cooler or a food-safe rubber trash can. Pour the cold brine over the pig and cover. Chill in a walk-in refrigerator for 2 full days.

(recipe continues)

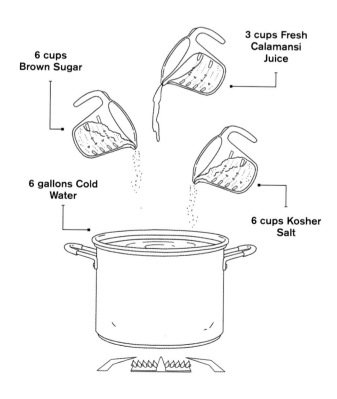

6 cups Brown Sugar

3 cups Fresh Calamansi Juice

6 gallons Cold Water

6 cups Kosher Salt

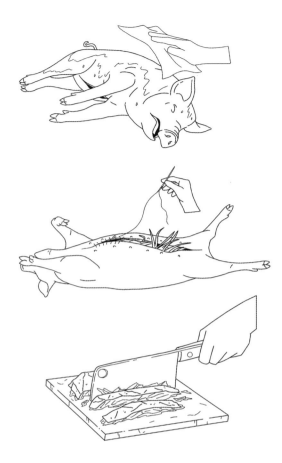

DAYS 4–6: PREP

Take your pig out of the brine, and pat dry—inside and out—with paper towels. The drier the pig, the crispier the skin, so go over it a few times till it's 100 percent dry. Discard the brine.

Then, liberally season the pig—inside and out—with the salt and pepper. It might look like a lot of salt, but remember, you have to cover and penetrate the entire flesh of the animal.

Stuff the cavity with the lemongrass, garlic cloves, onions, bay leaves, and lemons. Make sure all the ingredients are evenly distributed so the flavors are balanced when you roast the pig on the spit—no one section will taste more like one flavor than the other.

Sew up the cavity with butcher twine and a butcher needle, puncturing the flesh every ½ inch (see diagram).

Tuck the hind legs underneath the pig so they're touching its stomach. Wrap twine around the ankles three or four times to secure the legs. Repeat with the front legs.

Place the whole pig on a cooling rack set atop an unlined baking sheet. Your baking sheet will catch any drips from the roasting pig.

Refrigerate for 3 days, pulling the pig out every day and using paper towels to wipe off any excess moisture from the skin. Essentially, you're dry-aging the pork.

DAY 7: ROAST

Now, it's time to roast! Insert the pointy end of the spit through the mouth of the pig, piercing through the body of the pig and coming out the rear end. Take the two claws and clamp them to the pig to hold it in place. If your clamps aren't big enough, use a food-grade steel wire to securely fasten the pig onto the spit so it doesn't flop over as it spins. A lot of people, when they first do a pig, miss this step—you have to make sure the pig is secure on the spit, or else it won't roast evenly. It's better to test this 100 times before you even approach the flame.

Bring the pig to room temperature and cover it with cardboard or plastic wrap to protect it from the elements.

Meanwhile, build your fire. Fill each charcoal lighter with your hickory charcoal. Crumple up your scrap paper. Stuff the paper beneath the grate on your lighters. Using your stick lighter, carefully light the paper. The paper will catch fire and light the charcoal gradually. You'll see a huge buildup of visible fire, but don't touch it, as it's not ready yet. The charcoal will be ready when the fire has burned off and the charcoal is a glowing amber color.

Once your charcoal is ready, pour the hot charcoal into the back of the firepit. On top of the hot coal, throw 2 or 4 mesquite wood logs. That's more for flavor than for heat. Let that catch on fire, fully engulf, and then burn down. This will create a mass of embers—now, it's ready to go.

Put both ends of the spit on the part of the wall that's 4 hollow blocks high. Cook for about 1½ hours, rotating the pig every 10 minutes to make sure the skin doesn't burn. While this is happening, keep filling your charcoal lighters and throwing hot coal into the back of the firepit. Check your logs—if they're completely burned out, add another one. And watch your fire—with your fireproof rake, you want to pull your embers forward, beneath the pig. As the fire dies down, you'll be creating a bed of embers beneath the pig, creating even heat for roasting.

After your 1½ hours of roasting on level 4, move the pig down to the part of the wall that's 3 hollow blocks high. Cook the pig for 4 hours, rotating it on the spit every 10 minutes. Make sure that you're replacing the charcoal and checking the wood every 30 minutes. Test the heat by carefully waving your hand over the part of the wall that's 5 hollow blocks high—if you can't stand the heat, then it's perfect.

After 4 hours of roasting, take the internal temperature of the pig. It should be 118°F to 130°F. When it's reached that temperature, move the pig back up to the level 5 part of the wall. From this point on, don't add any more charcoal. The back wall will have absorbed a lot of the heat from the coal and will create an oven.

In a large bowl, mix the coconut water and liquid aminos together. With a large brush, paint the whole skin of the pig till the color is a beautiful golden brown. Repeat every 10 to 15 minutes for 1 hour.

Once the internal temperature of the pig is at 140°F to 155°F, your skin should be somewhat crispy. If it's not to your desired crispiness, heat up more coal and logs and get your fire blistering hot again. Rotate the pig constantly, searing the skin till it's at your desired crispiness. Don't baste while you do this, because you'll burn the skin. Pro tip: As much as you want to put direct heat onto the pig by putting it close to the coals, don't. It's super easy to accidentally burn the skin, and you'll ruin 7 days of hard work. Indirect heat—low and slow—is always the key for perfect lechon.

Meanwhile, line a table or counter (big enough to hold the pig) with banana leaves. Once your lechon is cooked through and the skin is perfectly crispy—I prefer a hard, shiny brown skin, with no bubbles—take the pig off the heat and let it rest on the spit on the lined table for 30 minutes. Then, pull out the spit and chop up your meat (see last step in diagram). Use your hands to pull the meat off the bones. For each serving, cut a piece of skin and serve it on top of the pork, along with some sarsa. Enjoy your lechon, know you've won at life, then rest.

Sarsa (Bread Crumb Sauce)

MAKES ABOUT 1 CUP

Sarsa—sold in a bottle under the name Mang Tomas—is an all-purpose sauce for lechon or roast chicken. In the Philippines, I had homemade sarsa once at a party. I remember it was pretty good. But I really fell in love with it later in life, when my Auntie Cita made it. She made hers with chicken livers, Progresso bread crumbs, brown sugar, and soy sauce. There was a minerality to it, along with a garlic-onion base, the brown sugar sweetness, a touch of vinegar, and the bread crumbs to thicken it. It was so good, and so complex. That sarsa is the heart of this recipe. I can never eat the Mang Tomas bottled version anymore. Sarsa has to be homemade.

½ **pound chicken livers, rinsed**

2 **tablespoons canola oil**

1 **small onion, chopped**

3 **garlic cloves, chopped**

2 **tablespoons Datu Puti cane vinegar (see sidebar; available at Asian markets and on Amazon)**

1 **tablespoon dark brown sugar**

¼ **teaspoon kosher salt**

¼ **teaspoon freshly ground black pepper**

½ **cup water**

¼ **cup plain bread crumbs**

Using a very sharp knife, cut the vein out of each chicken liver. Every liver has that vein, and it almost looks like a half-inch string of membrane. You can't miss it. Make sure you get rid of it because it's stringy. Then chop your livers into ½-inch chunks.

Heat a medium saucepan over medium-high heat until hot. Add 1 tablespoon of the oil and heat until you see the oil ripple, about 30 seconds. Cut the heat to medium. Add the chicken livers and cook, stirring, just until the livers are no longer red, about 3 minutes. Transfer to a plate and let cool to room temperature. Wipe out the saucepan.

Heat the saucepan over medium-high heat until hot. Add the remaining 1 tablespoon oil and heat until you see the oil ripple, about 30 seconds. Cut the heat to medium. Add the onion and garlic and cook, stirring constantly, until the onion is slightly translucent, 3 minutes or so.

Add the vinegar and cook, scraping up all the browned bits from the bottom of the pan. Add the sugar, salt, pepper, livers, and water and cook, stirring constantly and mashing the livers, for 3 minutes. Fold in the bread crumbs and cook, stirring, until the bread crumbs have absorbed the liquid, 1 to 2 minutes.

Throw the whole mix into a blender and blend on high until smooth. Pour into a ramekin and serve immediately. Or let it cool to room temp and refrigerate it in an airtight container for up to 5 days.

Filipino Cane Vinegar

Datu Puti vinegar is a staple in Filipino kitchens. Made from sugarcane, it has an astringent flavor that gives Filipino foods, like adobo, that distinctive tang. You can even buy Datu Puti cane vinegar together with Datu Puti soy sauce on Amazon— kind of like a Filipino starter pack.

CHAPTER 5

Auntie Cita

WHEN I WAS a baby, my parents were poor. We were actually poor my entire childhood. My parents are probably going to read this and disagree, but that's just their pride. In 1986, we were able to buy a home in Pico Rivera, but honestly, even crackheads were able to do that—and some of our neighbors were actual crackheads.

My dad's boss had passed away and ended up leaving the business to him. My mom worked as a bookkeeper, closer to home. As my dad's business started to take off and my mom focused on work, we had a little more money as a family, so my parents decided to hire a nanny to help take care of my brother.

They didn't hire just any kind of nanny—not Mrs. Doubtfire or some hot British au pair. They hired my Auntie Cita. She was my mom's cousin on my grandfather's side and was famous for making amazing Filipino food. Part of her deal with my parents meant that she could start a small catering business in the backyard.

So that's how our backyard became a dirty kitchen. Out went the picnic tables and mini basketball court. In went a couple woks and wok burners, a sink, a countertop deep-fryer, and a grill with stoves, arranged ad hoc style. Every year, my dad would buy a new grill for the dirty kitchen. I think it was his way of celebrating success. We had a coconut scraper, a huge can opener built into the patio columns, a can crusher, and big wok steamers for puto, kutsinta, and bibingka. Parts of our garage were used for food storage. My weekends went from chores and cartoons to learning how to be a prep cook and being a part-time babysitter. Auntie Cita taught me how to cut with a sharp knife and how to cook on a hot wok.

My knowledge of Filipino food went from basic to expansive. Egg rolls and noodles became whole hog stews and intricate traditional desserts. Coincidentally, my parents started to become super Catholic at this time. They started to attend weekly prayer meetings, which in turn generated more catering business for my aunt.

Every weekend, I was responsible for wrapping egg rolls, stirring stews, and shredding coconut meat. Weirdly, I loved the work. Stirring caramelized coconut milk and helping fill kutsinta molds made me happy. I remember tasting her bibingka with cream cheese—the mix of sweet and salty was a revelation. In reality, mixing flavors is the essence of Filipino food.

Those four years cemented my love and pride for Filipino food. The recipes that follow are straight-up Auntie Cita—wok master, cooking mentor, and reigning queen of the dirty kitchen.

The Dirty Kitchen

ALEXANDRA: Who was your first kitchen mentor?

ALVIN: Auntie Cita, the king of frying. She could make anything and everything. You name it, she would take it to the next level. She was a dainty woman, but super loud. She loved soap operas and skin care, but she would drink all night. I always remembered her laughing. She was a homie. She was down AF.

ALEXANDRA: What kind of food did Auntie Cita make?

ALVIN: She made sinigang and adobo, but amplified. She made killer turon, this sweet, sticky banana dessert. She introduced me to lechon kawali, the crispy, tender, deep-fried pork belly. Every Christmas, my family would have a big party with extended family. We'd always have the classics: pancit, jamonado, and pan de sal from Betsy's, arroz caldo in the Crock-Pot. Every year, Auntie Cita would make all the desserts by hand. She would make the sweet rice cake puto, the sticky, sugar-topped kakanin, bibingka with Philly cream cheese, the triple-layered sapin-sapin, the golden nuggets of kutsinta. For the entire week leading up to the holiday, tons of people would come by the house. Day in, day out, people would line up to pick up Christmas catering orders from Auntie Cita. Puto was mandatory in our house. Me and my cousins would top it with butter and American cheese, then blitz it in the microwave for 30 seconds. It was melty, savory, and sweet. To this day, that's Christmas to me. I remember my Grandpa Corny—a US Navy commissary chef—in the house making roast beef. Auntie Cita would be in the dirty kitchen, making lumpia sariwa and shaping the wrappers in a wok by hand.

Bibingka (Coconut-Rice Cake)

WITH PHILLY CREAM CHEESE

SERVES 6

The first time I met Auntie Cita, she brought this dish as a gift for my parents. It looked different from any other bibingka I had ever seen. It was unassuming: a round pie tin wrapped in banana leaves. I took a bite and it blew my mind. Every single mouthful had cream cheese. The texture was almost like cornbread with a really sugary topping. I tried it with a salted duck egg, and it was even better. The combination of salt, egg, and cream cheese was incredible.

Obviously and gratefully, my parents hired Auntie Cita. Over the years, she became the main caterer in our area. That bibingka with Philly cream cheese was her specialty. She made her own dry mix for the bibingka batter. She would line all these round cake molds with banana leaves, pour the batter in, and bake them off. Then, she would dip the bibingka in niyog, or freshly shaved young coconut meat, for that perfect textural touch.

On Saturdays, I was in charge of making niyog all day. *Niyog* as a word is kind of an onomatopoeia. It's the sound you hear when you scrape the coconut against the grater. I would sit on this little wooden stool with a cowboy spur at the end. I'd scrape half a coconut on that spur, and the coconut meat would fly off into this little plastic basin. And I would do fuck tons of coconut. Sometimes, you look at kids and you think, "How do they have so much energy?" I had that energy as a kid, so I would mow through cases of coconuts.

That niyog was the secret to this whole dish. You would dip the bibingka, scarpetta-style, into fresh, soft coconut meat. The bibingka was spongy, creamy from the cream cheese, and crispy. It was an explosion of flavor and texture. Auntie Cita made this dish every Saturday for six years. It made the house smell amazing.

---

1 large banana leaf (thawed, if frozen), cut into 2 (10-inch) rounds

5 tablespoons unsalted butter, at room temperature, plus more for greasing

1 cup glutinous rice flour, plus more for dusting

1 tablespoon baking powder

½ teaspoon kosher salt

1 cup muscovado sugar, plus more for sprinkling

3 large eggs

1 cup canned coconut milk

¼ cup heavy whipping cream

1 (8-ounce) block Philadelphia cream cheese, cut crosswise into 16 slices

1 cup Niyog (page 164) or any frozen shredded coconut

(recipe continues)

Preheat the oven to 375°F. Line a 10-inch springform pan with one of the banana leaf rounds. Butter the banana leaf and the sides of the pan, then dust with rice flour. Set the pan aside.

Sift together the rice flour, baking powder, and salt into a medium bowl. Don't just dump in the dry ingredients. Sifting is a magical process than makes pastries fluffier and helps prevent unwanted lumps.

In the bowl of a stand mixer fitted with the paddle attachment, cream the butter and muscovado sugar at medium-high speed for about 5 minutes, until the butter is creamy white. You're looking for buttercream icing texture. Scrape down the sides of the bowl.

Using the whisk attachment, add the eggs, one at a time, whisking at medium speed after each addition, until fully incorporated, about 1 minute. Scrape down the sides of the bowl after each addition. No gooey streaks; you want it to be one consistent mixture.

Returning to the paddle attachment, slowly incorporate the dry ingredients into the butter-egg mixture in three batches, mixing at medium speed. Make sure each is mixed well and incorporated before adding the next—about 15 seconds of mixing for each addition. Scrape down the sides of the bowl after each addition. With the machine running at medium speed, add the coconut milk and heavy cream in a slow stream. Beat until the consistency is like a pancake batter, about 2 minutes.

Pour the batter into the prepared pan; lightly tap the pan five times on the counter to distribute the batter and release any air bubbles.

Place the pan on a rimmed baking sheet and bake the bibingka until the top layer has set, 10 to 15 minutes. It should be pale and somewhat firm. Remove from the oven, top the pan with the second leaf round, and continue baking until the bibingka is set and just slightly jiggly in the middle, about 15 minutes. Adding the extra banana leaf will help flavor the bibingka and prevent the top from getting too brown.

Remove the pan from the oven; peel off and discard the banana leaf on top. Arrange the cream cheese slices decoratively over the top. Bake until a cake tester inserted into the center comes out clean, about 20 minutes. Let cool on a rack for 30 minutes. Release from the pan and peel off the leaf on the bottom; sprinkle more muscovado sugar over the top. Garnish with the niyog, slice into wedges, and serve.

Lechon Kawali (Wok-Fried Pork)

WITH CALAMANSI DIPPING SAUCE

SERVES 16, OR A TABLE FULL OF FRIENDS

Pico Rivera is right next to the San Gabriel Valley—SGV—home of Asian food in LA. Because of the proliferation of Asian markets there, skin-on pork belly was cheap and easy to find. My Auntie Cita noticed that and made lechon kawali a part of her menu. She would teach me how to use a fork to poke holes in the pork skin so it would become puffy and crispy.

My dad had a TurboChef air fryer, so we would use it to make lechon kawali. An air fryer is basically a hot-ass oven with a fan. I remember watching the lechon kawali through the glass as it cooked, seeing the oil bubble and ooze out.

The traditional method is to fry the pork in a wok. Today, I have a different technique for getting the crispy skin: I rub salt on my lechon kawali to exfoliate it. The more abrasive the salt is, the flakier the skin is going to be. I like to steam mine to render all the fat down. To me, perfectly cooked pork belly is a big sign of how good a chef you are. I take pride in my technique, which is my take on Auntie Cita's lechon kawali.

You will need a meat tenderizer with sharp teeth. Hit up Amazon ASAP and get one sent to you. If not, you can use a fork, but it will take 10 times as long.

---

1 (2-pound) center-cut, skin-on pork belly

1 cup kosher salt

Calamansi Dipping Sauce (recipe follows)

SPECIAL EQUIPMENT
Meat tenderizer

Use a meat tenderizer or fork to perforate the skin all over the pork belly. Rub the skin with a generous coating of the salt and then season the other side. Pretend you're exfoliating the pork belly. Set aside the remaining salt.

Set up a large wok or pot with a steamer insert. Pour 3 inches of water into the pot and bring to a rolling boil over medium-high heat. Reduce the heat to low, add the pork belly, cover, and steam for 1 hour. Remove the pork belly and let it cool on a wire rack for 30 minutes.

Meanwhile, preheat the oven to 450°F.

Rub the remaining salt all over the cooled pork belly skin. Treat this like a second exfoliation—because the skin has tenderized, the second pass will fill those perforations, creating nooks and crannies of salt and air. This is the secret trick to making the pork super crunchy when it roasts.

(recipe continues)

Place the pork belly on a rimmed baking sheet and roast, rotating every 15 minutes, until the skin reaches your desired crunchiness, about 1 hour. Remove from the oven, slice crosswise about ½ inch thick, and serve immediately with the calamansi dipping sauce.

Calamansi Dipping Sauce

MAKES ABOUT 1 CUP

3 garlic cloves, minced

1 tablespoon minced shallot

½ cup Datu Puti or Silver Swan soy sauce (see page 60; available at Asian markets and on Amazon)

3 tablespoons fresh calamansi juice (see Note, page 68)

In a small bowl, combine the garlic, shallot, soy sauce, and calamansi juice and whisk till combined. Serve right away.

The Calamansi Tree

ALVIN: We had fresh calamansi juice all the time growing up because we had our own calamansi tree. My grandpa brought it over in the '90s. Back then, it was just a seed he stuffed in a book. My family grew it from that, and when I was a kid, my grandpa would actually make me pee on the tree. After school, it was like, "Oh, I better pee on the fuckin' tree." Sure enough, our tree would bear so much more fruit than everybody else's trees. I would tell my friends, "It's because I pee on it." They would get so grossed out, but honestly, that's the secret.

ALEXANDRA: What else did you grow?

ALVIN: Mustard greens, tomatoes, and jalapeños, a guava tree, and a lemon tree. Many of my recipes rely on a backyard bounty or a very good market.

In the backyard, there was a little tiny brick wall that came like 18 inches up to my bedroom window. I used to sneak out, then my dad caught on. He put all the trash cans in front of my window. Then I realized I was dumb for sneaking out my window. My dad slept so hard, I could just walk out the front door. Facts!

Vegetarian Ukoy (Fritters)
WITH CHILE-VINEGAR DIPPING SAUCE

SERVES 6 TO 8

Ukoy is a crispy vegetable fritter, and it is my jam. As a kid, I was put to work shredding all the vegetables. I would shred carrots, sweet potatoes, onions, scallions, and bean sprouts into these giant mounds. In another bowl, I would mix the vegetables with chopped shrimp and rice flour batter. Auntie Cita would fry a scoop of that batter old-school wok style, and turn them into these really crispy, delicious fritters. They're so good with vinegar.

Today, I make a vegetarian version, and I shallow-fry it. Fry the ukoy in small mounds, like latkes! Or make a large pancake in the shape of a pan (easier to flip over).

1 cup mung bean sprouts

1 cup shredded sweet potato (about 1 small sweet potato, peeled and shredded on the large holes of a box grater)

1 cup shredded carrot (about 1 large carrot, shredded on the large holes of a box grater)

1 cup shredded parsnip (about 1 large parsnip, shredded on the large holes of a box grater)

1 cup thinly sliced scallions (about 10 scallions)

2 cups thinly sliced shiitake mushrooms (4 to 5 ounces)

1 (12-ounce) can plain seltzer

1 cup rice flour

Canola oil, for frying

Kosher salt

Chile-Vinegar Dipping sauce (recipe follows)

In a large bowl, combine the bean sprouts, sweet potato, carrot, parsnip, scallions, and mushrooms. Set aside.

In a medium bowl, whisk the seltzer with the rice flour until a thin batter forms. Add the batter to the vegetables and stir until thoroughly combined.

Heat 2 inches of oil in a large cast-iron skillet over medium-high heat to 350°F.

Working in batches, use a ½-cup measure to scoop the vegetable batter into mounds and lower them into the hot oil, no more than three at a time. Try not to move the ukoy; you want the mixture to stay intact. Shallow-fry the vegetable fritters like latkes or potato pancakes until crispy, golden brown, and delicious, 3 to 4 minutes on each side. Skim off any stray fried bits between batches.

Transfer the ukoy to a platter lined with paper towels to wick away the extra oil. Season with salt and serve immediately with the dipping sauce.

(recipe continues)

Chile-Vinegar Dipping Sauce

MAKES ABOUT 1 CUP

1 cup Datu Puti cane vinegar
(see page 137; available
at Asian markets and on
Amazon)

3 garlic cloves, minced

2 Thai bird chiles, stemmed and
thinly sliced

In a small bowl, whisk together the vinegar, garlic, and chiles. Serve right away or refrigerate in an airtight container for up to 1 week.

Pantry Chile Vinegar

MAKES 2 CUPS

This is super easy to make but needs time to marinate. It gives any dish a spicy zing, and it will last for weeks in the fridge. Enjoy with lumpia sariwa, lumpia Shanghai, or any pork dish.

8 serrano chiles

4 cayenne chiles

2 cups Datu Puti cane vinegar (see page 137; available at Asian markets and on Amazon)

Put the chiles in a 1-quart mason jar, then pour in the vinegar. Cover and let marinate at room temperature for at least 24 hours or up to 5 days at room temperature before using, then refrigerate for up to 3 weeks.

Lumpia Sariwa (Fresh Lumpia)

SERVES 6

I hated lumpia sariwa as a kid. It was like a Bloods and Crips thing: lumpia Shanghai versus lumpia sariwa. I remember even hating chickpeas, because Mom put them in lumpia sariwa.

Lumpia sariwa was typically made with carrots, onions, celery, bean sprouts, scallions, and chickpeas. Auntie Cita would make the wrappers in a wok from scratch, so I loved the wrappers. I loved the sweet sauce and the crushed peanuts, too. I just hated the vegetables. The dish tasted like earth. As a kid, I didn't really have toys or the Internet. I would play in sandboxes and get dirt in my mouth. All of that just reminded me of lumpia sariwa.

Then, after a lifetime of being a hater, I went to LASA in LA and tried their lumpia sariwa. Their version takes it to the top. It's such a special dish, so tasty and inspiring, that I decided to give it another chance. My version starts with a crepe wrapper. The ideal base is made of spring vegetables: garlic scapes, green garlic, scallions, torpedo onions, and chives. For texture, I add carrots or shredded bean sprouts. In the summer, you could use eggplant, zucchini, summer squash, and tomatoes. In fall, you could use kabocha squash, spaghetti squash, parsnips, or sweet potatoes. Because this dish is basically shredded veggies lightly cooked with salt, it's a great format. It's one of those dishes you can make all year round.

---

3 tablespoons canola oil

1 large yellow onion, thinly sliced

3 garlic cloves, minced

4 carrots, cut into matchsticks

1 cup sliced shiitake mushrooms

1½ cups cooked chickpeas or 1 (15-ounce) can, rinsed and drained

1 bunch scallions, sliced

3 cups mung bean sprouts

½ head napa cabbage, cored and sliced super thin

2 teaspoons dark brown sugar

1½ teaspoons kosher salt, plus more for seasoning

Heat a large wok over high heat until blistering hot. Add your oil, then cut the heat to medium and heat until you see the oil ripple, about 30 seconds. Add the onion and garlic and cook, stirring, until translucent, about 2 minutes. Add the carrots and cook, stirring, until softened, about 4 minutes. Add the shiitakes, chickpeas, scallions, bean sprouts, and cabbage. Season with the brown sugar and salt and cook, stirring, until the carrots are crisp-tender, about 4 minutes.

Add the soy sauce and fish sauce and scrape up all the fond from the bottom of the wok. Cook, stirring, until most of the liquid has evaporated, about 3 minutes. Remove from the heat, taste, and season with more salt if necessary. Let the vegetable filling cool slightly before you fill the lumpia.

Using tongs, add about ½ cup vegetable filling to 1 wrapper and roll it up tightly in a cylinder, leaving the ends open. You want to make

(ingredients and recipe continue)

¼ cup Datu Puti or Silver Swan soy sauce (see page 60; available at Asian markets and on Amazon)

1 teaspoon Rufina patis (Filipino fish sauce; available at Asian markets and on Amazon)

Lumpia Sariwa Wrappers (recipe follows)

Lumpia Sariwa Sauce (recipe follows), for serving

sure the wrapper is secure enough so the veggies don't fall out. Repeat with the remaining wrappers and filling.

Plate the lumpia sariwa with the seam side down and serve right away with the lumpia sariwa sauce.

Lumpia Sariwa Wrappers

MAKES 6 WRAPPERS

1 cup all-purpose flour

¼ teaspoon kosher salt

5 tablespoons unsalted butter, divided

3 large eggs

1½ cups whole milk

Sift the flour and salt together into a medium bowl. Set aside.

In a microwave-safe bowl, microwave 3 tablespoons of the butter in 10-second increments, stopping each time to stir. Do this until all the lumps are gone. The trick is to keep the light-yellow creamy color of the butter. Imagine liquid butter, not clarified butter. Set aside.

In a blender, blend the eggs and milk on high speed for 20 seconds, or until fully incorporated. Working in 3 batches, blend in the dry ingredients until each batch is fully incorporated. With the machine running at medium-low speed, slowly drizzle in the melted butter and blend until fully incorporated.

Heat a scant 1 teaspoon of the remaining butter in a large nonstick frying pan over medium heat until melted; swirl to coat the bottom of the pan. Add 6 tablespoons of the batter and swirl to coat the bottom of the pan. Cook the batter like a crepe until lightly browned on the underside, 1 to 2 minutes. Slide it onto a plate with the raw side facing up. Using the plate, flip the raw side of the wrapper onto the pan and cook until dry to the touch, about 1 minute. Transfer the wrapper to another plate and repeat with the remaining butter and batter. Cover the wrappers with a kitchen towel to keep them warm.

Lumpia Sariwa Sauce

MAKES ABOUT 3 CUPS

2 teaspoons canola oil

10 garlic cloves, minced

3 cups Homemade Vegetable
Stock (page 46)

1 cup smooth peanut butter

¾ cup dark brown sugar

¼ cup Datu Puti or Silver Swan
soy sauce (see page 60;
available at Asian markets and
on Amazon)

1 teaspoon Rufina patis
(Filipino fish sauce; available
at Asian markets and on
Amazon)

Kosher salt

Heat the oil in a medium, heavy-bottomed saucepan over medium heat until you see the oil ripple, about 1 minute. Add the garlic and cook, stirring constantly, until golden brown, about 2 minutes.

Add the vegetable stock, peanut butter, brown sugar, and soy sauce and cook, stirring and scraping down the sides of the pan, until the sauce is reduced by one-third, 15 to 20 minutes. The sauce should be thick enough to coat the back of a spoon.

Stir in the fish sauce and remove from the heat. Taste and season with salt. Let the sauce cool. Serve right away or refrigerate in an airtight container for up to 1 week.

Sweet Chile Sauce

MAKES ABOUT 2 CUPS

I ate lumpia a lot growing up, and then, in the 1990s, Vietnamese-style sweet chile sauce came into vogue. The sugary, vinegary, garlicky sauce was perfect with lumpia. I loved it so much, I started making my own sweet chile sauce from scratch. I would put it on everything. I'd glaze roast chicken with it. I'd eat jicama dipped in it as a summer snack. All my Mexican friends would eat jicama with chamoy, so this was my version.

I've always loved comparing Filipino food to Mexican food. When my Mexican friends had their champurrado, I'd bring my Filipino champorado to compare and contrast. In Filipino food, we have a dessert called puto, a sweet, glutinous rice cake. I'd bring it to lunch to stir the pot, because in Spanish, *puto* is a kind of curse word. You can look it up. Of course, I'd eat my puto with sweet chile sauce. It's so versatile, you can eat it with everything.

---

1 cup rice vinegar

1 cup sugar

¾ cup water

¼ cup Datu Puti or Silver Swan soy sauce (see page 60; available at Asian markets and on Amazon)

3 garlic cloves, minced

2½ tablespoons crushed red pepper

2 tablespoons cornstarch

In a medium saucepan, combine the rice vinegar, sugar, ½ cup of the water, the soy sauce, and garlic. Bring to a boil, then cut the heat to medium and cook until the sauce is reduced by one-third, about 15 minutes.

When the sauce looks like a thin syrup, add the crushed red pepper and let simmer for 5 minutes.

Meanwhile, in a small bowl, whisk together the remaining ¼ cup water and the cornstarch until all the lumps are gone. Slowly whisk this slurry into the saucepan. Cook, stirring constantly, until the sauce is thick enough to coat the back of a spoon, about 2 minutes.

Remove the pan from the heat, transfer the sauce to a small heatproof bowl, and let cool. Serve right away or refrigerate in an airtight container for up to 1 month.

Paksiw na Lechon
(Roast Pork Stew)

SERVES 8

Lechon kawali and crispy pata were Auntie Cita's specialties. But, the day after making lechon, we would take any leftovers and make paksiw na lechon. To "paksiw" means to cook and simmer in vinegar. I remember stirring pork liver, brown sugar, vinegar, garlic, onions, and Progresso bread crumbs to make the all-purpose lechon sauce in the backyard. That sauce would end up in the paksiw, and it would tie into everything. For this recipe, we would never use the kitchen inside the house. Instead, we would cook in the dirty kitchen outside. In the woks, we would make paksiw. It was savory, vinegary, and addictive, the ultimate dish for leftover lechon.

1 tablespoon canola oil

1 cup diced yellow onion (about 1 medium onion)

¼ cup minced garlic (about 10 large cloves)

1 cup Homemade Vegetable Stock (page 46)

¼ cup Datu Puti cane vinegar (see page 137; available at Asian markets and on Amazon)

1 cup Lechon Sauce (recipe follows)

1½ pounds leftover Lechon (page 131)

1 bay leaf

Kosher salt and freshly ground black pepper

Steamed Jasmine Rice (page 20), for serving

Heat the oil in a medium wok over medium-high heat until you see the oil ripple, about 1 minute. Add the onion and garlic and cook, stirring, until translucent, 2 to 3 minutes. Add the stock and vinegar and let it come to a simmer. Reduce the heat and simmer until the liquid has reduced a bit, about 5 minutes.

Add the lechon sauce, lechon, and bay leaf and continue to simmer until the sauce has thickened to a gravy-like consistency, 15 to 20 minutes. Remove and discard the bay leaf, then season to your liking with salt and pepper.

Remove from the heat, ladle the paksiw na lechon into bowls, and serve with rice.

(recipe continues)

Lechon Sauce

MAKES ABOUT 2 CUPS

2 tablespoons canola oil

¼ pound pork liver (available at Italian and Asian butchers), cubed

½ cup diced yellow onion (about 1 small onion)

2 tablespoons minced garlic

¼ cup white vinegar

3 tablespoons dark brown sugar

1½ cups Homemade Vegetable Stock (page 46)

⅓ cup plain bread crumbs

2 teaspoons kosher salt

1 teaspoon freshly ground black pepper

Heat 1 tablespoon of the oil in a medium frying pan over medium heat until you see the oil ripple, about 1 minute. Add the pork liver and cook, stirring, until firm and caramelized at the edges, about 2 minutes. Remove from the heat and set aside.

Heat a medium wok over medium-high heat until hot. Add the remaining 1 tablespoon oil and heat until you see the oil ripple, about 1 minute. Add the onion and garlic and cook, stirring, until the onion is translucent and soft, 2 to 3 minutes.

Cut the heat to medium, add the pork liver, and cook, stirring and mashing up the liver, until fully combined and fragrant, 3 to 5 minutes. Add the vinegar, sugar, and vegetable stock and bring it to a boil, scraping up all the fond from the bottom of the wok. Add the bread crumbs and cook, stirring, until the sauce has thickened, 3 to 5 minutes.

Transfer the sauce to a blender, add the salt and pepper, and blend until smooth. Let the lechon sauce cool before using.

Kutsinta (Filipino Mochi)

MAKES 24 TO 30 PIECES

Kutsinta are so uniquely Filipino. They're tiny, orange, gummy (or *makunat* in Tagalog) mochi made of glutinous rice flour, tons of sugar, lye water, and achuete (annatto seeds) for color. Kutsinta is a big deal in Cavite. You get judged by how good yours is. It can never be rubbery.

I remember Auntie Cita's hands would always be an amber color from mixing the achuete seeds with water. We would buy these sketchy bottles of lye water from the Filipino store. We had to drive all the way to Carson to get them. Lye water is caustic; it's the same ingredient that gives bagels and pretzels their chewy exterior. As a kid, I remember picking up a bottle and Auntie Cita saying, "Don't drink that, it's bad for you." I would say, "Why, if you're using it to cook?"

Auntie Cita would sit in the backyard for hours stirring the kutsinta. We had this gigantic four-level steamer, and she would fill the entire thing with kutsinta.

Honestly, there was nothing like getting a fresh kutsinta from the steamer, pushing it out of the mold like Jell-O, and dipping it into fresh coconut. It's mouthwatering, and so unique. It wasn't Mexican. It wasn't white. It was Filipino. It was me. My friends didn't like it, but I loved it. Today, it's a part of me, and it is on the menu at my first Filipino restaurant.

---

2 teaspoons annatto (aka achuete) seeds

1½ cups glutinous rice flour

½ cup all-purpose flour

1 cup packed muscovado sugar

1 tablespoon lihia (Filipino food-grade lye water; available at Filipino markets and on Amazon; see Note, page 161)

Niyog (page 164), for dipping (optional)

SPECIAL EQUIPMENT

2 (12-cup) silicone or nonstick mini muffin pans

In a small bowl, combine the annatto seeds with 1 tablespoon water. Let soak for 40 minutes. Strain out the seeds and discard; reserve the annatto liquid.

Grab two woks or pots, each large enough to hold a 12-cup mini muffin pan. Fit each with a steamer insert, pour in about 4 inches of water, and bring the water to a boil over high heat.

Meanwhile, sift together both flours into a large bowl and set aside.

Put the muscovado sugar in a medium heatproof bowl and add 1 cup boiling water. Whisk until the sugar is completely dissolved. Whisk in 1 cup cold water. Whisk this mixture into the flour in the large bowl. Carefully whisk in the lye water and the annatto liquid until fully incorporated. Your batter should be an amber color.

(recipe continues)

When the water in your pots is boiling, cut the heat to medium and place one muffin pan on each steamer insert. Whisk the batter again if it has separated; then, using a liquid measuring cup, carefully pour the batter into the muffin pans, filling the cups two-thirds of the way. Cover your pots and steam the kutsinta until set, 40 to 50 minutes. They should be firm to the touch but still chewy, like an aerated mochi.

Remove the muffin pans from the steamers and let the kutsinta rest on a wire rack until cool enough to handle with your bare hands, 10 to 15 minutes. Line a baking sheet with a silicone mat or parchment paper. Using a small rubber spatula, pop the kutsinta out of the muffin pans and let cool on the prepared baking sheet. Serve immediately as is or dip them in fresh niyog for a texturally bomb experience. If you have more batter, wipe out the muffin pans and repeat the steaming process.

NOTE:

Lye is caustic but becomes safe to eat when cooked. As a precaution, wear goggles, gloves, and an apron when using it.

Suman (Glutinous Rice Tamales)

MAKES 18 SUMAN

In Cavite, suman is a staple. It's a sweet, glutinous rice tamale. Growing up, I remember the smell of sticky rice cooking with coconut milk and hearing the metal spatula scraping the bottom of the wok. The coconut mixture scraping off the edge looked like a sticker peeling off. I used to wake up to those sounds and smells every time my aunt would make suman in the backyard.

With Auntie Cita, there were no recipe books. There were no exact measurements. She would start with about two bags of sticky rice soaked in water, then put the rice and coconut milk in a wok and cook it down. She rolled it into a banana leaf, tied it down, and steamed it.

When she pulled the suman out, it became a completely different texture. I would dip it in muscovado sugar mixed with shredded coconut and bite into heaven. When someone goes to the Philippines, I always ask them to bring back suman.

I grew up in a Mexican neighborhood, so tamales were a big deal during Christmas. I remember bringing suman to school and telling my friend, "This is the same thing. Yours is savory, mine is sweet." Back then, I had no idea about the parallels between Mexicans and Filipinos, and the impact of the galleon trade. Now, I realize that the story is the same: If you're poor, this is a gift that you can open. I still think of suman as a gift. Whatever suman is out there, I'll eat it. I love it all.

---

3 cups glutinous rice

1 (13.5-ounce) can coconut milk

¾ cup sugar

1 teaspoon kosher salt

3 large banana leaves (thawed, if frozen), cut into 18 (8 x 10-inch) rectangles

9 feet butcher twine, cut into 1-foot lengths

Niyog (page 164), for serving

Amboy Coconut Glaze (recipe follows), for serving

In a large bowl, combine the glutinous rice with 2 quarts of water. Let soak overnight at room temperature. (Soaking the rice will make the suman taste significantly better.) Drain the rice thoroughly and discard the water. Set the rice aside.

Heat a large wok over high heat until blistering hot. Add your coconut milk and heat for 1 minute. Add the sugar and let that dissolve, stirring constantly, about 2 minutes.

Add the rice and salt and cut the heat to medium-low. Cook, stirring constantly, until the rice is soft and has become a sweet, sticky paste— think extra-thick risotto—and starts to pull from the side of the wok, 12 to 15 minutes. Make sure you're checking the bottom of the wok so the rice doesn't stick and burn. Reduce the heat if the rice starts to stick. Remove from the heat and let cool for 30 to 40 minutes.

Place 1 banana leaf rectangle on a work surface so a long edge faces you. Place 2 tablespoons of the cooled rice mixture along that edge of the rectangle. Roll up that edge of the leaf away from you. Keep rolling till you reach the top of the leaf. Then, fold over both ends, tucking them under the body of the suman. Repeat with the rest of the rice mixture and banana leaves.

Take 2 suman packages and position them so the tucked ends are facing each other. Using 1 piece of twine, tie up the packages, binding each end of the suman. Repeat with the rest of the suman.

Pour about 4 inches of water into a wok or large pot fitted with a steamer insert and bring the water to a simmer over high heat. Add the suman bundles and steam until the rice is set to the consistency of a glue stick, about 1 hour. Pull them out, unwrap, and serve with fresh niyog and coconut glaze.

Amboy Coconut Glaze

MAKES ABOUT 2 CUPS

2 (13.5-ounce) cans
   coconut milk

2 cups loosely packed dark
   brown sugar

2 teaspoons kosher salt

In a medium saucepan, stir together all the ingredients and bring to a boil over high heat. Cut the heat to medium-low and cook, stirring constantly, until the sauce has reduced by half, 25 to 35 minutes. The sauce should be the color of caramel, and thick enough to coat the back of a spoon. Use immediately on suman, bibingka, ice cream, pancakes, or waffles—anytime you want a super-tasty dessert sauce!

Niyog (Shredded Fresh Coconut)

MAKES 30 TO 36 CUPS, DEPENDING ON THE SIZE OF THE COCONUTS

Niyog is freshly grated coconut meat. You make it using a coconut grater that looks like a wooden rocking horse for a kid, or an adult step stool. Growing up, I saw a lot of coconut graters made of reclaimed wood from broken patios. The structure starts with a saddle made of a 2 x 6-inch piece of wood that's about 3 feet long. It's 6 inches off the ground. Honestly, its quality depends on how nice your Lolo was who built it.

At the end of the stool, there's a spur that looks like a torture device from medieval times. It's sharp and spiky, and it would be nailed or screwed onto the edge of the stool. You would mount the stool like a horse, grab half a coconut, and start grating. You would spin the shell from the middle to the top. You would keep spinning it, and spinning it, and spinning it, till you saw the brown of the coconut shell. If you left any coconut meat in the shell, you would get in trouble.

It sounds crazy, but this coconut grater was a revered piece of furniture in my house. Why don't I have one? I should make one.

---

12 young coconuts

1 coconut grater (see page 166)

A lot of elbow grease

Place 1 coconut on a kitchen towel on your work surface. Using the spine of a heavy chef's knife, hit the middle of the coconut swiftly to crack it. Then, hit the blade at the crack of the coconut, extract the knife, and pull apart the two coconut halves with your hands. Reserve the coconut water to drink. Set the coconut halves aside. Repeat this process with the remaining coconuts.

Then, take your coconut grater outside. Place a large bowl underneath the scraper side to catch the niyog (coconut shavings).

Straddle the bench of the coconut grater. Take 1 coconut half and place it over the scraper, white side down. Scrape it from 12 o'clock to 6 o'clock, repeating until you see the brown of the shell. Repeat with the remaining coconut halves, transferring the niyog to another bowl as necessary.

Serve the niyog immediately, sprinkled over any dessert, or transfer to a resealable plastic bag and store in the refrigerator for up to 1 week or in the freezer for up to 3 months.

How to Make a Coconut Grater

First things first, go on Amazon and look for a Filipino or Thai or Malaysian coconut scraper.

Next, get a (7-foot-long) plank of 2 x 6-inch wood, preferably pine, and cut it into the following lengths:

- 1 (36-inch-long) plank for the bench seat
- 1 (32-inch-long) plank for the bench "spine"
- 2 (6-inch-long) pieces for the bench legs

You'll also need 15 nails and 3 screws.

Place the bench seat on a work surface. Position 1 bench leg flush to the end of the bench seat and hammer 3 nails through the bench seat to attach the leg. Repeat at the other end with the other bench leg.

Flip the bench over so the legs are pointing up. Position your bench spine lengthwise along the seat and perpendicular to the legs. Make sure the spine sits equidistant between the 2 legs, to create more support. Hammer 3 nails through 1 bench leg to secure the spine. Repeat for the other leg.

Flip the bench right-side up so the legs are on the ground. Hammer 3 nails through the bench seat to further secure the spine to the bench.

Pick your favorite end of the bench, and attach your coconut scraper using the 3 screws. That's it—you've got a coconut grater!

MATERIALS

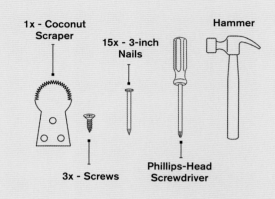

1x - Coconut Scraper

15x - 3-inch Nails

Hammer

3x - Screws

Phillips-Head Screwdriver

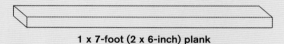

1 x 7-foot (2 x 6-inch) plank

PLANK CUT INTO PIECES

ASSEMBLE THE SPINE

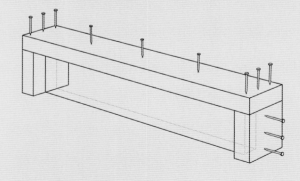

ATTACH THE SCRAPER

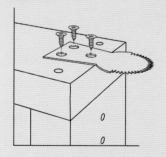

Bibingka Malagkit (Sticky Coconut-Rice Cake)

SERVES 12

This is the first bibingka I ever had. It's considered a treat for special occasions or parties. When I went to the Philippines last year—yes, I finally went back, it only took 16 years—they had it at the Manila Hotel. I ate it every morning. It's a dessert that I always crave.

In this recipe, you start by soaking sticky rice, then you cook it with brown sugar and coconut milk until it's soft. You put that mixture into a 9 x 13-inch baking pan or on a baking sheet. You top that with latik, which is coconut milk reduced down to a thick syrup. Then, you bake it off. You almost brûlée the caramelized topping. You can put a crunchy muscovado crumble on it. It's a slice of heaven.

When I was a kid, I would scrape off the coconut caramel sauce on top and just eat that.

2 cups glutinous rice

Butter, for greasing

1 large banana leaf (thawed, if frozen), cut into 3 (8 x 10-inch) rectangles

4 cups canned coconut milk

1½ cups loosely packed dark brown sugar

1 teaspoon kosher salt

2 cups Latik (page 169), plus more for serving

In a large bowl, combine your glutinous rice with 6 cups water. Let soak overnight at room temperature. (Soaking the rice will make the bibingka taste significantly better.) Drain the rice thoroughly and discard the water. Set aside.

Preheat the oven to 350°F. Butter a 9 x 13-inch baking pan.

Heat the rectangles of banana leaf directly over a low gas flame on the stove, turning frequently with tongs, until the leaves are soft and malleable but not burned, 10 to 30 seconds. They should turn a slightly darker, waxy color. If you don't have a gas stove, heat a large nonstick pan over an electric burner until hot. Working with one rectangle at a time, heat for 1 to 2 minutes on each side.

Line your buttered baking pan with the banana leaves, overlapping the long edges slightly and leaving 2 inches of overhang on the long sides of the pan.

In a large wok or heavy-bottomed pot, bring the coconut milk to a boil over high heat. Add your sugar and salt and cook, stirring constantly, until fully combined and slightly thickened, 2 to 5 minutes. Add your rice and cut the heat to low. Cook, stirring occasionally, until the rice has fully absorbed the coconut milk, 20 to 30 minutes.

(recipe continues)

Pour the mixture into the prepared pan, smoothing the rice evenly. Pour the latik on top.

Bake until the bibingka is firm to the touch and no longer jiggly in the center, about 1 hour. Remove from the oven, garnish with the latik solids, and let cool to room temperature on a wire rack, about 30 minutes.

Holding the edges of the banana leaves, lift the bibingka out of the pan. Cut into squares and serve with more latik on top.

Latik (Caramelized Coconut Milk)

MAKES ABOUT ½ CUP

Latik is this weird, caramelized, crunchy, oily coconut topping. I have a feeling someone made a mistake, tasted it, and said, "Huh, this is pretty good." Early on in my testing of Filipino desserts, I wanted to make the glaze that you would put on top of bibingka. I didn't know how to do it, so I just boiled a can of coconut milk. The solids separated from the oil and became this solid mass of coconut meat. I tried it and realized, "Man, this is Filipino!"

Now, I've refined it. I add coconut meat to give the coconut solids something to grab on to. The latik ends up sweet, tasting like ground caramel with coconut flavors. It's my favorite Filipino dessert syrup. You can put it on pancakes, waffles, doughnuts, coconut ice cream, suman, karioka (fried rice balls), or anything sweet!

---

1 (13.5-ounce) can coconut milk

1 cup Niyog (page 164)

1 teaspoon kosher salt

In a large saucepan, bring the coconut milk to a boil over high heat. Cut the heat to a simmer and cook, stirring occasionally, for 20 to 30 minutes, until the oil starts to separate from the milk solids.

Add your niyog and salt and cook over medium-high heat, stirring constantly, until completely caramelized and golden brown, about 10 minutes. Anything past golden brown will burn, so make sure you're watching the mixture carefully.

Once the coconut curds are golden brown, strain the mixture through a fine-mesh strainer into a bowl—that's your latik. (Reserve the solids to garnish your Bibingka Malagkit, page 167.) Let cool before serving, or refrigerate in an airtight container for up to 5 days.

CHAPTER 6

Sacred
Heart

AT FIFTEEN AND a half, I applied for a work permit and got my first job. I was a dishwasher at the Sacred Heart Retreat House, a convent for nuns in Alhambra. In the late 1990s, they didn't have automated dishwashers; they had one sink with three compartments. The water was always scalding hot, and I would walk away from work at the end of the night with chafed hands.

My "fondest" memory of the retreat house was working a busy 500-patron weekend where I was the only dishwasher. The nuns gathered around me singing hymns to help me through. I know you might think that it was a nice gesture, but not in my book. While they sang, I would think, "Maybe you could grab a sponge and help me get out of here!"

Working at Sacred Heart was one of the toughest gigs I've ever had. I wasn't just a dishwasher. I was also the janitor, prep cook, and some days the kitchen manager. By the time I was done there, I was pretty much running the show with my good pal Danilo. Imagine Tony Danza with a Filipino face—that's Danilo. He had no papers. He was a G, an immigrant straight off the boat. He didn't speak much English, but he was a devout Catholic. Working at the retreat house was an honor for him. I learned a lot from Danilo. He was poor, and he showed me how to work hard and not complain.

I saw things differently because of Danilo. He was married to a woman who was three times his size, and they had the cutest baby. His whole family lived in a tiny apartment in Monterey Park. He was always happy. He could've been painting a wall or washing cars. He was just happy wherever he was. I wish I could find him. He was my first-ever work friend, and he was always proud to be Filipino. He always used to tell me: "Be proud of who you are, Alvin."

In high school, I wasn't always gung-ho about being Filipino. The affluent Filipinos in school weren't my friends. They thought they were Crazy Rich Asians and drove Mercedes and BMWs to school. Next to them, I was always the hood Filipino. I wore Dickies white shirts, 501 Levi's, and fake Tommy Hilfiger. I drove a Corolla or a Civic.

In high school, I became more attached to Chicano culture. Everything I did was straight up from Pico Rivera. I would rather eat burritos and tacos than Filipino food. I'd race cars, play sports, and hang out with girls. Back then, going to a school dance was like clubbing. It was the thing to do on a Friday night after a football game. Other Filipinos didn't really do that, because their parents wouldn't let them.

As soon as I started driving, my parents had no control over me. I was a really bad kid. I would tell them I was coming home at 10 p.m., but I pushed it. I knew they would never let me sleep on the streets, so, I'd come home at 2 a.m. Some nights, I never came home. I would stay at some girl's house for two weekends. I did not give a fuck. It got to the point where I didn't care about school. My junior year, I got kicked out of Don Bosco Tech.

So, I moved to my aunt's house in Redlands. That lasted only a couple months because my cousins and I got in a fight. At 17, I started sleeping on friends' couches in Santa Fe Springs. I went to Pioneer High School for a week, then went to Santa Fe High. During my senior year, I went to three high schools and was in three yearbooks.

I had to graduate, so I wrote a paper for my final project called "Hip-Hop: A Ticket Out of the Ghetto." At the time, I was entrenched in the local hip-hop community. I was following rappers from the hood who became teachers at their local high schools. I learned that the correlation between rappers and thugs was not necessarily true. You could be a rapper and also be involved in the right sort of life—shout-out, Nipsey Hussle!

I aced the paper. It was one of the top three essays written that year. I ended up graduating with honors. After just four months at Santa Fe High School, I got to wear a sash as a distinguished student.

That whole time, I worked at Sacred Heart with Danilo. Even when I lived in Redlands, I'd drive over there and work on the weekends. Many times, I would drive Danilo home after work. On those rides home, we would talk about our dreams and our "one day" wishes. He would talk about how one day he wanted to buy a house for his family. Ultimately, he wanted to become an American citizen. I would talk about wanting to be a baller. When you're a kid, all you care about is being rich, or becoming Jay-Z. I wanted to make something of myself, I just didn't know how.

Danilo was the hardest-working dude I've ever met, to this day. There's no doubt in my mind that he made his dreams of owning a home and becoming an American citizen come true. The recipes that follow are inspired by those tough years, and by my friend Danilo—a proud Pinoy and captain of the Sacred Heart Retreat House.

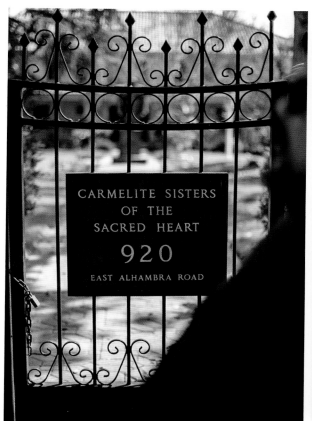

The Lord is found even among the pots and pans. *St. Teresa of Avila*

Limits

ALEXANDRA: Who was your role model growing up?

ALVIN: Ever since I could remember, I wanted to be just like my dad. He was my best friend as a kid. Compared to him, my mom was a diva. She would come home from work and go straight to bed. My dad would hang out with me and take me to Toys "R" Us. When people asked me in kindergarten what I wanted to be when I grew up, I drew a picture of myself with a key and a bench grinder. I wanted to be a locksmith, like my dad. But my dad said no, don't be like that. Be a scientist. Be something better than me.

My dad would crack jokes every day. Everyone respected him. He had tons of friends: his brother, his nephew, friends he grew up with, and neighborhood people. Every Friday or Saturday, they would come over to the garage to play mahjong and smoke cigarettes. My dad never smoked. Everyone would hang out for hours, drinking and talking about life. I would play ball, riding my bicycle down the street. Anytime I looked back, that garage always looked like home.

My mom was more introverted and devoted to the church. Once she got really active in the church, she got really popular. In the Philippines, my mom grew up with maids. In America, my dad did everything for her, except clean. I don't have many memories with my mom from when I was younger. She didn't help me with my homework because I didn't need it. My dad would ride bicycles with me in the park and come to my Little League games. He never missed a day. Then my dad became a business owner, and everything was different.

ALEXANDRA: What changed?

ALVIN: Everything. I never saw him again, not really, because he was always working. He started becoming more strict and more stressed. That's how I got to know my mom. When I was a teenager, we got closer. My mom would tolerate rap music, and I would tell her about girls I liked. I wanted my mom to drop me off at school, because I wanted to listen to music. My dad would never let me touch the radio, not anymore.

When I was 15, my relationship with my parents took a turn. Money and business had changed my dad, and it started to change our family. My parents started to become people from San Gabriel Valley. They no longer ate in their neighborhood. They started migrating toward the wealthier San Marino. They even changed their parish to Alhambra. They started to leave Pico behind, and that's when I started to rebel. I was born and raised as a kid from Pico Rivera. I grew up Catholic, had my First Communion and my first kiss in Pico Rivera. Pico was home, and I didn't want to leave it. My parents didn't matter, and school didn't matter. It was all about the block and my homies. That attitude shaped the next ten years of my life.

ALEXANDRA: How did that make you feel?

ALVIN: Like, damn. I had this chip on my shoulder. I wanted to show them I could do it on my own. So I started working, but I didn't have any idea of the magnitude of money. I didn't know what $100,000 was, or $1,000. Even if it was just $400 in my bank account, making money made me feel like I was on top of the world. That was my priority. Everything, including education, took a back seat to making money, and making it work.

ALEXANDRA: They wanted you to be better, when you were still trying to figure out how to be yourself.

ALVIN: Yeah.

Sinampalokan Manok
(Sinigang Packet–Roasted Chicken)

SERVES 4

I was fifteen and a half and working like a G at the retreat house with my pal Danilo. We'd make Filipino food for the nuns on the weekdays. I remember Danilo would always cook with his pinky up. It was the weirdest thing. The first time I saw Danilo make this recipe, I thought he was crazy. He would lay out rows and rows of chicken legs, rub the chicken with canola oil, then tear open a sinigang packet. He would look at me and say, "This is the secret," as he sprinkled sinigang-packet dust all over the chicken.

Every time I would have a break, I would go to the empty prayer hall, listen to Power 106 and eat my lunch. One day, I remember saving some of Danilo's sinigang-packet chicken for my lunch. When I ate it for the first time, it was so delicious that I made it that night for my parents. My dad ate it, and he was blown away. The combination of chicken, rice, and patis was a whole new way of eating sinigang. It was incredible.

---

1 (5-pound) whole chicken, cleaned, rinsed, and patted dry

Canola oil, for rubbing and greasing

1 (1.41-ounce) packet Knorr Tamarind Soup Mix (available at Asian markets or on Amazon)

1 tablespoon kosher salt

Preheat the oven to 350°F.

Rub the chicken all over with oil. Sprinkle the tamarind soup base in the cavity and all over the chicken exterior. Season the chicken with the salt.

Truss the chicken legs together and truss the wings, hugging the breast. You want to create a tight core to promote even cooking and browning.

Oil a cast-iron skillet large enough to house the bird. Place the chicken, breast-side up, in the skillet and roast in the oven, rotating every 15 minutes, until the chicken breasts reach an internal temperature of 155°F, about 1 hour 15 minutes. Remove from the oven and let the chicken rest for 15 minutes before carving and serving.

Danilo's Pancit Canton (Chinese-Style Noodles)

SERVES 6

I remember soaking pancit bihon rice noodles with my grandma. I would watch her run her fingers through the noodles. They weren't the long kind, more like fideos. When Danilo made his pancit, he used longer Chinese noodles with a thick gravy. It was night and day from the pancit I knew, which tasted like soy-flavored noodles with lemon, onions, carrots, and celery.

Danilo's pancit Canton was way more complex, like chow mein. It had sausage and pork in it, and it had cool lightning-looking carrots. He would make it in a big-ass commercial pot that you could tilt. On the weekends, we would make it for hundreds of people. I remember opening so many packets of egg noodles. I learned how to make a soy sauce gravy and how to let the onions, garlic, and marinade flavor the noodles.

When I first ate this dish, I realized: "Oh, these noodles are tight." They're unctuous, delicious, and completely craveable. It was the first time I was able to slurp noodles, because they were long. Then, I started noticing pancit Canton everywhere. You could get it at Salo-Salo Grill or Chow King. Pancit Canton became a new trend in the '90s.

Today, my pancit Canton nods to Danilo's, with added inspiration from Mongolian barbecue—mall-style. I cook the noodles like pasta, stir-fry them with the vegetables and cooked meat, and I'm done. It's super simple but super tasty!

1½ pounds fresh Chinese lo mein noodles

½ pound pork belly, sliced ½ inch thick

Kosher salt

¼ cup canola oil

1 large yellow onion, thinly sliced

3 garlic cloves, minced

1 cup Homemade Chicken Stock (page 44)

Fill a large pot with water and bring to a boil over high heat. Meanwhile, fill a large bowl with ice and water. Boil the noodles for 1 minute. Drain the noodles and plunge them into the ice bath for 3 minutes to stop the cooking. Drain and set aside.

Season the pork belly liberally with salt. Heat a large wok over high heat till it's blistering hot. Add the oil and heat until you see it ripple, about 1 minute. Lower the heat to medium. Add your pork belly and fry, stirring so it doesn't stick to the sides, until caramelized and most of the fat has rendered out, 8 to 12 minutes. Transfer the pork to a plate and set aside. Reserve 2 tablespoons of fat in the wok and discard the rest.

(ingredients and recipe continue)

AMBOY

6 tablespoons Datu Puti or Silver Swan soy sauce (see page 60; available at Asian markets and on Amazon)

1 tablespoon oyster sauce

½ teaspoon freshly ground black pepper

1 cup shredded napa cabbage

½ cup julienned carrots

4 scallions, thinly sliced

12 to 15 lemon wedges, for serving

Reduce the heat to medium-low. Cook the onion and garlic in the fat, stirring, until the onion and garlic are slightly caramelized, 8 to 10 minutes. Add the chicken stock, soy sauce, oyster sauce, and black pepper. Bring to a simmer and continue to simmer, stirring every few minutes, until the sauce reduces by one-third, about 5 minutes.

Add the cabbage, carrots, and scallions. Cook, stirring, until the cabbage and carrots are crisp-tender, 4 to 7 minutes. You don't want any of your veggies mushy.

Crank up the heat to medium. Add the reserved noodles and pork and cook, tossing, until everything is evenly distributed and the noodles are al dente, about 5 minutes. Divide among shallow bowls and serve right away with the lemon wedges.

Fried Calamari

SERVES 4

When Danilo would get frozen calamari, it was already cleaned, white, and pristine. It would look like a condom with tentacles. We would lightly coat it with rice flour to add to the crispiness, then we would deep-fry it. On the side, we would serve a garlic, chile, and vinegar dipping sauce. People would eat the crap out of it. We loved it. We would even have our own stash to eat on our break.

In high school, I would make fried calamari for my friends when we drank. It's such good drinking food. Some people will read this and say, "Oh, he was still in school and already drinking?" Yes, I drank in high school. We were very big on Coronas, and Mickey's malt liquor—when we wanted to get lit-lit—and we loved Miller Genuine Draft (MGD), because at the time they sponsored the Lakers, and the Lakers were winning. Shaq and Kobe. It was the best. It was that time.

I connect calamari and beer to my friend Cyrus's house. It was beautiful, had a pool, and was located on the ninth hole of the Candlewood Country Club. Tight. I still remember when Derek Fisher hit that 0.4-second shot. I was at Cyrus's house eating calamari.

Canola oil, for frying

2 cups rice flour

1 teaspoon garlic powder

1 teaspoon kosher salt, plus more for seasoning

1 (12-ounce) can plain seltzer

1 pound cleaned squid bodies, cut into ¼-inch-thick rings

1 lemon, cut into wedges, for serving

Pour 4 inches of oil into a medium pot and heat over medium-high heat to 375°F.

In a medium bowl, whisk together the rice flour, garlic powder, salt, and seltzer until a batter forms.

Working in batches, dunk the squid rings into the batter and let the excess drip off. Add to the oil and deep-fry, flipping as necessary, until golden brown, 3 to 5 minutes.

Use a spider to transfer the calamari to paper towels to drain and immediately season with salt. Plate the fried calamari and serve right away with lemon wedges, for freshness.

Filipino Spaghetti

SERVES 4 TO 6

This dish is not like Italian spaghetti at all—it's extremely weird, hypersweet, and often served at big family gatherings, like funerals. Danilo and I would make it for the nuns at Sacred Heart. I remember having to defrost tons of hot dogs for it and using crazy amounts of banana ketchup for the sauce.

Now, I try to make sense of it all. Instead of using sweet banana ketchup, I'll make a gastrique. In French cooking, you reduce sugar and vinegar into a syrup and you use that to tighten sauces. In my opinion, you can't use San Marzano tomatoes in this recipe. It's not an Italian dish. It's a strictly Filipino dish. You have to channel your inner Filipino to understand. I use Pomì tomatoes, which are on the sweeter side.

In this recipe, I use large chunks of onion. For me, if you can't see a big petal of onion, it's not Filipino spaghetti. I also throw in chopped garlic, a bit of sugar, soy sauce for depth of flavor, ground pork, and hot dogs.

I love Jollibee's fast-food rendition of Filipino spaghetti. I don't like the version I usually see at house parties. It's almost always a joke dish, overly sweetened and unappetizing on purpose—with cold shredded cheddar on top and room-temperature pasta that is always overcooked.

When I have really bad Filipino spaghetti, I just imagine a Betty Crocker postcard landing in the Philippines and being picked up by a lady who wants to make something that looks exactly like the picture on the card but lacks the ingredients to do it. So she makeshifts the recipe: "We don't have tomato sauce, but we have ketchup, so let's just use ketchup." It's a culture based on necessity.

In my experience, Filipino spaghetti is never mixed. That would defeat the customizability of it. I'll place a pot of spaghetti sauce next to the noodles, but that's as close to "mixing" as I go. Your ratio is your prerogative, so have as much as you want!

---

3 tablespoons canola oil

1 large onion, cut into 1-inch chunks

¼ cup chopped garlic (about 8 cloves)

1½ pounds ground pork

1 teaspoon kosher salt, plus more for seasoning

1 (6-ounce) can tomato paste

2 ripe bananas, diced

1 (26.46-ounce) box Pomì strained tomatoes

1 red bell pepper, roasted (see page 129), seeded, and chopped

½ cup sugar

½ cup rice vinegar

¼ cup Datu Puti or Silver Swan soy sauce (see page 60; available at Asian markets and on Amazon)

4 hot dogs, sliced at an angle

1 pound spaghetti, preferably Barilla

1 pound Edam cheese (rind removed and discarded) or 2 (7-ounce) cans Kraft pasteurized cheddar cheese, shredded, for serving

(recipe continues)

For the sauce, heat a medium Dutch oven or heavy-bottomed pot over high heat until hot. Add 2 tablespoons of the oil and cut the heat to medium. Add the onion and garlic and cook, stirring constantly, until the onion is translucent, 3 to 5 minutes.

Add the pork, breaking up the meat, and stir to combine. Season with the salt and cook, stirring constantly, until the pork has caramelized and is an even brown, 7 to 10 minutes.

Add your tomato paste and cook, stirring, for 2 minutes. Add the bananas and cook, stirring, for 2 minutes. Cut the heat to super low. Add your tomatoes and roasted red bell pepper and scrape up all the browned bits from the bottom of the pot. Simmer, stirring occasionally, until the sauce is reduced by one-third and thick enough to coat the back of a spoon, about 1 hour.

In a small saucepan, combine the sugar and vinegar and bring to a boil over high heat, stirring to dissolve the sugar. Once the sauce is bubbling, cut the heat to medium-low and cook until the gastrique is viscous, clear, and light yellow in color, 3 to 5 minutes.

Transfer the hot gastrique to your tomato sauce. Add the soy sauce and cook stirring occasionally, until the flavors marry, about 10 minutes.

Meanwhile, heat a small frying pan over medium heat until hot. Add the remaining 1 tablespoon oil and heat until you see the oil ripple, about 30 seconds. Add the hot dogs and cook, stirring constantly, until crisp and caramelized around the edges, 3 to 5 minutes.

Throw the hot dogs into the tomato sauce and continue to cook over low heat, stirring occasionally, until the flavors marry, 5 to 10 minutes.

While the sauce is cooking, fill a large stockpot with water and bring it to a rolling boil over high heat. Season generously with salt. It should taste like seawater. Add your spaghetti and cook according to the package directions, stirring occasionally. Drain the spaghetti.

Divvy up the spaghetti into bowls and serve with the sauce. Sprinkle on as much shredded cheese as you desire, and serve hot and weird!

Thursday-Night Retreat House Chicken

SERVES 4

This is what we used to feed the nuns on Thursday nights: roast chicken marinated in Italian dressing. It was the day before all the retreats happened, so we just wanted to chill. We knew we were going to get our asses kicked Friday, Saturday, and Sunday, so this dish emerged: low-key, delicious, and simple. Back then, we didn't even make the dressing—we used Hidden Valley!

2 pounds bone-in, skin-on chicken parts or one whole chicken

⅔ cup Homemade Italian Dressing (recipe follows)

2 teaspoons kosher salt

½ teaspoon freshly ground black pepper

Steamed Jasmine Rice (page 20) or Sacred Heart Retreat House Fried Rice (page 186), for serving

Preheat the oven to 375°F. Line a rimmed baking sheet with a silicone mat, foil, or parchment paper and set it aside.

Meanwhile, put the chicken in a large bowl. Add your dressing and toss to coat the chicken evenly. Let marinate at room temperature for 30 minutes.

Transfer the marinated chicken to your baking sheet, skin-side up, spacing the pieces about 1 inch apart. Sprinkle the salt and pepper over the top of the chicken.

Pop it in the oven and bake until the internal temperature reaches 155°F for the breasts and 165°F for the thighs, about 15 minutes. The skin should be a crispy, golden brown. Let it rest for 15 to 20 minutes. Serve with your choice of rice.

Homemade Italian Dressing

MAKES 2 CUPS

½ cup red wine vinegar

1 tablespoon minced red onion

1 tablespoon minced garlic

1 tablespoon Dijon mustard

1 teaspoon kosher salt

1 teaspoon freshly ground black pepper

1½ cups extra-virgin olive oil

Combine the vinegar, onion, garlic, mustard, salt, and pepper in a blender and blend on medium speed until fully incorporated, about 30 seconds. Add the olive oil and blend on high until fully incorporated, about 20 seconds. Use a spatula to scrape all the good stuff from the sides and lid of the blender, and mix it into the dressing. Use right away or transfer to an airtight container and refrigerate for up to 1 month. Shake well before using.

Sacred Heart Retreat House Fried Rice

SERVES 4

Danilo and I wanted to make fried rice at Sacred Heart one weekend. We didn't have jasmine rice, so we used medium-grain white rice. We didn't have Filipino soy sauce, so we would use Kikkoman. We did have a lot of frozen vegetables, the kind you get in plastic packs—carrots, green beans, lima beans, and peas—and being a creative Pinoy, Danilo just made it work. You can make Filipino food out of pretty much anything. The Pinoy soul of it all is the garlic and soy sauce.

Making fried rice is an art. In this recipe, you use day-old rice instead of fresh rice because it's not as sticky. You mix your rice with soy sauce before putting it into the pan so that all your grains are evenly brown. You heat the garlic perfectly, so it almost melts into the rice. Then, you get the rice hot so that the moment the egg hits the rice, it begins to cook. Because the egg is being cooked by the radiating heat of the rice, you end up with the fluffiest egg ever.

In my opinion, you're doing it wrong if you have large chunks of egg in your fried rice. Every bite should have a piece of rice and a fleck of egg.

---

4 cups cold Steamed Jasmine Rice (page 20)

¼ cup House Toyomansi (page 71)

1 tablespoon plus 1 teaspoon canola oil

4 teaspoons minced garlic (see page 110)

4 large eggs

2 cups frozen vegetable mix, preferably carrots and peas

Kosher salt and freshly ground black pepper

1 teaspoon thinly sliced fresh chives (see page 110)

Crumble the cold rice into a medium bowl. Add your toyomansi and use your hands to mix it with the rice to thoroughly coat every grain until the rice is an even brown. Set aside.

Heat a large pan over medium-high heat until hot. Add the 1 tablespoon oil and heat until you see the oil ripple, about 30 seconds. Add the garlic. Cut the heat to medium and cook, stirring, until the edges of the garlic just crisp up, about 20 seconds. Add the rice and cook, stirring constantly, until the garlic is incorporated and the rice is hot throughout, about 3 minutes.

Once your rice is super hot, make a well in the center. Add the remaining 1 teaspoon oil. Crack the eggs into the well, then swirl with a wooden spoon to beat the eggs and incorporate them fully into the rice. Stir constantly until the eggs are cooked all the way through, 3 to 5 minutes. The mixture will feel wet at first, but it will progress to feeling dry. Keep stirring until the egg is flecked through all the rice and the rice is super fluffy, about 2 minutes.

Fold your frozen vegetables into the rice and cook on medium until they are warmed through, about 3 minutes. Season to your liking with salt and pepper. Serve hot in bowls with a sprinkle of chives on top.

My First Steak Ever

SERVES 1 HUNGRY PERSON

In high school, my mind was blown by medium-rare Delmonico steak at Norms, a neighborhood chain diner. It was $4.99, and I would order it all the time with my friends. At home, I made my own version by chopping 30 garlic cloves, rubbing those on a steak, and cooking it up on the grill in the backyard.

If you're grossed out by the smell of garlic, or if you're going to make out with someone who is offended by it, don't attempt this recipe, because this is going to make you smell, for sure.

1 (12-ounce) **New York strip steak**

4 teaspoons **olive oil**

1 teaspoon **kosher salt**

1 teaspoon **freshly ground black pepper**

2 teaspoons **minced garlic**

2 tablespoons **canola oil (for cooking in a pan; omit if grilling)**

Steamed Jasmine Rice (page 20), fried rice (pages 109, 186, and 333), or warmed Pan de Sal (page 83), for serving

Put your cold steak on a plate and drizzle the olive oil over both sides. Rub the olive oil lightly into the meat. Season with the salt and pepper, about ½ teaspoon of each on each side of the steak. Sprinkle the garlic on each side of the steak, and tamp it down by hand into the meat so it's evenly coated.

Let your steak hang out, uncovered, marinating in all that goodness, till it reaches room temperature, 30 to 40 minutes. That way, it will cook more evenly. Otherwise, it's easy to accidentally cook the outside super well-done while leaving the inside super rare.

If you're doing this up on a grill, place your steak with the tip pointing at 10 o'clock on the hottest part of the grill for 1 minute. Then, flip your steak and keep it at 10 o'clock for another minute. Flip your steak again, placing the tip pointing at 2 o'clock on the hottest part of the grill for 1 minute. Then, flip it back and keep it at 2 o'clock for another minute. This will give you a rare steak with perfect, sexy grill marks. (If not, drizzle the steak with a little olive oil to get grill marks.)

Now, if you want to take that rare steak to medium, place it on the coolest part of the grill at 2 o'clock for 1 minute. Flip it, place at 2 o'clock for another minute, and pull it off the grill. Or, to take that medium steak to well-done, place it on the coolest part of the grill at 2 o'clock again for 1 minute. Flip it, then place at 2 o'clock for another minute. Repeat for 1 minute on each side, then pull it off the grill.

If you're doing this on the stovetop, heat a large cast-iron pan over high heat till it's blistering hot. Add the canola oil, cut the heat to medium, and heat until you see the oil ripple, about 30 seconds.

Place your room-temperature steak in the hot oil and sear it on both sides: 2 minutes per side for a rare steak, 3 minutes per side for medium-rare, 4 minutes per side for medium, and 6 to 8 minutes per side for well-done.

Whether grilled or pan-seared, transfer the steak to a cutting board and let it rest for 10 minutes. Then, slice it ½ inch thick and serve either with rice or in a hot pan de sal.

CHAPTER 7

Weekend Heroes

—

THE LAST YEAR of high school was a blur. Those days were covered in kush clouds and malt liquor. I can't believe that I was able to graduate on time. Shout-out to 18-year-old me for getting through it all!

I had no intention of going to college. I wanted to work. My dad's construction business was taking off, so I asked if I could work for him. To be clear, my dad never wanted me to work with him. He never wanted me to follow in his footsteps, so when I asked him for a job, he knew exactly what to do.

On my first day working for Quality Building Interiors, my dad sent me to work in Palm Desert. I was working in 106-degree heat with a dude who didn't speak English. My job was to break up a sidewalk with a jackhammer. I worked for three days in the blazing sun. After the third day, I told my dad I didn't want to work for him anymore. I thought I would try out college.

I started college as a freshman in 2001. The first week of school, our country suffered a devastating act of terror. The threat of World War III was in the air.

I started school in a new world full of uncertainties and what-ifs. We couldn't even open our mail because we thought anthrax could be in our packages. A lot of my friends enlisted in the military. I was tempted to, but, ultimately, I wanted to hustle. Like a squirrel stashing away nuts for the winter, I wanted to stack as much money as possible in case someone tried taking everything away from me. So I hit the streets and sold some things: weed, fake designer bags, and stolen DVD players. I wanted security. Education was not a priority.

College Boy

ALEXANDRA: What was your worst job ever?

ALVIN: When I was in junior college in Whittier, I worked at a telemarketing place. I was basically doing collections in Irwindale, and it was the worst. It was boring and sterile, and took no talent.

ALEXANDRA: What was your best job ever?

ALVIN: I loved selling cell phones! One night, I was walking down Hollywood Boulevard when the Hollywood and Highland area was still a new thing. Some people were promoting a party for Schick razors at a club called Level 3, so I went. There was this dude drinking at the bar, and he had a cool-ass phone. I asked him about it. He told me about this new company called T-Mobile, and this phone called a Sidekick. He was looking for someone to work with, someone enterprising to sell his product. I said, "Tell me more."

So I got my business license and started a cell phone company at 18. To market it, I bought the most expensive business card I could find. On the card was my name and my number. I'd hand it to people at the club and say, "If you ever need a cell phone, just call me."

The guy from the club would give me new Sidekicks, I'd make a commission off the sale, and that was it. It was easy-peasy $8,000 commissions. I sold Sidekicks and paid my taxes. It was my first experience running a business and it was profitable. I felt like I was rich.

ALEXANDRA: Did you work any other jobs in college?

ALVIN: At the same time I was selling cell phones, I was also a nightclub promoter. Back then, I was driving a big car I couldn't afford, popping Cristal at the club, and full-on faking it till I made it.

I'd drive around and hit all the shopping areas on Melrose and Fairfax. Every week, I'd get new shoes and new shirts. I spent money as fast as I made it. I wanted to be Jay-Z so bad.

I would hang out at the Nacional in Hollywood. It was the kind of place that attracted hip-hop heads, skate geeks, and street-fashion impresarios. It was a fraternity of dudes doing things.

I would sit and smoke, the youngest guy among legends. All around, everyone was drinking, rolling, and getting high. The babes and rappers all came through. Every night of the week, I would be out at a different club. Mondays were reggae nights in Hollywood, Tuesdays were Taco Tuesdays in Fullerton, Wednesdays were backpack hip-hop in Atwater Village, Thursdays were back in Brea at a club, Friday nights were the Nacional in Hollywood, and Saturdays were at Boardner's.

After a while, I found myself heading down to the kitchen all the time. I would hang out with the staff cooks while everyone was upstairs getting shit-faced. I would spend more and more money on food. I'd hit BOA Steakhouse, then Madeo for Italian food. I would go to all the LA celebrity hot spots. I was eating at places like a millionaire, except that I wasn't. But I loved it, because it was different. It was inspiring.

ALEXANDRA: When did you start getting into cooking food at home?

ALVIN: After college. I finished my degree, got a real job in Fullerton in construction, and hated it. I spent the entire time at work looking up recipes. All I wanted to do was cook. The advent of the gastropub was upon us, and I was obsessed.

I became a hard-core home cook. Friends would come over, and I would cook for them. It was good times and the best part of Fullerton. I learned how to braise meat and how to properly fry chicken. I wanted to impress my childhood friend Mark.

He had just finished culinary school and was venturing into fine dining. I had no idea there was a hierarchy in the kitchen, so I thought Mark was a legit chef. Looking back, he was just starting out as a cook. I would always ask what he thought about different recipes. He would look at me like: "You better pay your dues."

When you're a home cook, everything you're doing is seen as mostly for fun. But I was serious. I became obsessed with learning the mother sauces. Back then, my theory was that anything tasted good if the sauce was good. Now, as a chef, I know there's so much more.

ALEXANDRA: It makes sense that you started with sauce. Filipino food is so sauce-heavy, sometimes I feel like the antithesis of Filipino food is dry food. Take our concept of sabao.

ALVIN: Exactly. Sabao is so unique. It's something between soup and sauce. It's a whole genre in Filipino food. You can have a whole meal that's just sabao and rice.

When I started learning how to cook, I started with the mother sauces, which are kind of the French equivalent of sabao. They're their own genre. I learned emulsification and how to make fresh mayonnaise and hollandaise. I learned how to use a roux to thicken animal and vegetable stocks. It became a gravy called velouté. I made béchamel, tomato sauce, and sauce Espagnole, which is a mix of tomatoes and gravy.

For me, that Spanish sauce brought the mother sauces full circle. It's similar in concept to Filipino food. You take a stock, mix it with tomatoes, then thicken it with a roux. Dishes like mechado and afritada are based off those kinds of sauces, except we use potatoes as a thickener instead.

ALEXANDRA: How did your cooking evolve from there?

ALVIN: In the beginning, I didn't have any money. But the minute I started to make money, I'd blow $300 on ingredients and cook all weekend. I was hella into movies. I'd watch *The Godfather* and *Goodfellas* and make the red sauce straight from the movie. I'd buy steaks and pork chops and learn how to prepare them. My favorite dish was steak au poivre. I'd make fried chicken over and over again. I'd make kung pao chicken and honey-walnut shrimp. I'd ruin food, make decent food, and then master the dish. I discovered heavy cream and put it in everything. I learned how to take steak drippings and turn them into a pan sauce. It felt like magic.

I loved making Italian and French food. For me, Italian food was level-two gourmet. It was one step up from American food, with classics like pot roast and mashed potatoes. I loved making pasta. I learned how to salt water and cook pasta perfectly al dente. I learned how to build flavor by making sauces. When I was able to buy real Parmigiano-Reggiano, it changed my life. I started shredding it and putting it in everything. Before umami was even a thing, I realized Parmesan cheese made everything taste better. I had this overall curiosity about food. And I had the means to explore it because I had money from my construction job. I started doing holiday dinners. I was serious. I wanted to cut perfectly. I kept my knives sharp. In a Filipino household, a sharp knife is hard to find.

ALEXANDRA: What kind of knives did you get?

ALVIN: I got whatever I saw on *Top Chef,* usually Calphalon or Henckels. More than anything else, it made me want to become a chef so bad. I started upgrading my kitchen equipment and got better knives, good tongs, and a wooden cutting board. I started to accept and love food. It became my world.

The Blueprint

Once college was over and it was time to enter the real world, I only had a couple options for moving forward: I could continue my dad's construction business or work for one of his competitors. Besides cooking, that's really all I knew how to do. I could cost out materials and labor, and bid on projects. I'm not going to lie, I had a passion to be a general contractor. I've renovated many offices and homes. My specialty was flooring, and on the weekends my team and I would do residential renovations. I even worked on homes in Beverly Hills, but fifteen years ago, a lot of our construction projects were with big national banks—the same banks that asked for billions of dollars in bail-out money and left my generation with high tuition bills and no sight of an American dream. So every day I went to work, and every day I would generate work orders for tens of thousands of dollars for stuff that didn't really need to be done. It was all vanity, taking fairly new office spaces and then totally renovating them on the taxpayer's dime. It wasn't what I wanted to do. I made good money, but my heart was not in it.

As a result, I would rush through work for the first few hours of the day so I could spend the rest of it searching for recipes online. I deposited my checks on Friday and headed straight to the grocery store to buy food so I could cook all weekend. If my commission checks were high, I would buy a commercial smoker or All-Clad pans. I wanted to be the best home cook out there. Sometimes on my lunch break, I would head to Barnes & Noble, grab a cookbook, and read all about pasta and sauces.

Eventually this gourmand lifestyle was all I could think about. It got to the point where I would take weekend trips to various culinary schools, from New York's Culinary Institute of America to the Art Institute of Las Vegas. Months went by and my infatuation for amazing food grew stronger and stronger. The recipes I was developing were getting tighter and more refined. I needed more. I wanted to be a chef!

The recipes that follow are the ones I worked on right before I went to culinary school. These are the dishes that converted me from home cook to culinary student. Cheers to these recipes. Not only did they widen my horizons, but they marked the beginning of a whole new life.

Hennessy Steak au Poivre

SERVES 4

I watched Food Network; my go-to shows were *Iron Chef, Iron Chef America,* and *Good Eats.* I got really into steak. On Friday, I would go to Costco and buy a five-pack of rib eyes (or filet mignon, if I was feeling bougie). Friday night, I would cook one rib eye, and maybe screw it up. Saturday, I would make a good one. Sunday, I would learn how to make an au poivre sauce with Hennessy. I would use cream, beef stock, a little bit of brandy or cognac, and peppercorns. A week later, I would still have two more rib eyes, but I would have no more cream left. I'd just have Hennessy. I'd ask myself, "What would happen if I just deglazed the pan with Hennessy?"

Looking back, it was how I learned technique. It was my first foray into making actual alcohol reduction sauce, and it was delicious.

STEAKS

4 (1-inch-thick) filets mignons (12 to 14 ounces each)

Kosher salt and freshly ground black pepper

1 cup canola oil

SAUCE

2 tablespoons canola oil

½ cup minced shallot (about 1 large shallot)

½ cup Hennessy V.S cognac

1 cup heavy cream

1½ tablespoons coarsely ground black pepper

Kosher salt

PREPARE THE STEAKS: Preheat the oven to 350°F.

Season each steak all over with salt and pepper. Set aside.

Heat a heavy-bottomed skillet over medium-high heat until smoking, 3 to 5 minutes. Coat the pan with ¼ cup of the oil and heat until you see the oil ripple.

Add 1 steak to the hot oil. (Cook only one steak at a time; more than that, and you won't get that perfect sear.) It should sizzle when it hits the pan. Cook till the steak is seared to a beautiful brown, 3 to 4 minutes on each side. Transfer to a plate and repeat with the remaining oil and steaks.

Insert a meat thermometer into the center of each steak; if it reads between 110°F and 118°F, then let it rest for 5 to 20 minutes. If the temperature reads any lower than 110°F, transfer the steaks to a wire rack set over a rimmed baking sheet and pop them in the oven. Roast the steaks, checking every 3 minutes, until the internal temperature reaches 118°F. This should take 7 minutes max. Take the steaks out of the oven and let them rest for 5 to 20 minutes.

(recipe continues)

Dump the used steak oil but reserve all the bits stuck to the pan. This is called the "fond." It's super tasty and very important.

MAKE THE SAUCE: Heat the canola oil in the steak pan over medium heat for 1 minute. Add the shallot and cook, stirring, until translucent, 2 to 4 minutes.

Remove the pan from the heat and add the Hennessy. Return the pan to medium heat—be careful, because the alcohol may catch on fire. This is normal; once the alcohol is cooked off, the flame will go out. The result will be a more concentrated sweetness and complexity in the sauce. Cook, scraping up all the fond from the bottom of the pan with a wooden spoon, until the alcohol has cooked off, 1½ to 2 minutes.

Add the cream and black pepper and let the sauce simmer, stirring constantly to thoroughly mix the cognac and cream, until the sauce thickens enough to coat the back of the spoon, 3 to 5 minutes. Taste the sauce and add salt to your heart's desire.

Transfer each steak to a plate, smother with the sauce, and serve immediately.

Sunday Gravy

SERVES 8 TO 12

My favorite kind of movies were always the ones with gangsters—whether they were the Bloods and Crips of Compton or Michael Corleone and the mafia. On HBO's *The Sopranos,* the mobsters would have family dinners on Sunday. Even for them, it was important to eat food and share it with people you loved. This Sunday "gravy" is what I made. For my take on the iconic red sauce, I render chicken fat to braise sausages and ground beef. Then I add tomato paste and canned tomatoes and let it cook for a long time, until the sauce is unctuous and the tomatoes become super sweet. Some cayenne pepper gives it a kick of heat. This sauce is a throwback to my roots. It's the foundation of an endless bowl of pasta that a family can eat all day long.

½ **pound ground beef**

1½ **tablespoons canola oil**

4 **bone-in, skin-on chicken thighs**

¼ **pound sweet Italian sausage, casings removed**

¼ **pound hot Italian sausage, casings removed**

1 **large yellow onion, diced**

16 **garlic cloves, chopped**

1 **tablespoon sweet paprika**

2 **teaspoons dried oregano**

1 **teaspoon cayenne pepper, plus more if desired**

3 **tablespoons tomato paste**

2 **cups Homemade Chicken Stock (page 44)**

6 **(28-ounce) cans whole peeled San Marzano tomatoes**

Kosher salt and freshly ground black pepper

3 **pounds spaghetti, cooked, or 4 loaves crusty bread, toasted, for serving**

Take your ground beef out of the fridge and let it come to room temperature. Meanwhile, heat a large Dutch oven or heavy-bottomed pot over medium-high heat until hot. Add the oil and swirl to coat the pot evenly. Heat until you see the oil ripple, about 1 minute. Add the chicken thighs, skin-side down. Cut the heat to medium-low and do not touch the thighs until the skin releases from the bottom of the pot, 10 to 15 minutes. You might have to reduce the heat to get a nice crust on the skin. The trick is to slowly render the fat from the chicken so it melts and helps release the skin from the pot.

Flip the chicken and cook until browned on the other side, 12 to 15 minutes. Transfer the chicken to a plate and reserve it for another use. Reserve all the chicken fat in the pot.

Turn up the heat to medium-high. Add the ground beef to the pot and cook, breaking up the meat and stirring frequently, until the beef is browned and caramelized, 5 to 7 minutes. You want the ground beef to get nice and brown. If it's grayish in color, your pot may be too small, which crowds the meat. Or, your meat may be too cold, which lowers the temperature of the pan when you cook it. Or, your heat simply wasn't high enough. Make sure you cover all the bases when browning meat, and the difference will be tremendous.

(recipe continues)

Using a slotted spoon, transfer the ground beef to a medium bowl and set aside. Reserve all the beef fat in the pot. Add the sausage and cook, stirring and breaking it up into small pieces as it cooks, until the sausage is caramelized, 5 to 7 minutes. There should be a lot of meat goodness ("fond") stuck to the bottom of the pot, and that's a great thing. Using a slotted spoon, transfer the sausage to the bowl with the ground beef and refrigerate until ready to go into the sauce. Reserve all the fat in the pot.

Reduce the heat to medium. Add the onion and garlic to the pot and cook them in the delicious, fond-y fat, stirring, until the onion is a bit translucent, 3 to 4 minutes. Add the paprika, oregano, cayenne, and tomato paste. Cook, stirring, until the tomato paste is lightly toasted, about 2 minutes. Add the chicken stock and scrape up all the fond from the bottom of the pot.

Cut the heat to super low. Add the tomatoes and their juices and cook, stirring occasionally, until the tomatoes completely break down, about 6 hours. Super low heat will prevent the sauce from over-reducing and scorching the bottom of the pot. Occasionally skim any fat off the top of the sauce. Taste your sauce—your tomatoes should be sweet. If the tomatoes are still tart, cook for up to 2 more hours until they mellow out.

Once the tomatoes are stewy and perfect, return the ground beef and sausage (but not the chicken, which you can use for something else now) to the pot and cook for 30 minutes. This is a good time to cook your pasta or toast your bread. Season the gravy to your liking with salt and pepper.

Serve the Sunday gravy over spaghetti or simply eat it with hot, toasted bread.

Godfather (or Sunday) Gravy

ALVIN: I called this the Godfather Sauce because it's based on the recipe from the first *Godfather* movie. It's right after Don Corleone gets shot, right before all five families go to war. Clemenza is teaching Michael Corleone how to make sauce. He just dumps the entire container of sugar in the sauce. It's not a little bit of sugar. Or in *Goodfellas*, Henry talks about how they made the gravy and used a razor blade to thinly slice the garlic.

ALEXANDRA: Did you ever cut the garlic like that?

ALVIN: With a razor? Oh, absolutely. This next scene, also from *Goodfellas*, is my favorite. Henry talks about braising the beef, pork butt, and veal shanks for the tomato sauce and making ziti with the gravy. Just that shot of the meat! It makes me want to eat. Movies and scenes like this were so amazing, they made me want to cook right away.

I used to watch movies like them every day. I would fall asleep to them. They meant so much to me. To this day, they influence what I cook and what I crave.

Also, coming from hip-hop culture, gangsters are the shit. So, if gravy is what Michael Corleone eats, then I want to eat it. When he becomes the leader of the organization, that's how I feel. I relate to it. It's epic and romantic. That's why I really focused on perfecting my red gravy sauce. I still make it to this day.

ALEXANDRA: What do you put in it?

ALVIN: This recipe takes an entire day. I start off in the morning searing all my meat. I sear off chicken, ground beef, spicy Italian sausage, and sweet Italian sausage. Then, I put all that meat aside. I have all the great bits in the bottom of the pan. I cook the onions and garlic. Then, I'll use chicken stock to deglaze all that, throw in the tomatoes, and cook it for 6 to 8 hours. Tomatoes release pectin when you cook them down. They lose any sourness and they become sweet like a jam. So instead of adding sugar, I let the natural sugars develop.

After the sauce is simmered down, I'll add the meat back. I'll cook that down some more, so the flavors start to marry. I used to make this gravy on Sunday and started calling it Sunday Gravy, and friends from culinary school would come over for it. These days, while the gravy is cooking, I chill. Angela, my girlfriend, does laundry. I might do household chores. For me, this gravy is a celebration of the end of the week with family. That's really the heart of it.

Mother Sauces

Mother sauces are the foundation of most sauces in French cuisine. I was obsessed with learning how to make them from scratch. I started with emulsions—a mayonnaise and a hollandaise-style sauce—which is basically egg beaten into fat. Then I picked up béchamel, which is a combination of milk and roux. I learned how to make a velouté, or a gravy, by using water, chicken bones, and roux. I determined that tomato sauce was just straight up tomato, garlic, and onion. Last, I mastered sauce Espagnole, which is stock thickened by tomatoes and a roux. To me, sauce Espagnole is Filipino food. Now I make a buttery roux in adobo, instead of thickening adobo with potatoes, or cornstarch and water. Butter has more flavor than cornstarch and water, and any chance I have to add more flavor to a dish, I will take it.

If you know how to make all five mother sauces, everything else is easy. Master the basics, and then you have the foundation to create any sauce you can imagine!

Emulsion: Hollandaise Sauce

MAKES ABOUT 2½ CUPS

To make an emulsion, you basically whip air into fat. Then, you whip more fat into those air bubbles. Some of the sauces in this book, like Homemade Italian Dressing (page 185) and Bring Out the Best Mayo (page 59), are emulsions. For this basic hollandaise, I cheat: I like technology, so this recipe requires a high-speed blender. Serve your hollandaise over vegetables or eggs Benedict.

4 large egg yolks

1 tablespoon apple cider vinegar

¼ teaspoon chili powder

1 pound (4 sticks) unsalted butter, melted

Kosher salt

In a high-speed blender, combine the egg yolks, vinegar, and chili powder. Blend at medium-low speed until you see little bubbles in the mixture, about 1 minute.

With the blender running at medium speed, slowly stream in the butter and blend until the butter is fully incorporated and the sauce reaches a nice, thick, butter-mayo-like consistency, about 2 minutes. (For these 2 minutes of blending, you want to go as slow as possible so you don't overwhelm the yolks and break the emulsion. You're basically injecting the butter into the bubbles of the egg yolks.)

Once the butter is fully incorporated, season the hollandaise with salt and pour it into a gravy boat. Serve right away.

Béchamel

Your first foray into learning béchamel is probably mac and cheese. When I didn't know how to cook, I thought mac and cheese was melted cheese on macaroni. When I tried it, I got this cheesy, oily, gross mess, because when cheese separates, nothing will ever put it back together. It becomes two separate entities, like oil and water.

When you add a roux, that chemical composition pulls the fat and milk solids from the cheese so it all sticks together and doesn't separate. It's a good reason to learn béchamel: You can make great mac and cheese.

---

4 cups whole milk

1 cup Roux (recipe follows)

1 teaspoon kosher salt

Heat a medium saucepan over medium-high heat until hot. Add your milk and bring it to a boil.

Whisk in the roux, a third at a time, until fully incorporated. Cut the heat to medium and cook, whisking constantly, until the mixture is thick enough to coat the back of a spoon, about 30 seconds. Season with the salt.

Cut the heat to low and cook the béchamel, whisking occasionally, until the raw flour taste is gone and the sauce has thickened, about 45 minutes. Use right away or let cool to room temperature and refrigerate in an airtight container for up to 3 days. Reheat gently before using.

Roux

MAKES 2 CUPS

1 cup (2 sticks) unsalted butter

1 cup all-purpose flour

Melt the butter in a small, straight-sided pan over medium heat. Cut the heat to medium-low, whisk in the flour, and cook, whisking frequently, for 10 minutes, or until the flour smells like popcorn.

Use right away or let cool to room temp and refrigerate in an airtight container for up to 2 weeks.

Velouté

MAKES ABOUT 1 QUART

Don't be fooled by the fancy French name. Velouté is just continental-style gravy: broth or stock thickened by a roux. Vegetable stock velouté is perfect with steamed vegetables and rice, while one made with chicken stock is perfect for roast chicken or to ladle on mashed potatoes. Beef stock velouté is amazing with roast beef. Sauces make dishes awesome. Learn every kind of sauce out there. Pair it with your favorite vegetables or proteins and your recipe game will reach new levels.

4 cups Homemade Chicken Stock (page 44), Beef Stock (page 45), or Vegetable Stock (page 46)

1 cup Roux (above)

1 teaspoon kosher salt

Heat a medium saucepan over medium-high heat until hot. Add your stock and bring to a boil.

Whisk in the roux, a third at a time, until fully incorporated. Cut the heat to medium and cook, whisking constantly, until the mixture is thick enough to coat the back of a spoon, about 30 seconds. Season with the salt.

Cut the heat to low and cook the velouté, whisking occasionally, until the raw flour taste is gone and the sauce has thickened, about 45 minutes. Use right away or cool to room temperature and refrigerate in an airtight container for up to 3 days. Reheat gently before using.

Tomato Sauce

MAKES ABOUT 1 QUART

Homemade tomato sauce is perfect for pasta, and in Amboy cooking it's what makes tomato-based stewy dishes like Mechado (page 126), Putahe (page 128) and Kalderetang Chickpeas (page 313).

4 cups canned tomato puree

1 cup diced onion (about 1 medium onion)

¼ cup minced garlic (about 10 large cloves)

In a large stockpot, combine the tomato puree, onion, and garlic. Bring to a boil over high heat. Cut the heat to low and cook, stirring occasionally, until the tomato sauce has reduced by half, 2 to 4 hours. It should move from a tart, sour flavor to a sweet, savory flavor. Use right away or let cool to room temperature and store in an airtight container in the refrigerator for up to 1 week or in the freezer for up to 3 months.

Sauce Espagnole

MAKES ABOUT 1 QUART

If you mix velouté and tomato puree, you've got sauce Espagnole. This is a lost and forgotten style of sauce. Mix it with peas and potatoes and you'll have an awesome side dish. Pour sauce Espagnole over a roast leg of lamb and you'll have a kickass Sunday supper.

4 cups Homemade Beef Stock (page 45)

1 cup canned tomato puree

1 cup Roux (page 207)

1 bay leaf

1 teaspoon kosher salt

Heat a medium saucepan over medium-high heat until hot. Add your beef stock and tomato puree and bring to a boil.

Whisk in the roux, a third at a time, until fully incorporated. Add the bay leaf, then cut the heat to medium. Cook, whisking constantly, until the mixture is thick enough to coat the back of a spoon, about 30 seconds. Season with the salt.

Cut the heat to low and cook the sauce, whisking occasionally, until the raw flour taste is gone, about 45 minutes. Remove and discard the bay leaf. Use right away or let cool to room temperature and refrigerate in an airtight container for up to 3 days.

Lasagna

SERVES 8

I grew up eating Stouffer's lasagna because my great-uncle would make it all the time. It was the kind of lasagna that you take out of the freezer, put in the oven, and it's ready to go. Growing up, lasagna was super comforting and homey. When I started cooking, I would see these cool lasagna baking pans, and I would want them so bad. But then I would have to justify buying them somehow. Finally, I said, "Fuck it. I'm going to stop buying Stouffer's and start making my own lasagna." I loved it because it was so indulgent. It's this big block of pasta with meat sauce, ricotta, mozzarella, and Parmesan. It's the ultimate comfort food. At first, I would buy the noodles dry. Then, I started to make my own pastas. It's simple: All you need is flour, eggs, and salt.

Pro tip: Make two of these lasagnas at a time. Eat one and freeze the other. Later, you can take a lasagna out of the freezer, pop it in the oven, and have dinner. It's better than Stouffer's any day.

Kosher salt

**12 Lasagna Noodles
(recipe follows)**

**12 cups Sunday Gravy
(page 201)**

**4 cups whole-milk ricotta
cheese**

**4 cups shredded low-moisture
mozzarella cheese**

1 cup freshly grated Parmesan

Preheat the oven to 375°F.

Bring a large stockpot of water to a rolling boil over high heat. Season generously with salt. It should taste like seawater. Add your noodles and cook, stirring, until al dente, about 1 minute. Drain and set aside.

Ladle 1 cup of the gravy into a deep 9 x 13-inch baking pan, spreading it evenly to cover the bottom of the pan. Lay 3 lasagna noodles in a single layer over the sauce. Top with another 2 cups of the gravy, spreading it evenly over the noodles. Spread 1⅓ cups of the ricotta evenly over the gravy. Sprinkle 1 cup of the mozzarella evenly over the ricotta. Spread 1 cup of the gravy over the mozzarella. Repeat these layers (3 noodles, 2 cups gravy, 1⅓ cups ricotta, 1 cup mozzarella, 1 cup gravy) two more times. Then lay on the remaining 3 noodles in a single layer and top with the remaining 2 cups gravy.

Bake the lasagna for 30 minutes. Pull the pan out of the oven, scatter the remaining 1 cup mozzarella and the Parmesan evenly over the top, and pop it back in the oven until the cheese looks nice, 7 to 10 minutes.

Pull the pan out of the oven and let the lasagna rest for 30 minutes at room temperature. Then cut into it and enjoy!

Lasagna Noodles

2½ cups all-purpose flour,
   plus more for dusting

1 teaspoon kosher salt

4 large eggs

Sift the flour and salt together into a large bowl. Mound the flour on a clean, dry work surface.

Make a well in the center of the mound. Pour the eggs into the well and beat the eggs with a fork. Slowly incorporate the flour into the eggs with the fork to make a dough. Knead until the dough is shiny, about 10 minutes. Form the dough into a ball and press your thumb into the center. If the dough springs back, it's ready to go. If not, keep kneading. Transfer the dough to a bowl, cover with a damp towel, and let rest for 1 hour.

Cut the ball of dough into 4 equal quarters. On a floured work surface, roll 1 piece out with a rolling pin into a rectangle that's ⅛ inch thick. Cut the rectangle into five 4-inch-wide strips. Dust the strips with flour so they don't stick to each other. Repeat with the remaining dough. Use right away or stack on a baking sheet with a piece of parchment paper between each noodle. Cover with plastic wrap and chill for up to 1 day.

Spam Chips and White Bean Puree

MAKES 20 TO 30 CHIPS AND SERVES 8 TO 10 AS AN APPETIZER

Experimenting with Spam is one of my favorite things to do. When I was in culinary school, I would use Spam to practice French cutting techniques, one of which was slicing ham paper-thin. I tried this with Spam and then crisped it up in a pan. I found out that they became crispy chips. I quickly made my favorite Italian white bean dip so I could scoop it with the Spam chips. Then I served it at a Super Bowl party, and it was an instant hit.

1 tablespoon canola oil

1 (12-ounce) can Spam, sliced lengthwise ⅛ inch thick

White Bean Puree (recipe follows), for serving

Heat a medium frying pan over medium-high heat until hot. Add your oil, then cut the heat to medium and heat for 30 seconds.

Set a wire rack over a rimmed baking sheet and set aside. Add 6 Spam slices to the pan in a single layer and fry until crisp, about 1½ minutes on each side. Transfer to the wire rack and let cool for 5 minutes. Repeat with the remaining Spam. Serve right away with the white bean puree.

White Bean Puree

MAKES ABOUT 1 QUART

4 cups dried cannellini beans

1 onion, quartered

1 carrot, quartered

2 celery stalks, quartered

½ cup minced garlic (about 20 large cloves)

1 cup extra-virgin olive oil

1 teaspoon kosher salt

Put the beans in a large bowl and cover with plenty of water. Let soak overnight.

Drain the beans and discard the liquid. Transfer the beans to a large stockpot and add a gallon of fresh water, along with the onion, carrot, and celery. Bring to a boil over high heat, then cut the heat to medium-low. Cook, stirring occasionally, until the beans are soft, about 45 minutes. Drain the beans and discard the liquid and vegetables.

Transfer 3 cups of the beans to a food processor. (Reserve the remaining beans for another use.) Add the garlic, olive oil, and salt and process until smooth. Transfer to a bowl and serve right away as a dip for Spam chips, or spread on top of toast or bagels.

Death Row Meal

ALEXANDRA: If you could only eat one dish ever again, what would it be?

ALVIN: It's my death row meal: Spam, eggs, and sinangag, or garlic fried rice. For me, the eggs have to be over easy because I like to use the egg yolks as a sauce.

ALEXANDRA: It's cool that's your death row meal because it's a classic Filipino breakfast. That's Spamsilog.

ALVIN: Yeah! I don't need caviar or lobster. Give me Spamsilog and we're good.

I like to cook the Spam crispy on medium-low heat. I'll cook it till the Spam goes from pink to maroon, and it gets a nice craggly texture. I like cutting the Spam ¼ inch thick, almost like a thick credit card. Sometimes, if it's crispy enough, I use the Spam to scoop up my rice and egg. I'll eat it like chips.

ALEXANDRA: That's awesome. When I grew up, we would cut Spam into thin slices, spread each side with a little brown sugar, and put it in a pan. It's so good.

ALVIN: I've had it like that, and I love it. It's like jamonado glazed with brown sugar and pineapples. I feel that a lot. Honestly, Spam is so versatile. It can be your main dish. You can put it in pan de sal and it becomes a sandwich. You can dice it up, put it in fried rice, and now you have Spam fried rice. Or you can dice it up, put it in noodles, and now you have Spam pancit. It's an awesome part of Filipino food.

Braised Pork Shoulder

WITH FRESH TORTILLAS

SERVES 8 TO 10

If you don't know how to braise meat properly, you should learn immediately. It will change your life. When I was younger, I loved fried food. As I got older, grilled food took over. Now, I have more patience. I'm learning how to cook with low heat, so braised meats have become the undisputed way to eat protein.

I'll sear a pork shoulder and get it nice and caramelized. Then, I'll cook it submerged in water, with some onions and garlic, in a super-low oven for several hours. The result is divine—super-tender, falling-apart meat.

It's the most Catholic thing to eat. You put all this hard work into it, and you enjoy it after. So many Filipino dishes are a braise. We make one-pot wonders. Honestly, most of our food is that way because you can start it, go to work, come back, and have food. Filipino households are not like American households—there's always someone at home, especially in the Philippines. You can leave your dish on the stove and go to work. Then, you have your mom, nanay, lola, lolo, or kuya watch over it. There's always someone there. In Filipino culture, the entire tribe takes care of the food. Everything is family: family style, family prepared. That's why the one person who doesn't pull their weight is the one that gets treated poorly. There's always the *tamad,* or Tito Boy. There's always the kid who's *bunsod,* who doesn't pull their weight. Every family has one. Don't be that guy!

In my opinion, the best way to eat pulled pork is with fresh tortillas. Just get a fresh tortilla, add pulled pork, a slice of onion, a little cilantro, some Tapatío sauce, and call it a day. Or, you can make a quesadilla. Open it up when the cheese is melty, and shove some shredded carnitas in there for a fantastic experience.

Learning how to braise meat is tough. You have to let the kitchen gods do their thing. You have to wait for it to be perfect, and then eat it in that window. To test the meat, take a fork, give it a twist, and if that pork has no resistance at all, it's ready!

---

6 tablespoons canola oil

2 pounds boneless pork shoulder

2 onions, quartered

30 garlic cloves, peeled

Kosher salt and freshly ground black pepper

Extra-virgin olive oil, for drizzling

Fresh Tortillas (recipe follows), for serving

Salsa or hot sauce, for serving

Chopped white onion and fresh cilantro, for serving

(recipe continues)

Preheat the oven to 250°F.

Heat a large, straight-sided pan over high heat until hot. Add the canola oil and heat until you see the oil ripple, about 30 seconds. Cut the heat to medium. Place the pork shoulder in the pan flat-side down and sear until caramelized, about 4 minutes per side.

Transfer the pork to a large Dutch oven. Scatter the onions and garlic around the pork and pour in enough water to submerge the pork shoulder. Cover and braise in the oven until the pork is fork-tender, about 6 hours.

Remove from the oven. Transfer the pork to a large bowl. Strain the braising liquid and use in place of the chicken stock for an all-pork-based version of Amboy Adobo (page 243). Discard the solids. Using two forks, shred the meat into bite-size pieces. (Alternatively, use your hands when the pork is cool enough to handle.) Season the pulled pork with salt, pepper, and olive oil.

Transfer the pulled pork to a platter. Allow guests to make tacos with the tortillas, pulled pork, salsa, onions, and cilantro.

Fresh Tortillas

MAKES 20 TO 24 TORTILLAS

2 cups masa harina
½ teaspoon kosher salt
1½ cups water

In a large bowl, whisk together the masa harina and salt. Microwave the water for 30 seconds on high (or heat in a small pot) until warm, then stir it into the dry ingredients. Knead with your hands until the dough is smooth and feels tacky but not sticky, 3 to 5 minutes. Set the dough aside.

Cut 2 rounds from a large resealable plastic bag, each about 7 inches in diameter. You will use them to line your tortilla press.

Heat a cast-iron pan over medium heat until hot.

Meanwhile, pinch off about 2 tablespoons of dough and roll it into a ball. Repeat with the remaining dough.

Place 1 plastic round on the bottom plate of your tortilla press. Place 1 ball of dough in the center and top it with the second plastic round. Close the tortilla press and press down gently to make a thin tortilla of even thickness. (Alternatively, do this with two heavy pans and the plastic rounds.) Carefully peel off the plastic rounds and gently lay the tortilla on the cast-iron pan. Cook until lightly browned in a few spots, 1 to 2 minutes on each side. Transfer to a plate and cover with a kitchen towel to keep warm. Repeat with the remaining balls of dough.

Pulled Pork Adobo

SERVES 4

I love braising pork shoulder. I made pulled pork everything—pulled pork BBQ, pulled pork tacos. Sometimes instead of tortillas, I would crave rice. I would take that pulled pork and toss it in the quintessentially Filipino dish, adobo. I was so Filipino, it was inevitable. Today, I even put the pulled pork adobo into a pan de sal! It's awesome, and so Amboy.

1 pound leftover pulled pork from Braised Pork Shoulder (page 215)

2 cups adobo sauce from Amboy Adobo (page 243)

Steamed Jasmine Rice (page 20), for serving

In a medium saucepan, combine the pork and adobo sauce over medium heat. Cook, stirring, until thoroughly combined and the liquid reduces slightly, about 10 minutes.

Remove from the heat, ladle the pulled pork adobo into bowls, and serve with rice.

Biscuits and Gravy

SERVES 6

Growing up, I always loved biscuits. My first memories of making them were buying a Pillsbury tube, popping the top off, cutting up the dough, and throwing them in the oven. They were good, but they were never as good as the biscuits at McDonald's, KFC, or Popeyes.

In 1999, I watched a video of Alton Brown on *Good Eats*. He made biscuits with his grandma, and I made his recipe. For the first time, I learned how to make a white milk gravy. From then on, I fell in deep, deep love with biscuits and gravy.

Now, I have the perfect biscuit recipe. To go with it, I'll make gravy with breakfast sausage and sometimes bacon. I'll render out the fat, get the good bits, and season it up with onion and garlic powder. Then I'll thicken it with either a béchamel or cheese. Once it coats the back of a spoon, it's ready to go. You throw it on top of fluffy, fresh-baked biscuits, and it's some of the best breakfast in the world.

---

225 grams (2 sticks) unsalted butter, chilled

550 grams (about 4 cups) bread flour, plus more for dusting

30 grams (about 2 tablespoons) baking powder

8 grams (about 2½ teaspoons) kosher salt

2 grams (about ½ teaspoon) baking soda

250 grams (about 1 cup) well-shaken buttermilk

50 grams (about ¼ cup) heavy cream

50 grams (about ¼ cup) Clarified Butter (recipe follows), for glazing

Country Gravy (recipe follows), for serving

Preheat the oven to 350°F. Line two rimmed baking sheets with parchment paper and set aside.

In a large stainless steel bowl, shred the chilled butter on the large holes of a box grater. Freeze the butter in the bowl until ready to mix with the dry ingredients.

Meanwhile, sift together the flour, baking powder, salt, and baking soda into a medium bowl.

In a liquid measuring cup, whisk together the buttermilk and cream until combined.

Transfer the dry ingredients to the bowl with the shredded butter. Using your hands, toss together to lightly coat the butter with the dry ingredients.

Make a well in the center of the butter and flour mixture and pour the wet ingredients into the well. Using your hands, slowly mix just until a soft, crumbly dough forms. Do not overmix the dough.

(recipe continues)

On a lightly floured work surface, pat the dough out into a rectangle. (The dough will be crumbly, but will eventually come together after rolling.) Use a bench scraper to keep the rectangle together. Cut the rectangle into thirds, then stack the thirds of dough on top of each other. Roll the dough out to about 1¼ inches thick. Cut into 3-inch squares. (Alternatively, use a 3-inch biscuit cutter to stamp out—without twisting the cutter—biscuit rounds as close together as possible. You can reroll the scraps and stamp out more biscuits. They just won't be as tender.)

Place the biscuits on the prepared baking sheets. Spacing doesn't matter. Bake for 15 minutes. Rotate and swap the pans and quickly glaze the tops of the biscuits with the clarified butter. Bake until the biscuits are golden brown on the tops and sides, 12 to 15 minutes. Don't be tempted to open and close the oven while baking or the biscuits won't get a full rise.

Transfer the biscuits to wire racks to cool for 10 minutes. For each serving, plate 2 biscuits and top with the gravy.

Clarified Butter

MAKES ABOUT 1½ CUPS

1 pound (4 sticks) unsalted
butter

Melt the butter in a small, heavy saucepan over super low heat. Cook until the browned milk solids separate from the butter, 45 minutes to 1 hour. Remove from the heat.

Fill a large bowl with cold water. Pour the melted butter into the water and refrigerate until the butter re-solidifies, about 2 hours. The clarified butter will rise to the top of the water during this time. Use the warmth of your hands to melt the layer of clarified butter from the top and immediately skim it off into a bowl. Melt the clarified butter before using or refrigerate in an airtight container for up to 1 month.

Country Gravy

MAKES ABOUT 3 CUPS

1 tablespoon canola oil

1 pound bulk pork breakfast
sausage or links, casings
removed

1 teaspoon onion powder

1 teaspoon garlic powder

1 quart Béchamel (page 206;
if you don't have a full quart,
make up the difference with
whole milk)

Whole milk, as necessary

Kosher salt and freshly ground
black pepper

Heat a medium Dutch oven over high heat until hot. Add the oil and heat until you see the oil ripple, about 30 seconds. Cut the heat to medium. Add the sausage and cook, stirring and smashing into little pieces with a wooden spoon, until caramelized, 6 to 8 minutes.

Cut the heat to low. Add the onion powder, garlic powder, and béchamel and cook, whisking constantly, until thickened, 15 to 20 minutes. If the gravy is too thick for your liking, whisk in milk to reach your desired consistency. Season the gravy with salt and pepper and serve right away. Or refrigerate in an airtight container for up to 2 days. Reheat gently and whisk in more milk, if desired.

Portland Runaway

THERE'S THIS SCENE in the movie *Blow* where Johnny Depp is in jail with this dude. The guy says, "I am El Mágico, I am the dreamer." When I saw that movie, I knew that's who I was. You know those people who are dreamers but never do anything about it? I was the opposite.

For most of my life, I had to hide who I was from my parents. I became almost pathological. My parents were church-going, God-fearing people, so I had to be a completely different person with them. When I wasn't with them, I smoked weed. I drank. I would drive drunk. It all stemmed from having to hide all the time. That's the thing about being Filipino. You have to hide any part of yourself that your parents would disapprove of. It all goes back to that respect. My parents wanted me to be a doctor, a nurse, an engineer, or an accountant. They were like any Filipino mom and dad. They wanted me to do well in school and be that guy.

I hustled to keep up with my American friends who had more than me. I would sell or trade my toys with my rich friends so I could get the freshest Nikes. Then, I would keep my shoes at school so my parents wouldn't see them. I had baggy pants, but I only wore them at school. I would hide who I was all the time. I couldn't be myself around my family.

AMBOY

My first real girlfriend was the daughter of my parents' best friend. My parents played us out like we were the next royal couple. At first, I liked her, even loved her. But then, we grew apart. My parents wanted me to keep it going, so I did, just to make them happy. It didn't last. We broke up and it hurt like hell, but I was happy it was over.

I went to college just to prove to my parents that I could. I took a job at a construction business—sat in a cubicle so a white dude could make money—because my parents thought I should. Then I realized that a four-year college degree in business wasn't what I was passionate about. Making money for the same dude that everyone else was slaving for made me sick. I hated life. I did everything my parents wanted me to do, and I wasn't happy. I've never been the type to drown in my sorrows. I've always been the type of dude who says, "Fuck it, I'll start all over again." So I did.

I turned my desk job into a "how to get out" project. Every day at work, after I'd secured contracts, after my boss went out to survey a job, after I put in the service orders, sent it for approval, and received my hourly plus commission, I would look up culinary schools in the area.

In 2009, I even tried becoming a cook without going to culinary school, but no one would hire me. There was no room in an LA kitchen for a privileged suburban kid with a construction management resume and a college degree. Even entry-level positions turned me away.

This is about the time I began cooking all-nighters, when I was becoming obsessed with cooking. I was 26, but things weren't turning fast enough. I was having my quarter-life crisis. I'd go to Vegas with friends, wake up early, and check out the culinary school there. I toured schools in New York and Pasadena. Finally, on a visit to Portland, Oregon, to visit a friend, I found the one. That weekend, on a tour of the Oregon Culinary Institute before I was even enrolled, an instructor taught a bunch of prospective students—me included—how to make brownies, and they were the best brownies I ever made. The place clicked. The curriculum, the instructors, the class size—everything was perfect. Even the rent made sense. I couldn't stop thinking about it for weeks. I signed up for Pell Grants and student loans.

Then, I left.

I was so close to my friends and family, and I left. I was dating a girl, and I left. I didn't tell anybody, because I knew if I did, they wouldn't let me leave. They probably all hated me, and it was selfish, but I had to do it for me. So the time came . . . for Portland!

I moved in secret. I packed my SUV with all my belongings and headed north. It took two days. I got to Portland and settled in my friend Jeni's house by the airport.

Oregon! There were so many white people. Everyone was so nice. I remember the first weekend there, I went to Target with Jeni and a salesclerk in a red shirt was following us around. I finally snapped and told her I wasn't going to steal anything, so she could leave us alone. She just smiled. She said she was there to help me find anything I needed. I was so embarrassed. I apologized and immediately knew I was in a totally different world.

Culinary school was the best time I've ever had in a school setting. I was a smart-ass. I never missed school. I was the first person to raise my hand. I was the person who did all the homework. I was the most prepared for exams.

I wanted to be a cook so bad. But just as in LA, Portland restaurants weren't looking for inexperienced cooks. So, I decided to work for free. I volunteered to peel carrots, wash dishes, and clean bathrooms at every top restaurant in Portland. I just wanted to get my foot in the door. Luckily, I was due two years of severance pay from my job in Fullerton. That gave me just enough to survive.

The effort paid off. I helped everyone, and my reputation spread. I started working a paying job at Jake's Grill as a cook. I moonlighted as a barista at a coffee shop off Burnside. Later, I staged at Castagna, Olympic Provisions, and Ten01. I began to spread myself thin. This never ended. It was how I learned to live. I juggled three different jobs and school. In my free time, I would cure meats and sharpen knives. Come to think of it, not much has changed.

Looking back, I just want to say thank you. Thank you, Portland. Thank you for being a kind city I could evolve in. Thank you for not chewing me up and spitting me out. Thank you for transforming me from a kid dreaming about food to a cook with skills I will carry for the rest of my life.

This is the story of my escape to Portland, and my time in cooking school.

The Reality of Being a Cook

ALEXANDRA: What was culinary school like?

ALVIN: Back then, Oregon Culinary Institute was fairly new, around two years old. I liked that it was very focused on the reality of being a cook. There weren't posters of famous chefs. You walked in, and you could tell it was all about learning how to cook. At that school, no one ever told me, "Hey, you're going to be famous one day."

ALEXANDRA: Do you think you knew a lot compared to the people you went in with?

ALVIN: I went in there thinking, "I have a sophisticated palate. I eat at really expensive restaurants in Beverly Hills, and this is Portland. They don't know what they're talking about." I had a chip on my shoulder purely because I cooked a lot, and I knew what fancy ingredients were.

In reality, I learned so much in Portland. We would get tested on our knife skills once a week. I would take that so seriously. On the first or second test, I wanted to do so well, I went to Home Depot and I bought four 2 x 1-inch blocks, and I cut each one 12 inches long. I cut grooves in each block at ⅛, ¼, ½, ¾, and 1 inch. At night I would run my fingers through these grooves on my coffee table, so that my muscle memory would develop on how far the distances were. I would run my knife through the grooves so that I could train my wrist. I did this every day for years. Now, if I dice up an apple, they come out in perfect squares.

ALEXANDRA: So you literally learned the distance—how to measure—by feel?

ALVIN: Yeah! I trained my eyes, my hands, and my wrists. People thought I was crazy, but I knew I wanted to be a specific kind of chef. I didn't want to just be a cook. When you change your life and your career, you have the opportunity to be the best that you can be. I was super passionate about it. I've always had that in me. If I'm going to dedicate my time to it, I want it to be great. During culinary school, I would learn how to make sausages. So I would take everything out of my apartment and just hang sausages. People would come over, look around, and say, "Yo, Alvin, what the fuck?"

In my Portland apartment, I had the world's tiniest kitchen. I had a dining room area, but since I lived by myself, I turned the dining area into a test lab. So I bought a stainless steel table, a mixer, and a food processor. I had all these gadgets.

ALEXANDRA: What would you test?

ALVIN: In school, we had this one term where we learned how to break down pigs. We had six pig heads left over. So I decided to make this Filipino dish called sisig with my friends Dave and Lung. Someone had told us that if you use pineapple juice, it'll tenderize the meat. Lung and Dave went to the grocery store across the street to buy the stuff. So I decided to take all the meat off the head. They came back with pineapples and pineapple juice, and we started to cook it. The problem was the pineapple juice tenderized the meat so much, all the fat and meat started to disintegrate. We were left with these huge, gross, oily flecks of meat. We totally failed. But we had five more heads, so we kept trying. That's what we did. We tried. We tried and we tried and we tried. We wanted to be the Navy SEALs of the restaurant game. We wanted to be those guys.

In culinary school, there are three terms before graduation. Our first term had thirty students. Our second term had fifteen. We graduated with seven. Aside from me, it was Lung, the butcher; Zan, who is now the executive chef of the best restaurant in Portland; and Dave, who won a StarChefs Rising

Star award (Cleveland) in 2016. It was probably the most decorated class of chefs that had ever graduated, purely because of how dedicated we were outside of school.

ALEXANDRA: What was your hardest job during culinary school?

ALVIN: Catering, hands down. I worked at a catering company that also had a restaurant. It was pretty big and like a higher-end version of TGI Fridays. I was stuck working in the hotel. Everyone got married there, so we had to cater weddings every weekend. During the week, I would prep for five hundred to a thousand people.

I highly recommend working for a catering company because you really get to master your skills as a cook. Think about all those hours that you put in trying to learn how to cut an onion. I had to cut cases of vegetables. I had to break down cases of meat. For me, it was fundamentally one of the best jobs I could have during culinary school, because it made me sharper.

ALEXANDRA: Take me through your life in Portland. Where was home?

ALVIN: I rented a place right by school in northwest Portland. It was also right by Providence Park stadium, and a block away from my favorite bar, the Marathon. I literally went there twice a day. It had cheap beer and terrible junk food. I still go there to this day. If you talk to anyone I knew from Portland, they know where to find me. It was our after-work spot.

It was also where I realized I was exotic. All the girls that hit on me were super white. They would say, "What are you? You're not Mexican." At the time, I was getting professional haircuts. I was super self-conscious of my image. I had this parted hairstyle, really slicked back, creased-up flannels and jeans, Red Wing boots, real Portland suave.

PORTLAND RUNAWAY

People may argue that some white men have an Asian fetish. I think I can argue that some white women have a "colored dude" fetish. Girls would literally say, "We should date, because you're different." I would go on dates with them, and we would do this weird arts and crafts shit. I was just an experiment for them. Back then, I never took women seriously. I became a player because I lived on top of a bar called the Bitter End. It was this Portland Timbers bar that everyone went to. Plus, I had weed, and I was culturally ambiguous. It created this amazing situation. At 2 a.m., I knew I could hit on chicks, so I would just go downstairs to the bar like the sleaze that I was.

I lived in a prewar building with a clawfoot bathtub. I had one of those sinks with separate hot and cold taps. It was just a classic old apartment. I went to yard sales, bought books I didn't read, and scattered them all over my apartment. I wanted it to look like all I did was cook, read books, and smoke. I had a gravity bong right there. *Kitchen Confidential* was my bible, and I was living in that style.

Was this an alter ego? In LA, I was hip-hop Alvin: one-carat diamond earrings on each ear, fitted cap, sneakers, and a T-shirt. In Portland, I became hipster Alvin. When you came to my house, I had wine, cheese, and a microbrew. I was the one older guy in my class, and I had a car. All of this made me so much more than I was in LA. It helped my confidence, and it helped me become a chef.

When I went to work, I was confident. When I went to the bar, I was confident. It was the first time in my life everything felt right. It was the greatest feeling in the world. LA offered none of that. While I was away, Lola Pacing had passed away. My entire family had grown apart. I'd strained my relationship with my brother—he had wanted to go to culinary school, too, but couldn't yet because he was still in high school.

Everyone I knew said, "You've changed." I didn't know if I'd changed, or if I'd become myself.

But I knew that the freedom to choose—that mental space that Portland gave me—helped me understand what I wanted in life. I wanted to be a chef. By any means necessary. And I wanted to be the best cook in the kitchen of any kitchen I worked at.

So, I worked harder. On the weekends, I'd take photos of recipes in books I couldn't afford, just so I could learn them. At work, I would climb the walls during cleanup so I could clean the vents no one else wanted to touch. I was that guy. I made sure my chef had coffee. To me, it wasn't being a kiss-ass. It was showing my commitment.

Castagna

After culinary school, I got an externship at the best restaurant in Portland. It was called Castagna, and the chef was a Portland culinary school alum. He had gone to Spain to work at Mugaritz. He had worked at El Bulli. At the time, Spain was the best culinary country in the world.

He was the kind of chef who would encapsulate yogurt so it would look like a ball. When you would bite into it, it would burst in your mouth. He would make a piece of lamb belly look like rocks. It was very avant-garde and artsy. I was good enough to get that kind of internship. It was a learning experience. My entire culinary school career, I had wanted to be a fine-dining chef. Castagna was as fine dining as you could get in Portland. It was 8 to 12 courses, white tablecloths, a glass for water, and a wineglass.

I was working from 8 a.m. to 2 a.m. every day for free. Because of the long hours, I finished my externship quickly. Then, I was at a crossroads. Did I want to continue making this kind of food? I thought long and hard and realized I wasn't passionate about it. Even though I could do it, I didn't want to spend all day cooking beef to make it look like something different. I didn't want to get the freshest carrots at the farmers' market, then put chemicals on them to treat them differently.

At Castagna, they were trying to blow people's minds with that philosophy: "Oh, it looks like a carrot, but it's not!" I didn't like that. It encouraged the development of a gamer-style chef. The cooks would spend all night trying to figure out how to win the avant-garde game—basically, the crazier the better. You would make foams and dusts. You would find the rarest herbs by foraging them yourself. It was cool, but ultimately not what I wanted to do.

I wanted to make food that anyone could identify, on a highly executed level. I wanted a piece of beef to look like a piece of beef. Even though I could cut a potato into the shape of a football, you still knew it was a potato. I didn't want to treat food any other way. At the end of the day, a potato was a fucking potato.

I liked that idea, so I ended up getting a job at

Ten01. Both chefs had worked for Thomas Keller. Michael Hannigan was Thomas Keller's sous chef, and Colin Stafford was his junior sous chef. They both ended up in Portland because their spouses got relocated there. I was so excited to work for them. *The French Laundry Cookbook, Under Pressure, Bouchon, Ad Hoc at Home*—those were my bibles in culinary school. At Thomas Keller's restaurants, he used green tape to label his food. Everyone had a white chef's coat, a blue apron, and green tape. I wanted to live that life. I wanted to be part of the green tape gang.

Chef Colin Stafford

The biggest culinary mentor I had in Portland was chef Colin Stafford. He was the sous chef at Ten01. He was the guy who said, "Alvin, take your time, do it right. Make everything perfect." One time, I was rushing because I was going to meet a girl after work. I cleaned up my station. You're supposed to clearly label all your food. That day, I scribbled everything. Colin took photos of it all and sent them to me while I was on this date. He said, "Alvin, what the fuck? This looks like shit. I'm not going to call you chef anymore."

Colin taught me how to do everything. He refined my skills. He turned my school lessons into professional skills. He showed me how to cut through herbs, otherwise all the flavor goes into your cutting board. If you slice instead of chop, you're slicing the cell walls. Then, the flavor stays in the leaves. He taught me how to sear meat and how to sous vide. I spent a lot of time with that dude.

One time, I was overusing Saran wrap and he made me cost it out. That was when I realized each foot of Saran wrap costs 10 cents. That's not cheap! He would give me creative freedom, but I would always have to cost it out. Those are things that you need to learn to be a chef. Now, he's the executive chef for East Hampton Grill here in New York. It's a Hillstone restaurant, which is one of my favorite restaurant groups. To this day, Colin and I still message each other. He has a family now. Even though he wasn't my executive

chef, I learned so much from him.

If I had to describe Colin, I would say the dude is white as hell! He's blond and blue-eyed. He would always reference *Top Gun*. He would always say, "Talk to me, Goose!" I was like, "What?" He would say, "Have you never seen *Top Gun*?" Dude, I've seen the movie, but I don't reference it! It's funny, because now I do that. At the time, I never understood why he liked *Top Gun* so much. Later, I watched it, and I realized that those airmen are like cooks. They're brothers. Every restaurant that I make, the team that I build is like that.

Chef Colin helped me gain the confidence and the bravado that you need as a chef. If you have any type of insecurity, it comes through in the food.

You can tell that there's something missing. This guy's holding back. Or, you can tell if there's over-confidence, where they're doing too much.

Colin made everything good. His pâté of rabbit and chicken livers was so good. It's a finesse dish. He taught me to be a finesse chef. To me, finesse means you're super fast and also high quality. That was the game changer in my career. Chef Colin would say, "Take bigger steps, you'll be twice as fast!" So I would do that. I would take bigger steps. I would work faster. He lit a fire within me that I never knew I had.

The recipes that follow are the ones that I made in culinary school, and after—missing Filipino food, and remembering home.

Filipino by Way of France

ALEXANDRA: Did you miss Filipino food when you were in Portland?

ALVIN: Of course. But in Portland, I wasn't Filipino. In Portland, I was "exotic," this brown guy. At Ten01, as much as I loved my chef there, he thought I was Mexican the whole time. In the beginning, I would make the food for family meal that I missed. I missed Pico Rivera nachos and carne asada. So the first few months at Ten01, I was making Mexican food. I guess that's why he thought I was Mexican. But then I started making Filipino food, and I really got into it.

ALEXANDRA: Were there Filipino restaurants in Portland at the time?

ALVIN: If there were, I never went to one. To get Filipino ingredients, I had to drive an hour away. I got really into making Filipino food at home and for my friends at work. Because I was in culinary school, I would make French-style adobo. I would thicken the sauce with butter. I added parsley, chives, and all these French herbs. I would make bistek, but use hanger steak, cook the onions separately, and make a demi-glace.

For family meal at work, which I was often in charge of, I would make embutido, the Filipino meatloaf with hard-boiled eggs. It's basically a roulade. I would use caul fat, which is this fat liner that pigs have. It looks like a spiderweb of fat. I would take that spiderweb, use the pork mixture on top, layer hard-cooked eggs in it, and roll it with mushrooms. I would sear it off so the outside would be crispy, then I would finish it in the oven so the inside would be juicy. I would put a pineapple-soy glaze on top, and people would ask, "What is this?" I would say, "It's a Filipino dish."

I liked to turn a lot of our Filipino dishes into vegetable dishes. I did a ratatouille with an adobo glaze. I would season tomato, zucchini, red onion, yellow squash, and eggplants with oil and garlic. I would layer them in a casserole and pour soy sauce and vinegar over that. I would cook it, and it would get melty. It was fantastic over rice. I also used to make and sell longanisa. I had a sausage stuffer at my house. Ratatouille-style adobo with longanisa and garlic fried rice is so good.

I was making French food every day, so all my Filipino food was done with French technique. At work, we were making blood sausage. I would dice pork belly and pork shoulder, sear them off, and deglaze the fond on the bottom with water. Then, I would add pig's blood and heavy cream. That's a classic French sauce. We would add heavy cream and butter until the sauce would get thick and beautiful. Then, I would make a gastrique with vinegar and sugar. I ended up with a sweet-and-sour flavor. Then I put pickled jalapeños on top. I was making dinuguan, and for me, dinuguan has to have that spice.

When I made this version of dinuguan for my chef, it blew his mind. His cooking is super French in style, so he said, "What the fuck is this?"

So I started to get juiced up about Filipino food, because I was excited that he liked it. I knew the line cooks would like it because at the time, cooking with blood, snout, ears, and tails was the hottest thing in the culinary world. I was badass for doing it. So I was able to be a woke Filipino in the white world of Portland, just by cooking food.

ALEXANDRA: It makes me think of our friend Charles Olalia. So many people we know trained in the French style of cooking, so there is a sort of "Filipino by way of France" theme going on.

ALVIN: Yeah, it's nuts. It's literally where everybody trained.

ALEXANDRA: Did you ever go to Powell's? It's endless.

ALVIN: I love Powell's! I've literally spent days there. It's where I found a lot of used Filipino cookbooks. I would never have the money to buy the $50 book, but I would sit there and read the entire thing or take photos of recipes I wanted to test.

AMBOY

Embutido (Pork Meatloaf)
WITH PINEAPPLE GLAZE

SERVES 8 TO 10

When you work at a restaurant, family meal is made from the scraps of whatever we make on the menu. It's always the undesirable cuts of meat or vegetable cuts that aren't perfect or weren't weighed properly. Making ground-meat dishes like burgers or Bolognese is very common. When it was my turn, I made embutido.

I started by flavoring ground pork with thyme, chives, and shallots and finished with a pureed glaze that would go on top. I've since streamlined those steps into this recipe.

Cooking the eggs perfectly, while not undercooking or overcooking the meat, is difficult. When I mastered it, it was one of my proudest moments in culinary school.

4 cups cubed stale, crustless white bread (about 6 slices)

½ cup whole milk

½ pound sliced bacon, coarsely chopped

½ pound ground pork

½ pound ground beef

2 tablespoons dark brown sugar

2 teaspoons kosher salt

4 Hard-Cooked Eggs (page 125)

1 cup Pineapple Glaze (page 121)

Steamed Jasmine Rice (page 20), for serving

In a large bowl, combine the bread and milk and let soak for 1 hour at room temperature.

Pulse your bacon in a food processor just until finely chopped. Measure out ½ cup of the ground bacon and add it to the bread mixture. Reserve the rest (if any) for another use. Add the pork, beef, brown sugar, and salt and mix with your hands until evenly combined. Let this mixture—aka "farce"—sit for 2 hours at room temperature. (This is a good time to hard-cook the eggs and make the pineapple glaze.)

Preheat the oven to 375°F. Line a rimmed baking sheet with a silicone mat.

Spread the farce onto a large sheet of plastic wrap and pat it out into a 9 x 13-inch rectangle; it should be about ½ inch thick.

Place the peeled eggs in a row, lengthwise, across the middle of the farce rectangle. Roll the farce tightly around the eggs using the plastic wrap so you get a long rolled meatloaf with eggs in the center. Remove the plastic wrap and transfer the embutido to the prepared baking sheet.

Bake, brushing the embutido with the pineapple glaze every 7 minutes, until the internal temperature of the meat reaches 155°F, 30 to 35 minutes. Remove from the oven, slice crosswise, and serve with rice.

Dinuguan (Pork and Blood Stew)

WITH CREAM AND PICKLED JALAPEÑOS

SERVES 8

At Ten01 we made a French dish with pork blood. I used the leftovers to make dinuguan, and my chefs loved it. That's when I told them I was Filipino. They said, "Dude, I thought you were Hawaiian, if anything." I felt weird. It felt like a compliment, but then again, it was weird that people didn't know what Filipinos were. That's when I knew the world was black and white. Coming from California, you don't know that. You think everything is as mixed as LA, and it's not. Portland is white. Aspen is white. Connecticut is white as fuck. I was driving through Arizona when Bush was still president, and there was a protest of basically white people against people of color. It was supposed to be anti-terrorist, but it was just racist. Thankfully, I was just driving through, but that's the world we live in.

Enjoy this recipe for dinuguan, the Filipino dish my white chefs loved for family meal!

- **2 tablespoons canola oil**
- **1 cup diced yellow onion (about 1 medium onion)**
- **3 tablespoons minced garlic (about 8 large cloves)**
- **1 pound pork belly, cut into 1-inch cubes**
- **1 teaspoon kosher salt, plus more for seasoning**
- **1 pound boneless pork shoulder, trimmed of excess fat and cut into 1-inch cubes**
- **¼ cup Datu Puti cane vinegar (see page 137; available at Asian markets and on Amazon), plus more if desired**
- **1 cup pork blood (available at Asian markets and specialty butchers)**
- **½ cup heavy cream**
- **Freshly ground black pepper**
- **2 cups sliced pickled jalapeños, drained**
- **Steamed Jasmine Rice (page 20), for serving**

Heat a Dutch oven or other heavy-bottomed, straight-sided pot over high heat until hot. Add the oil and heat until you see the oil ripple, about 30 seconds. Cut the heat to medium.

Add the onion and garlic and cook, stirring constantly, until the onion is translucent, about 3 minutes. Add the pork belly and cook, stirring occasionally, until caramelized and most of the fat is rendered, 10 to 15 minutes. Stir in ½ teaspoon of the salt. Transfer to a plate and reserve the pork fat in the pot. Add the pork shoulder and cook, stirring occasionally, until caramelized, 5 to 8 minutes. Stir in the remaining ½ teaspoon salt. Return the pork belly and onion to the pot.

Add the vinegar and cook, scraping up the browned bits, for 2 minutes. Cut the heat to low. Add the pork blood and cook, stirring constantly, until the stew is slightly thickened, about 3 minutes.

Add the cream and cook, stirring, until the stew is very thick, like a velvety gravy, 8 to 10 minutes. Season generously with pepper. Taste and season with additional salt, if necessary. Also check the balance between the earthiness of the blood and the tanginess of the vinegar. You want to have a nice zing. Stir in more vinegar, if desired.

Transfer the dinuguan to shallow serving bowls and garnish with the pickled jalapeños. Serve with rice.

Amboy Adobo

The traditional way of making adobo is super fast and super easy. But, as a young cook, I didn't like how you would quickly sear chicken and end up with a somewhat tough meat. I didn't want to stray from what's traditionally in adobo, but I did want to use a different technique. It wasn't till I began to master sauces in school and play with French basics that I figured out the answer.

I would start by brining my chicken so it would stay tender, then sear it skin-side down until perfectly brown. I'd throw in whole garlic cloves and let that simmer until the garlic softened. Then, I deglazed the pan with my homemade chicken stock. I added my Datu Puti soy sauce and cane vinegar and tasted it. If something was missing, I'd throw in a bay leaf or a couple peppercorns.

At that point, the sauce was still very watery, so I used beurre manié, a mixture of butter and flour, to thicken it and add a rich velvety-ness and depth of flavor. Then I basted the seared chicken with the adobo sauce to infuse the two together.

The result is a refined version of an adobo. The chicken skin stays intact and crispy because it is seared. It's moist in the middle and saucy thanks to the thick adobo sauce. When you eat it with rice, that thick sauce almost becomes a gravy. A thin sauce isn't bad at all, but this amplified version appeals to me more. It has a rich, super-salty, super-umami flavor. Enjoy it with hot rice!

BRINE

- 2 gallons water
- 2 cups kosher salt
- 2 cups loosely packed dark brown sugar
- 1 cup fresh calamansi juice (see Note, page 68)
- 4 bone-in, skin-on chicken thighs (about 3 pounds total)
- 4 bone-in, skin-on chicken drumsticks

ADOBO SAUCE

- ¼ cup canola oil
- 16 garlic cloves, peeled
- 3 quarts Homemade Chicken Stock (page 44)

BRINE THE CHICKEN: Combine the water, salt, brown sugar, and calamansi juice in a large stockpot and bring to a boil over high heat, stirring occasionally. Boil for 3 minutes, then remove from the heat. Let the brine cool to room temperature, then refrigerate until very cold, about 2 hours. Add the chicken to the brine and refrigerate for 8 to 12 hours.

Remove the chicken from the brine and pat dry with paper towels. This is vital: The chicken must be completely dried before we start cooking.

MAKE THE ADOBO: Heat a large Dutch oven or cast-iron pot over medium-high heat until hot. Add the oil and heat until it sizzles. Carefully add the chicken thighs, skin-side down, in a single layer and spaced apart—if you crowd them, the cooking surface will cool and you won't get that nice crispy chicken skin. Cook the chicken until the skin is golden brown, about 5 minutes. Test that the chicken can

(ingredients and recipe continue)

¾ cup Datu Puti cane vinegar (see page 137; available at Asian markets and on Amazon)

½ cup Datu Puti or Silver Swan soy sauce (see page 60; available at Asian markets and on Amazon)

2 bay leaves

3 to 6 tablespoons Beurre Manié (recipe follows)

Kosher salt and freshly ground black pepper

4 cups Steamed Jasmine Rice (page 20), for serving

move easily from the pan; if there's any resistance, the chicken isn't done yet. The chicken actually talks to you!

When the skin is nice and crispy and releases easily, cut the heat to medium and flip the chicken. Cook until the internal temperature reaches 155°F, 10 to 12 minutes. Transfer the chicken to a plate. Repeat with the drumsticks. Reserve all the chicken fat in the pot.

Afterward, there should be delicious bits of chicken ("fond") on the cooking surface. Those right there are our best friend. Do not in any way burn that fond. Add the garlic to the pot and cook for 2 minutes, stirring constantly. Add the chicken stock and scrape up all the fond from the bottom of the pot. Add the vinegar, soy sauce, and bay leaves. Crank up the heat to bring the liquid to a boil.

Cut the heat to a simmer and return the chicken and any accumulated juices to the pot. Let the chicken braise until some of the meat pulls from the bone, about 1½ hours. Transfer the chicken to serving plates.

But wait, you're not finished! To prep the sauce, fish out the bay leaves and discard them. Smash the garlic cloves or, if you want to get fancy, use an immersion blender to crush the garlic in the adobo sauce. At this point, you've reached adobo status. But we can take it up a notch. Turn the heat up to medium again and bring the sauce to a boil. Whisk in the beurre manié, 1 tablespoon at a time, until the sauce reaches your desired thickness. Once you get to the consistency that you like, taste the sauce and season with salt and pepper.

Ladle the finished sauce over the chicken, and boom, you've got Amboy-style adobo. Serve hot with rice.

Beurre Manié

MAKES ABOUT 10 TABLESPOONS

½ cup (1 stick) unsalted butter, at room temperature

¼ cup all-purpose flour

In a small bowl, smash the butter into the flour with a fork until fully incorporated. It should look like a soft cookie dough. Use the beurre manié right away or wrap tightly in plastic and refrigerate for up to 2 weeks. Bring to room temperature before using.

The Evolution of Bistek

SERVES 2

When I was growing up, my dad always made bistek, but it was never my favorite dish. It was always super well-done. The onions were either too mushy or too crunchy. They were never cooked perfectly. Along with adobo, it was one of the first dishes I started to make over.

When I was younger, I used London broil. I would sear it off like a steak and cook it medium-rare. I would slice it thin, then top it with onions that I cooked separately with soy sauce and calamansi juice. That improved the onions. And as I got older, I started to use better cuts of meat, like rib eye. I would still make them on a backyard grill. Recently, I started making bistek in a pan, using New York strip or skirt steak. I'd give it a hard sear and baste it in butter. I'd deglaze that with demi-glace and create a nice pan sauce with calamansi or lemon juice, soy sauce, and sometimes butter. I'd serve it rustically on a cutting board, sauced like a steak and covered with onions.

This recipe is super American, but the flavors are so Filipino. It's like a crazier bistek. To make authentic Filipino food, you have to nail the flavors and the textures. Presentation can be anything, but you have to hit those senses.

---

2 tablespoons canola oil

1 (1½-pound) skirt steak, at room temp

1 large onion, sliced

1 cup Homemade Beef Demi-Glace (recipe follows) or store-bought beef demi-glace

2 tablespoons Datu Puti or Silver Swan soy sauce (see page 60; available at Asian markets and on Amazon)

1 tablespoon fresh lemon juice

1½ teaspoons kosher salt

1½ teaspoons freshly ground black pepper

Steamed Jasmine Rice (page 20), for serving

Heat a large sauté pan over high heat. Add the oil and heat until you see the oil ripple, about 30 seconds, then cut the heat to medium. Add the steak and sear until well browned and caramelized, about 4 minutes on each side. Transfer the steak to a cutting board and let rest for 20 minutes. Reserve all the fat in the pan.

Meanwhile, increase the heat to high and add the onion to the pan. Cook, stirring, until translucent, about 5 minutes. Cut the heat to medium. Add the demi-glace and cook, scraping up all the browned bits from the bottom of the pan, until the demi-glace is reduced by half, about 10 minutes. Add the soy sauce and lemon juice and cook, stirring, until the onion sauce is the consistency of a loose gravy, about 2 minutes. Season with the salt and pepper.

Slice the steak against the grain into ½-inch-thick strips and plate. Spoon the onion sauce over the steak and serve right away with rice.

Homemade Beef Demi-Glace

MAKES ABOUT 1 CUP

4 cups Homemade Beef Stock (page 45)

In a medium saucepan, bring the stock to a simmer over medium-high heat. Cut the heat to maintain a simmer and cook until the stock reduces to 1 cup, 3 to 4 hours. Use the demi-glace right away or refrigerate for up to 3 days.

Ratatouille Adobo

SERVES 4 TO 6

Ratatouille became my favorite vegetable dish to make because of the movie. Yeah, the one with the rat. The whole motto of *Ratatouille* is: Anyone can cook. That always appealed to me. When you think "chef," you think of some French dude in a tall toque with a neckerchief. In this movie, the chef is a rodent, the lowest of the low. I always thought, "That's kind of how minorities are treated." I remember when Ricardo Zarate became famous. He was the first popular brown chef in LA. He showed what was possible. That's why I was so excited about *Ratatouille*. I don't think we're rats, but I do think we are the underdogs of the culinary world.

Ratatouille made sense to me. It's a no-brainer. You're slowly baking all these vegetables that have a lot of water in them. As you cook it in the oven, it almost naturally stews in itself. I would start with shaved tomatoes, eggplant, zucchini, summer squash, and onions. I shingled them in a casserole dish, with garlic beneath or in between the shingles. Then, I drizzled soy sauce and vinegar over the whole thing.

Canola oil, for greasing

2 tablespoons minced garlic

3 plum tomatoes, sliced into ¼-inch-thick disks

1 large zucchini, sliced into ¼-inch-thick disks

1 large yellow squash, sliced into ¼-inch-thick disks

1 Japanese eggplant, sliced into ¼-inch-thick disks

2 small white onions, sliced into ¼-inch-thick disks

1 cup Amboy Adobo Glaze (page 306)

Grease a 2-quart oval baking dish with oil and scatter the garlic evenly over the bottom of the dish.

Alternating the tomatoes, zucchini, yellow squash, Japanese eggplant, and onions, stack the vegetables upright going clockwise in the dish until it's completely filled.

Pour the adobo sauce in the dish so it seeps into the veggies. Let sit for about 20 minutes at room temperature.

Meanwhile, preheat the oven to 400°F.

Cover the dish tightly with aluminum foil and bake for 40 minutes. Cut the oven temp down to 350°F, remove the foil, and bake until the vegetables are tender and lightly caramelized, 50 minutes to 1 hour. Remove from the oven and let it rest for 20 minutes before serving.

Longanisa (Sweet Sausage with No Casing)

SERVES 6 TO 8

I grew up eating chicken longanisa because my parents thought it was healthy. When I finally ate pork longanisa, I was transported to a whole other world. It was textural and phenomenal.

When I moved to Portland, I worked at Olympic Provisions. I interned there for fun and for free, and I learned how to mix the fat and the meat together, and how to press the sausage. Everyone says that people don't want to know how sausage is made. I totally dug it.

My first foray into making my own sausages at culinary school was longanisa. I did it the old-school way, where I used nitrates to keep it red. There's a chew you get with longanisa. I experimented with different ratios and spice blends, and I finally made one that I liked. It was sweet, garlicky, peppery, and so addictive. My friend Lung and I would make it, and then I started selling it to my coworkers. Enjoy with garlic fried rice and sunny-side-up eggs for classic breakfast vibes.

1 pound ground pork

½ pound ground pork fat (ask the butcher for this)

½ cup minced garlic (about 20 large cloves)

¼ cup loosely packed dark brown sugar

½ cup ice water

2 tablespoons Shaoxing wine

1 tablespoon Datu Puti or Silver Swan soy sauce (see page 60; available at Asian markets and on Amazon)

1 tablespoon Datu Puti cane vinegar (see page 137; available at Asian markets and on Amazon)

2 teaspoons kosher salt

2 teaspoons sweet paprika

1 teaspoon freshly ground black pepper

Canola oil, for frying

Garlic Fried Rice (page 109) or fried eggs, for serving

Place a large stainless steel bowl in the freezer while you prep your ingredients.

Remove the bowl from the freezer and add the ground pork, pork fat, garlic, brown sugar, ice water, Shaoxing wine, soy sauce, vinegar, salt, paprika, and pepper. Mix thoroughly with your hands until the pork fat is evenly distributed throughout. Transfer to an airtight container and let marinate in the refrigerator overnight, or preferably up to 3 days.

Using your hands, shape the meat into meatballs or small patties.

Heat a large sauté pan over medium-high heat until hot. Add just enough oil to coat the bottom of the pan and heat until you see the oil ripple, about 30 seconds. Working in batches, add the longanisa to the pan in a single layer and cook until caramelized and cooked through, 2 to 4 minutes per side. Transfer to plates. Pour off the fat in the pan, wipe out any charred bits, and repeat the process with the remaining longanisa. Serve with garlic fried rice or with fried eggs for breakfast.

CHAPTER 9

The Death of Ten01

TEN01 WAS MY dream restaurant job. I dedicated my life to those people. I would say, "Just tell me when I'm doing something wrong. I don't even want to know when I'm doing something right."

It was 2010, and they hired me as a prep cook. After a month, I worked on salads and cold apps, then on meats, then as a saucier. Next thing I knew, I was the chef de partie, the lead chef on that line. I was on top of the world. I finally got this rapport with my chefs, and we started to work as a team. It was one of the best French kitchens in Portland at the time. Six months into the job, it was New Year's Eve. We were preparing for three hundred people, and we had a special. It was a surf and turf, a strip steak with a butter-poached lobster. It took us a month to prepare for this huge night. We all wore dress shirts and ties underneath our chefs' coats. We were ready.

You can still see my scars from that night because of how many steaks I flipped. At midnight, we all cheered for the new year. I looked around, and thought, "Everything in my life is falling into place. All my hard work from culinary school, all this training, is paying off." I was the happiest dude in the world.

I slept through New Year's Day—the restaurant was closed—and showed up for work on January 2, with everyone else. Except everything was gone.

The entire restaurant was empty. There were no tables and no chairs, the kitchen had been gutted, and they took out all the appliances. The bar had no liquor and no kegs. Our lockers were gone. There was a folding table in the middle of the room with all of our possessions on it. We met the owner of the restaurant, this bald guy in a suit. He handed us our last checks.

It was awful. We all went to the bar after, and some of us cried. "How the fuck am I gonna pay rent? What am I gonna do?" We were blindsided. I guess the place was mismanaged, and they didn't want to tell us. They thought we were going to steal all the stuff.

I think I was a little better prepared than the others, even if it was a blow. I had read *Kitchen Confidential* by Anthony Bourdain. I knew how turbulent it would be to become a chef. Also, I'm from LA, where nothing is promised—if you're born and raised in Los Angeles, you know that. Every day, you see people move to LA. They think they're going to be something special, and nothing happens. People fail hard all the time.

My 27th birthday was eight days away, so I packed my bags again. I'd worked at the best kitchens in Portland. There was nowhere else to go there. I decided to go back to LA.

This is the story of that in-between time, moving from Portland to LA—when I was figuring out what I wanted to cook, and what kind of chef I wanted to be.

Stage City

Dave LeFevre from Water Grill was opening up a new restaurant in Manhattan Beach. I asked him if I could come work for him, and he said yes, but it would be three months before they opened. So I started looking for a job in the meantime.

I staged in Napa for a week at the French Laundry. I staged at Bouchon in Yountville. Then, I went back to LA. I worked at Hatfield's for fun for two weeks. I worked at Spago.

I was getting these really cool culinary gigs for a month, and then I got a call from a gastropub in Pasadena. They had three different locations, and they were looking for a solid sous chef.

So I interviewed. I make the dude a burger. It was the kind of place that doesn't hire chefs. They hire a dude, and they teach him how to cook a burger. I go in wearing a blue apron, which at the time signified that you were from a specific kind of restaurant. I had a clean mustache and a clean haircut. I come in and this dude was totally wowed by me. He gave me a job and a consultant fee at the same time. He thought I was going to save the restaurant.

Strangely, it didn't need saving. They made so much money off beer, they thought that maybe they finally found someone who would take over the kitchen and make good food. I'm an asshole because I kind of lied to them. I was only there for two months, and then I left to open Manhattan Beach Post with Dave LeFevre.

My relationship with Dave is interesting, because he's a corporate chef. He hires a big army to do work. I was used to working from 8 a.m. to 2 a.m. every day with a lean crew, where everyone was doing everything, owning everything. Dave didn't like that. He didn't like that I was so hands-on, or that I knew a better way to do things. He didn't like how much I knew, and he didn't like my style of cooking. I was a perfectionist. I wasn't going to sell food that I wasn't proud of.

Dave wanted fast. He wanted me to be faster and faster. Every day he'd say, "Hey, you need to get faster." I would say, "Yo, it doesn't matter how fast you want it. I'm putting it out on time. You're complaining about a minute or two, not 20 minutes." That's the sign of a weak cook. If it takes you

20 minutes to do something that should take two minutes, something is wrong.

I think Dave was picking on me because he saw how dedicated I was. I'm sure it was his way of managing me to become better. But it didn't work for me, because I had a chip on my shoulder. In my head, I was better than half the people there. Dave LeFevre was a big-city chef. I was a small-city cook. I felt like Dave never gave me credit for what I had done. He always just saw the mistakes.

MB Post opened in spring 2011. We quickly moved into brunch and started making eggs. I loved learning it, because I had never worked breakfast for any other restaurant. I would go out to eat to try to get ideas from other restaurants, and there was nothing. At the time in LA, breakfast was just pancakes, waffles, and omelets. It was this diner, greasy-spoon-style breakfast. There wasn't anything new.

After six months, I ended up leaving MB Post. I did not leave nicely. It ended with me and Chef LeFevre getting into this huge argument in the walk-in. The next day, I said, "Fuck you, I'm not coming back." I think I even did it through email.

So, now what would I do? I didn't have years and years of experience, but I had a few years of experience working for free. I had the great experience working my dream job at Ten01. I felt like I checked off a lot of the boxes of what I could do.

I knew for a fact that I couldn't open my own restaurant. I just didn't have the experience. I hadn't even gotten to the point where I was running someone else's restaurant. I was like a trained assassin. I would go in, do my job, kill it, and then leave.

Building Eggslut

ALEXANDRA: How did you come up with the idea for Eggslut?

ALVIN: I knew one thing: I could make a fuckin' sandwich. This was the same time that food trucks were blowing up in Los Angeles. So I did it. I opened a food truck in August 2011, just weeks after I left MB Post.

The first menu at Eggslut was very ambitious—a fancy egg menu. Since then, I've learned that when you create a menu, it's not necessarily what you want to cook—it's what people want to eat. That first menu had a caramelized leek tart with my own pie crust . . . that I heated up in a toaster oven. I would do a quenelle of crème fraîche. It was Alvin show-off food, not customer food. And it wasn't selling.

I had to step into the shoes of my customer: I'm rolling in a truck with four wheels, an '86 Chevy step van, where you have to turn the car on in order for the refrigerator to stay cold. So eating an egg and leek tart with a really delicate crust and a quenelle of whipped crème fraîche, with the smell of gas on

Sunset Boulevard—it made no sense. The ambiance of a food truck is street food. I was bringing elevated brunch food onto the street. Disconnect.

But it took a few more beats to figure that out. I made a dish called the Bone Mi, which was my take on the Vietnamese banh mi. But instead of using traditional Vietnamese French bread, I was using a custom-baked brioche. It was a very delicate sandwich with pickles, cilantro stems, jalapeños, sliced pork belly, and a fried egg. There was so much going on, and the bread wasn't strong enough to hold it all. You made a mess while you ate it. Again, not smart street food.

Then, one morning, I was given a chance to team up with Intelligentsia Coffee in Silverlake. We made a breakfast burrito, and everyone loved it. Then we got kicked out of that spot. Then some other coffee guy found out about us, and invited us to park in front of his place, Coffee Commissary on Fairfax.

That represented a turning point, but we didn't know it. We were three months in, and I'd burned through nearly all my money. My best friend at the time—let's call him "Nicky"—had to leave the truck to go back to school. I was alone.

ALEXANDRA: That sounds bad.

ALVIN: I thought I was regressing. And right about that time I got a phone call from Chef Matt Lightner from Portland. He was moving to New York and was going for a Michelin star. I thought, maybe I should move to New York.

I'm sure that if I pursued it, I would have been offered a job. It was that kind of kitchen. They knew how I worked, so they would hire me. I thought about it a lot. Should I get paid X amount of dollars per hour? Or not get paid at all, and pursue a dream?

ALEXANDRA: What was the moment you chose Eggslut?

ALVIN: It was the day the Eggslut logo got slapped on the truck. I started to cry as I was driving it. Because I felt something, you know? I felt it. I knew that Eggslut had something. Sometimes you just know it. And when I was in my food truck, I felt it. This was it. This is what I was going to do. This is what I was made to do. For 27 years of my life, I needed to find that peace, and I finally found it. I had to do whatever I needed to make it survive.

ALEXANDRA: What made you believe in the concept?

ALVIN: When I was growing up, I would go to New Jersey a lot to visit my family. We would take the PATH train over to Wall Street in the morning. I would always go to this street cart and get a bacon, egg, and cheese on a kaiser roll. I loved it. I still eat those today. I have to have two a week, at least. I always wondered why they didn't have anything like that in LA. So, one day, I made a bacon sandwich, and I thought, "This is what I like to eat for breakfast. Why can't I do that?" So I did it. I made a regular bacon, egg, and cheese with brioche. And for a twist, I offered turkey sausage that I made out of ground turkey. It helped, at that point, that I didn't have enough money to buy a ton of food, and I only had myself on the truck. I was the cook and the cashier.

The "evolved" menu offered options 1, 2, and 3: 1 meant bacon, 2 meant sausage, 3 meant "Slut." So, a person could get bacon, egg, and cheese. Sausage, egg, and cheese. Or the Slut—coddled egg, potato puree, baguette. Customers would shout it out to me, I would make it, give it to them, and take money in exchange. I could do it all at once. And it fucking worked.

That's how I learned that fancier ingredients and higher technique didn't matter, not when it came to a food truck. What mattered was the simplicity of the food—as dictated by the location: the street. The pavement was my ambiance, my setting. Desperation put me on a fast track to menu-development-by-feel.

Once the truck was on solid ground, I could change up the menu again. And the dishes got so good. The Madame was a French ham sandwich topped with a cave-aged Gruyère cheese sauce and a fried egg. I got really great bread from La Brea Bakery, when it was still Nancy Silverton's. I would go to Campanile every day to pick up brioche for other sandwiches. It fancied things up, but not too much.

Cooking pork belly skin-side down on the griddle on the truck took hours. We didn't have an oven. We used a pot on top of a charbroiler so we could do the Sluts. We didn't really charbroil anything, so we used the grill as a stove. It was great.

We made our own pickles for the banh mi. We sourced all the best ingredients. In a sense, it had all the integrity from my fine-dining days. Mind you, I never cooked in a casual restaurant my entire career. The first casual restaurant I ever cooked at was my own.

The Bullshit

That truck would break down every other day at the start. One time, the brakes went out. At 4 o'clock in the morning. We were on Fairfax and Melrose, where we'd parked. We could start but we could not fucking stop. So we let it coast. We stopped pressing the gas, and ran three red lights. Thankfully, there were no cars on the street. I slowly maneuvered the truck toward the sidewalk so the tires could rub on the curb and slow it down. Finally, we stopped. We put blocks underneath the tires, and we waited for the tow truck to pick us up.

The only problem was that the tow had to come from the guy who leased us the truck. And he said, "We can't pick you up until 3 p.m." That was 11 hours in the future. So we just opened right there. We had to. We couldn't lose a day of business.

One time, after a Saturday event, we broke down on the 101 near Glendale Boulevard, right around Historic Filipinotown. I managed to park it on Glendale and Temple. I called our lease guy again so someone from his yard could come get it. At the time, I didn't have a car, so I didn't have a ride home. There was no Uber then. My employee that day had to take off because it was his son's birthday. He couldn't wait with me at the truck, so he had his wife pick him up. I slept inside the truck until it got picked up the next day.

You know that thing they say about parents who develop sudden superhuman strength to protect their children in extreme circumstances? It's the same thing with a brand you create. When you care that much for a business, you will do anything to protect it.

We went through a lot over those two years. I was the sole owner of the business and worked on the truck every day it was open. We would drive that shoddy hunk up and down the Hollywood Hills to do private parties and catering events. One night, we catered a Young Hollywood party. I never went inside, but my guys passed food in from the truck. Then they'd come back and say, "Dude, those kids are all half-naked." I would say, "Yeah, I'm not going in there." I'd reached a point where I cared more about business than half-naked people.

Some nights, we would cook in the Hollywood Hills and all our power would shut off. So, we would cook in the dark because the gas would still work. We all had our cell phone flashlights on. That was so illegal.

One time, the truck rolled off a driveway right before a party started when the emergency brake failed. Another time, in Agoura Hills in the middle of summer, I was on for the entire service, and after we sold the last sandwich, I passed out on the concrete from heat exhaustion and fatigue. That's what I had to deal with.

Now, we have seven locations. That truck became a restaurant with two-hour waits. And all that trouble—nearly going broke, sleeping in the truck, shot brakes—all that was essential to the process. My pride is in the toil. And I take that pride with me to every restaurant I work on and open. I started from the bottom and learned what it takes to make a brand work.

I let go of workers who don't care about the business. When you've worked 30 days straight, it's hard to hear complaints from anyone. I know the sacrifice it takes to make something successful.

Now, when I'm on a new frontier opening a brand-new restaurant, I know what to do.

The Rise of Eggslut

"Walking down Fairfax in the absurd sunshine of an LA winter, we happened upon a food truck. I am incapable of passing one without stopping for a bite, but this one called out to me with a particularly loud voice. It wasn't the name—Eggslut—but the description of their signature dish: A coddled egg on top of potato puree with gray sea salt and chives. A well-coddled egg is a beautiful thing, and when the chef said, 'This will take a while; we coddle them to order,' I was hooked. As anyone would be. This is a perfect way to start the day—a tender egg, held together with no more than a wish, on top of buttery pureed potatoes. The crunch of salt, the snappy bite of chives. Heaven in a spoon. And so rich it made three of us deliriously happy for the rest of the day."

—RUTH REICHL, RUTH REICHL.COM, JANUARY 26, 2012

THERE IT IS! The blog post that legendary food writer Ruth Reichl wrote in 2012 about my coddled egg dish at Eggslut. This blurb changed the rest of my life. I went from an under-the-radar food truck in West Hollywood to the hottest food truck in LA. One day, we had a hundred followers on Instagram and the next day we had ten thousand. It was remarkable. No one cared about our truck before. We were just a couple of guys cooking for the homies on the block. And then . . .

The blurb eventually propelled us to a commercial kitchen at Red Studios in Hollywood, and then to a full-fledged brick-and-mortar at Grand Central Market.

But first, the truck. And the sweat. Eggslut was my master's degree in culinary school. After those first lean months, I settled into a groove. I put together my five-man crew: Nicky, Teddy, Dave, Christian, and me. We worked seven days a week, trying to make magic.

Nicky ran the register and was the star of the truck. He knew everyone, and everyone loved him. He had a steel trap for a brain and remembered everyone's name, especially the names of the beautiful women.

Teddy was the OG, true mero-mero. When he started, he was inexperienced, but he had a heart of gold. I was especially hard on him because he wanted to be the best, so I didn't cut him any slack. I thought, "If I let this kid think that the restaurant life is easy, he's gonna think that he can skate through fine-dining kitchens later on in his career. And he'll be dead wrong." I was a strict chef, a certified dickhead. I remember a customer telling me that he would come to the truck all the time just to watch me yell at my kitchen staff. I regret it all. Today, I'm a completely different dude. I apologize, y'all.

Dave was my ace. He was the definition of a copilot. He was my boy. We were friends all through culinary school, and he came down to LA to help me make it happen. I'm forever indebted to the guy. If it wasn't for all his hard work and leadership, I don't think Eggslut would've made it past the truck.

Christian was my first-ever apprentice. He worked for Keep Company, a shoe store on Fairfax where we parked the truck. He ate breakfast at the truck every day. One day, he told me that he wanted to pursue a career in the restaurant world. I said if he worked for me for a year and still wanted to cook, he would have the bearings to continue his culinary journey. The dude made it work. He was always late, but he worked his butt off! Next thing you know, Christian enrolled in Oregon Culinary Institute and left for Portland. He became a great cook. Eight years later, he and I are still working together in New York.

Everything was gravy! I brought on my cousin as a business partner, and he was our extra hand on the truck. Lord knows we needed it. Homeboy was a skateboarder and unemployed graphic designer and bummed about where his career was headed. He was like a brother to me. I couldn't bear seeing him so depressed. He was thinking about becoming a respiratory therapist at his mother's request. I said, "Fuck it! Put some money down, and I'll give you a part of this business." He was my bro, so why not give him a piece of the pie?

I'd give him that chance again, despite what would later happen between us. I'll leave it there. It's not jolly. Honestly, Eggslut becoming big changed everything. Ted, Dave, and Christian are the only ones who used their knowledge and experiences gained from the truck to better their careers and make something for themselves.

This is the story of Eggslut, and how we built a million-dollar restaurant from nothing.

The Truck

ALEXANDRA: Who was the most interesting person who ever came and ordered from the truck?

ALVIN: Seth Rogen used to come to our truck and order bacon, egg, and cheeses. I would never charge him, but he would always tip. We would take his tip money and put it in an envelope. We called it the Seth Rogen Emergency Fund. We had over $300 in tips from him in there. One day, the tire popped on the truck, and we needed money to fix it. So we used his money. He literally saved the truck.

ALEXANDRA: What were the best times on the truck?

ALVIN: We were all friends on the truck. Going to work every day was fun. We loved creating new specials. At the time, Carly Rae Jepsen's song "Call Me Maybe" was really popular, so we created a special called Call Me Caprese. It was heirloom cherry tomatoes, mozzarella pearls, whipped ricotta, prosciutto chips, and a poached egg.

When Chris Paul got traded to the Lakers and then got nixed from the NBA, we did a CP3. That special was three cremini mushrooms, three scrambled eggs, and Parmesan cheese. It was fun and it would sell because it referenced the current news cycle. Everyone would read it and laugh. We were very good at that on the truck.

We met so many friends on the truck. My friend Justin and his wife, Tattiya, came to the truck on one of their first dates. They ended up getting married and we did Sluts at their wedding. They had a baby, and then their baby came to Unit 120. To me, having those friendships and seeing that evolution of life is the greatest thing about having a restaurant. You have customers for life when you do this, and that's why you do it. It's a business, but it's more than that. It's a living and breathing thing.

ALEXANDRA: Were there any chefs you admired who visited the truck?

ALVIN: Jon Shook and Vinny Dotolo would eat at our truck. Chef Ludo Lefebvre would eat at our truck. When we were on the West Side, and when we were on Fairfax, pretty much every chef in the area ate at our place.

There was this guy named Alan Weiss. Alan was one of the first gourmet food purveyors in LA. When Wolfgang Puck arrived from Austria to cook in California, Alan said, "Wolfgang, I'm going to show you around LA." He was that guy. He was already in his 60s when we met. When he came and saw my truck, he was so impressed. He asked me where I got my ingredients. I said I went to stores and sourced them individually. He said, "You don't need to do that anymore. You know Alan Weiss." He gave me his card and said, "Call me." He had his guys deliver all our food to wherever we were from that point on.

After, Alan started mentoring me on the food industry in Los Angeles. He would take me to Vegas and show me the Vegas food industry. He was my guidance counselor and friend, and he was also the biggest food purveyor in Los Angeles. He passed away in 2015, but I still have his voicemail on my phone. I never deleted it. It's worth sharing:

ALAN WEISS: "Hey, Alvin, Alan Weiss. So I need to talk with you about eggs. I saw over the weekend you had some Sunrise instead of Michael and Sons. The eggs from Sunrise are at the same prices that Michael and Sons used to be, which is $39. It's $11 cheaper than what Michael and Sons would be. Michael and Sons just jacked their costs up to me, about $16 a case. So there's that issue. And then, for some reason, they've stopped ordering orange juice from me. Let me know what I need to do. If I need to push back to their court, I'll do that, but let me know what's going on, and I'll get that taken care of. Oh, and then, also, if I can get an idea of what time you guys would like your delivery at Grand Ramen, I can set that up in the system. Please give me a call, Alvin. And hey, I've got some chefs coming into town from Vegas for a hockey game. I believe it's January 19. And these are guys from Guy Savoy. And I'm wondering if you wanna go to a hockey game. I'm gonna do another chef thing. Anyway, gimme a call. Talk to ya, bye."

ALVIN: That's when we were first starting our ramen place. It was supposed to be at Grand Central Market. That voicemail was right before he died. That voicemail tells you who he was.

He would say, "These guys are gouging us for eggs, I can get you better eggs. Your ramen place is opening up, let's talk about that. I have friends you need to know." He was one of the most influential people I've ever met. He took care of us everywhere he went. It's so different now that he's gone. I'm sure Alan had a ton of stress. He was the kind of guy that had a heart attack on Friday and was back to work on Monday. It got to the point where he said, "Alvin, I can't eat your eggs anymore. The doctor said I need to chill." So I would just make him a salad.

Alan would visit us at least twice a week. We would talk forever about eggs. He indulged me because he knew I had a grand scheme when it came to food. He knew that I wanted to do more and more. He knew I could partner up with him later, and we would do amazing things together.

Jim Jannard, the founder of Red Digital cameras and Oakley, was another great friend. He loved our sandwiches so much that he let us use the restaurant on his movie lot, Red Studios. Our first-ever commissary kitchen for Eggslut was on that Cahuenga lot. We were basically there to be his private catering company and do whatever other work the truck business required. The days of prepping the Nita—our pulled pork sandwich—illegally in my house were over, because now we had a health department–approved restaurant. Jim charged me just $400 for rent for a 1,500-square-foot restaurant. It was insane. We owe you, Jim.

Insta-Fame

ALEXANDRA: When success hit at Eggslut, what did it look like?

ALVIN: Babes. I remember going out to the bars after work—the Varnish, the Association, Cole's. I'd be drinking and people would put two and two together. There's the Eggslut guy and his crew. Ding! Let's just say there were epiphanies breaking right and left. I think the babe thing was a big deal for Nicky. I was a little bit more focused on business than women.

ALEXANDRA: Describe Nicky as a person.

ALVIN: Seriously, he was the friendliest dude. He would pretty much do anything for you. He knew I'd be a crankypants when I got to work in the morning, so he'd already have a cup of coffee waiting for me. It was cold brew with two shots of espresso, no sugar, no milk. He knew the way I liked my coffee, just straight up. He knew it got rid of my red eyes. He was that dude. He'd read your mind to try to ease your pain.

As a server, he faked it till he made it. He'd never been formally trained. He would keep his ear to the counter, and he would find out if anyone had problems. One time, he overheard this guy complaining that he felt like he ordered the wrong thing, and he might want to try something else. Nicky made it for him and comped it on the house. He would solve problems. "Hey," he would say, "now you can try both."

People would show up just for him. They would call him by name. He was short and dark-skinned, with super-long, luscious black hair. He would wear the dingiest, lowest-cut V-necks, the tightest jeans, and thousand-dollar sneakers. Of course, he never paid a thousand dollars for them. He was the guy who had the plug for everything.

Some days, he would come in with perfect French braids. Probably he hung out with some girl the night before who did his hair. He would have a manicure and a pedicure. Also girl's doing. But he was also very cocky and very arrogant. He knew that we were the shit, therefore he acted like the shit. He had that chip on his shoulder. We all did.

All my line cooks would go out at night thinking they were the best because they worked at one of the busiest restaurants in the city. When you told people you worked at Eggslut, it came with perks. Oh, you work at Eggslut? Cool, here's an extra shot. Oh, you work at Eggslut? Cool, here's 20 percent off. In 2013, when we had the restaurant, we were literally the guys in downtown. There was no one else who could compare.

We had a reputation. We would go to Sam's Hofbrau, the strip club. As soon as we walked in, all the girls on stage would scream, "Alvin and Nicky are here!" It was stupid. It felt so cool at the time, but I don't think I'd ever do it again.

Continental Club opened up at the same time as Eggslut. That was our spot in downtown LA. I would go there every day. I knew the bouncer, so I never had to wait in line, and I never had to follow the dress code. If I called the owners, and they were there, I would have a bottle of Jameson with my name on it for free. It was a crazy time.

We were the architects of cool. We were hanging out with restaurant people and architects and designers and movie producers and photographers. All the movers and shakers hung out together. We were all tried-and-true downtown cats.

The recipes that follow are from the OG Eggslut truck—when we were building our brand, working like crazy, and falling head over heels in love with LA.

Bacon-Leek Tart

SERVES 1

This recipe was inspired by a fantastic dish I learned at MB Post. It had a really fluffy, eggy custard with caramelized leeks and bacon. You would put it into a pie dough, like a tart, and bake it off and serve it topped with a quenelle of crème fraîche and a seasoned arugula salad on the side. It was one of my favorite dishes on the menu at MB Post, and I prepped it every day.

When I made the first menu for the truck, I wanted to make my version of it. To keep it simple, I nixed the whipped crème fraîche and the salad. I wanted people to eat the tart like a pizza. I made the pie crust fluffier, more like a biscuit. I made the same custard, but I used no-brand, applewood-smoked bacon. At MB Post, we were using baller $30-a-pound bacon.

On the truck, we would make the tarts in a toaster oven. Then, we put them on the griddle and let them come to temperature. I'd slide that on a paper plate, and it was the best fancy breakfast pizza you could have.

---

1 disk Tart Dough (recipe follows), chilled

All-purpose flour, for dusting

4 ounces slab bacon, cut into ¼-inch cubes

¼ cup minced leeks, white and tender green parts only (from 1 small leek)

½ cup Egg Custard (recipe follows)

2 teaspoons freshly grated Parmesan cheese

SPECIAL EQUIPMENT

1 (5-inch) tart pan

Pie weights

Preheat the oven to 350°F.

Place the chilled tart dough on a lightly floured work surface. Flour your rolling pin and roll out the dough to a round that's ⅛ inch thick, turning the dough a quarter turn after each roll. Roll the round onto your rolling pin, then unroll over a 5-inch tart pan. Without stretching the dough, ease it into the pan and push it into the corners. Cut off the excess by rolling the pin over the pan. Prick the bottom with a fork 15 to 20 times.

Line the tart crust with parchment paper, add baking weights (dried beans work the best), and blind-bake the dough for 15 minutes. (Blind-baking means baking a crust before you put the filling in.) Remove the parchment and baking weights and bake the dough for 10 more minutes, or until pale golden. Remove the pan from the oven and let cool on a wire rack for 45 minutes. Leave the oven on.

Meanwhile, heat a medium sauté pan over medium heat until hot. Add the bacon and fry, stirring, until the bacon is crisp and most of the fat has rendered, 3 to 5 minutes. Transfer the bacon to a plate lined

(recipe continues)

with paper towels to wick away the excess fat. Transfer the bacon to a small bowl, stir in the leeks, and set aside.

Place the cooled tart pan on a rimmed baking sheet. Pour ¼ cup of the egg custard into the tart shell and bake for 10 minutes. Remove from the oven and scatter the bacon and leeks over the top of the tart. Pour in the remaining ¼ cup egg custard and bake until the crust is golden brown and the filling no longer jiggles, about 15 minutes.

Remove from the oven and sprinkle the Parmesan over the top of the tart. Let cool on a wire rack for 20 minutes before serving.

Tart Dough

MAKES ENOUGH DOUGH FOR FOUR 5-INCH TART SHELLS

1 cup (2 sticks) unsalted butter, chilled

2½ cups all-purpose flour, plus more for dusting

1 tablespoon sugar

1 teaspoon kosher salt

¼ cup vodka

¼ cup ice water, plus more as necessary

In a large stainless steel bowl, shred the butter on the large holes of a box grater and freeze for 1 hour.

Add the flour to the bowl and use your hands to toss together so the flour barely coats the butter. Add the sugar, salt, vodka, and ice water and toss with your hands just until all the flour is incorporated and the dough pulls from the side of the bowl. You don't want to overmix the dough. If the dough is too dry, add more ice water, 1 teaspoon at a time, until the dough just comes together.

Turn the dough out onto a floured work surface. Divide into 4 pieces. Wrap each piece in plastic wrap and pat the dough into a disk. Let the dough rest in the refrigerator for at least 1 hour, but preferably overnight.

(recipe continues)

Egg Custard

MAKES ABOUT 2 CUPS

4 large eggs

2 cups heavy cream

Fill a large bowl with ice and water. Set the ice bath aside.

Bring 2 inches of water to a simmer in a medium saucepan over medium heat. Reduce the heat to maintain a simmer.

In a medium heatproof bowl—large enough so the bottom of the bowl does not touch the water when set over the saucepan of simmering water—whisk together the eggs and cream until incorporated.

Set the bowl over the saucepan and whisk constantly for 4 to 6 minutes, until the custard is thickened to the consistency of pancake batter. Do not stop whisking or the custard will get lumpy.

Transfer the bowl to the ice bath to stop the cooking. Use the custard right away or refrigerate it in an airtight container for up to 2 days.

The Madame

SERVES 2

This was my take on the croque madame, a classic brunch dish and very, very French. At the time, it was extremely Alvin Cailan. It was a dish we made at Bouchon, back when I staged everywhere and never got paid. Everyone wants free labor, and I was the guy to give it.

Looking back, the food I made in my early years was so pretentious. When I first started my culinary career, I was working for all the best restaurants, so I wouldn't eat shit. You would never, ever see me eating fast food. At home, I made all my food from farmers' market ingredients. I was that guy. Everything I made was mega-French in preparation. I was using hella butter. I'd make tons of sauces and put crazy avant-garde spins on dishes. I would lacquer steaks with coconut charcoal—before that was cool—so when you'd cut into them, you'd find a 36-hour sous vide piece of meat. Mind you, I did this at home. It would take me three days to make dinner.

My croque madame was made with a cheese sauce of cave-aged Gruyère, La Brea bread, and French ham from Whole Foods. We served what was basically a fancy ham and cheese melt on a compostable paper tray, and it was delicious.

---

4 teaspoons unsalted butter, at room temp

4 slices pain de mie or other firm white sandwich bread

8 slices ham

2 thin slices Gruyère cheese

2 teaspoons canola oil

2 large eggs

1 cup Mornay Sauce (recipe follows)

Thinly sliced fresh chives, for garnish (optional)

Spread ½ teaspoon butter on both sides of each slice of bread. Toast in a large frying pan over low heat until golden brown on each side. Transfer to a work surface.

Divide the ham between 2 slices of bread. Top the ham with the Gruyère. Close the sandwiches and set aside.

Heat the oil in a large nonstick pan over medium-high heat. Crack your eggs into the pan and cut the heat to super low. Cook sunny-side up until the whites are set and the yolks are runny, 2 to 3 minutes. Jolt the pan with high heat until the eggs bubble up. Slide a spatula underneath and transfer 1 egg to each sandwich.

Plate the madames, smother with Mornay sauce, garnish with chives, and serve right away.

(recipe continues)

Mornay Sauce

MAKES ABOUT 2 QUARTS

1 cup (2 sticks) unsalted butter

1 cup all-purpose flour

6 cups whole milk

1 cup shredded white cheddar cheese

1 tablespoon kosher salt

Melt the butter in a medium saucepan over medium heat, then cut the heat to medium-low. Add the flour and cook, stirring, until the mix resembles wet beach sand, about 10 minutes. Cut the heat to low and continue to cook until the mixture smells like popcorn, 10 to 20 minutes. Add the milk and cook, whisking, until the sauce has thickened, about 4 minutes. Add the cheese and cook, whisking, until the cheese is fully melted and incorporated, about 2 minutes. Season with the salt.

Remove from the heat and use the cheese sauce right away or let cool to room temperature and refrigerate in an airtight container for up to 1 week.

The Bone Mi

SERVES 1

I love banh mi sandwiches and quirky names, so that's how the Bone Mi was born. These are my guilty pleasures. I can go for banh mi with head cheese, but I'm also a sucker for BBQ chicken banh mi with that sweet flavor that all Filipinos love.

From 2010 to 2011, pork belly banh mis reigned supreme. Everyone loved them. It was the height of pork belly mania, so I knew it was going to sell. Honestly, if I used baguette, it would have probably sold even more. I put ours on custom-baked brioche. I felt that it had to be brioche because brioche is fancy. Also, brioche is an egg bread, so it made sense. It was on-brand. (Now I use bacon instead of belly and Vietnamese baguette instead of brioche because it's easier to source.)

---

4 slices bacon

1 (10-inch) banh mi baguette (available at Vietnamese bakeries)

2 tablespoons Bring Out the Best Mayo (page 59)

¼ cup Pickled Daikon and Carrots (recipe follows), drained

3 or 4 fresh cilantro sprigs

6 thin slices jalapeño

6 thin slices cucumber

1 teaspoon canola oil (optional)

1 large egg

Kosher salt

Sliced fresh chives, for garnish

Heat a frying pan over medium heat until hot. Add the bacon in a single layer and fry, flipping every 30 seconds so it doesn't grossly curl up, until the bacon is cooked to your desired crispness, 4 to 7 minutes. Transfer to a plate lined with paper towels and set aside. Reserve 1 teaspoon of the bacon fat to fry your egg, if desired.

Split the baguette lengthwise, leaving a hinge. Open up the baguette and toast the split sides in a toaster oven or in a 400°F oven until slightly crisped, 3 to 5 minutes.

Slather 1 tablespoon of the mayo on each of the split sides of the baguette. On the bottom half of the baguette, layer on the bacon, pickled daikon and carrots, cilantro, jalapeños, and cucumber.

Heat a small frying pan over medium-high heat until hot. Add the oil or reserved bacon fat and swirl to coat the pan. Crack your egg into the pan and cut the heat to super low. Cook sunny-side up until the white is set and the yolk is runny, 2 to 3 minutes. Jolt the pan with high heat until the egg bubbles up. Slide a spatula underneath and transfer the egg to the banh mi. Season with salt and garnish with chives. Close the sandwich and serve right away.

(recipe continues)

Pickled Daikon and Carrots

1¼ cups rice vinegar

1 cup water

½ cup sugar

1½ teaspoons kosher salt

1 small daikon (about ½ pound), julienned

3 carrots, julienned

Combine the vinegar, water, sugar, and salt in a medium saucepan. Bring to a boil over high heat, stirring to combine. Remove from the heat and pour into a large heatproof bowl. Add the daikon and carrots, toss to combine, and let the brine cool to room temperature. Cover and refrigerate for at least 4 hours or up to 1 week.

The Nita

SERVES 1

When we first started making the Nita, we had to do it illegally because there was no way to do it on the truck. I would braise the pork at my house and then sell it from the truck, a no-no. Every day, I would come home at seven o'clock at night. I would braise the whole pork shoulder so it would be ready by the time I woke up. Then, I would throw it into my employee's car when he picked me up for work.

The Nita was inspired by chile verde, so I made my own green sauce. The final sandwich is pulled pork, green sauce, cotija cheese, and a fried egg in brioche. It was one of our best-selling lunch and dinner sandwiches on the truck.

1 teaspoon unsalted butter, at room temp

1 brioche bun, split

1 teaspoon canola oil

1 large egg

3 ounces pulled pork from Braised Pork Shoulder (page 215)

¼ cup Nita Green Sauce (recipe follows)

2 ounces cotija cheese, crumbled

Spread ½ teaspoon butter on each of the split sides of the brioche. Toast in a frying pan over low heat until golden brown on each side. Transfer to a plate.

Heat a small frying pan over medium-high heat until hot. Add the oil and swirl to coat the pan. Crack your egg into the pan and cut the heat to super low. Cook sunny-side up until the white is set and the yolk is runny, 2 to 3 minutes. Jolt the pan with high heat until the egg bubbles up. Slide a spatula underneath and transfer the egg to a plate.

Pile the pulled pork onto the bottom of the brioche bun, top with the sauce, then sprinkle the cotija cheese over the sauce. Top with the fried egg, close the sandwich, and enjoy.

(recipe continues)

Nita Green Sauce

MAKES ABOUT 1 CUP

1 cup fresh cilantro leaves

1 cup fresh flat-leaf parsley
leaves

2 garlic cloves, peeled and
lightly smashed

1 teaspoon red wine vinegar

1 teaspoon crushed red pepper

½ cup extra-virgin olive oil

Kosher salt

Combine the cilantro, parsley, garlic, vinegar, crushed red pepper, and oil in a blender. Blend at the highest speed until smooth. Season with salt and serve right away or refrigerate in an airtight container for up to 1 week.

The Major Leagues

IN 2013, MY team and I announced that we would be opening a brick-and-mortar spot. We signed up to be one of the first tenants of the renovated Grand Central Market. I was honored to be a part of the new generation of that market. When I was a kid, I used to go there and eat pupusas. It was the perfect transition from a food truck because the location was right on the street. We were located at the east entrance, front and center. We were on Broadway, in the heart of downtown LA.

We designed the restaurant in Photoshop and nickel-and-dimed every vendor. At the end of the day, we got it built for less than 60 grand. We pulled off a business miracle. It took us six months, but we made it happen!

When I began to order the food for our opening weekend, I thought we'd serve five hundred people in three days. On the truck, we had been doing about 120 sandwiches a day, so it made sense. On opening day, there was already a line around the block at 8 a.m. It was insane. We ran out of food by noon, so we had to work all through the night to prep for the next day. From that day on, we had a line waiting for our sandwiches. I was told by one of the OG taco vendors that the line would last only a week because the space was cursed. Well, six years later, we still have a line out the building.

AMBOY

In 2014, I cooked for the StarChefs Rising Stars Award, an award that three of the four chefs I worked for before Eggslut had won. When I "tried out" for Antoinette Bruno, the StarChefs head who chooses the winner, I was so scared. I loved StarChefs. I followed all their moves on social media, and I subscribed to their magazine. When I finished cooking for Antoinette, I ran to the bathroom and barfed. It was the most important meal I had cooked up until that point. I honestly thought I fucked it all up. When it comes to cooking, I'm a perfectionist. I didn't feel confident after that meal.

Six months went by. I didn't hear from her, so I chalked it up to the game. I just didn't make it happen. One day, I was beat after service. As I sank in my chair drinking lukewarm Gatorade, I got a phone call from Antoinette. She said she'd been meaning to call me. She was at home washing dishes and was reminded that she owed me a call. My heart sank, and I felt the Gatorade coming up.

Then she said, "Alvin, you won! You're LA's Rising Star Concept Chef!"

Out of nowhere, tears started to pour out of my eyeballs. She asked me if I was happy, and I answered, "I can't believe this is happening." The icing on that cake was that the girl I had a crush on—now, the love of my life—witnessed it all. She saw the roller coaster of emotion I suffered in a five-minute phone call. But I ended on top of the world.

That year, Eggslut won a slew of awards. Our momentum grew, and our popularity was through the roof. This was the rise of downtown LA. There were cool bars popping up everywhere. The Ace Hotel was the place to be, and since I was the chef and owner of Eggslut, I had juice everywhere.

This is the story of Eggslut the restaurant—the highs and the lows, what I built and what I lost, and the reality of success. The recipes here are the ones birthed from sacrifice.

The Best Friend

ALEXANDRA: You told me once that your friends are your family. Who was your best friend?

ALVIN: A guy I'll call "Nicky." He and I would put in the hours. Based on the sheer happiness of working together, we got through four years of 60-hour workweeks. Forever I thought he'd be my best man. That's how serious it was. Together, we created the DNA of Egglsut.

And for a long while, it worked. LA nightlife engulfed us. It swallowed us whole, and we loved it. We would party all night long and be at work at 5 a.m. We had each other's backs. Nicky would pick up a fifth of vodka at the liquor store and mix it with orange juice, and we would do brunch. Then, at the end of a service, Nicky would run up to the liquor store and get everyone Gatorade. He would pass them out and say, "Good job."

ALEXANDRA: What changed?

ALVIN: It couldn't last. Things started to fall apart. I'm over here taking business meetings with the CEO of the Cosmopolitan Hotel, and he's running my restaurant jacked off God knows what. He was dedicated and loyal to Eggslut. When I opened Ramen Champ, we grew apart. I think he resented me because I left. Eggslut was no longer my only priority. I had bigger and richer friends. I was rolling in a Tesla, and Nicky was still stuck at Eggslut working a 15-hour grind. He just got lost in it. Every single person he hung out with downtown was doing coke. Every single one of the bartenders and waiters was washed up. Everyone was a junkie. To this day, he hates me. We can't even be in the same room. He was never properly compensated, and he should have been. He should have been.

ALEXANDRA: When was the last time you saw him?

ALVIN: The last time I talked to him, I had given up a lot of my power in Eggslut to get freedom. I had a meeting with him. I said, "Yo, fuck that place. Come with me. I'll buy you an S2000." That was his favorite car. He then was passive-aggressively fired, to the point where he just never showed up again. He didn't want anyone else to run Eggslut, because we created that DNA. When you showed up to Eggslut, we knew your order. We knew your name. It was a glory time.

ALEXANDRA: Where is he now?

ALVIN: No one knows. I heard he's dabbling in coffee. Every time you see him, he's all fucked up. He's still cool with my cousins from Jersey, which is better than my standing. My great-aunt, our neighborhood nanny when we were kids, when she died, I wasn't even invited to the funeral. I'm pretty sure he was. Out of my whole block, the block that I love—out of all my homies growing up—I became the evil one. I'm in New York. I'm in SoHo. I have a restaurant here, and they're still there. It sucks.

Some of my homies still talk to me. Some don't. Some resent me. They'll say, "I'm so proud of you." Then they get together and talk shit. The thing is, I'm still working 15-hour days. I'm still wearing the same Birkenstocks I've worn forever. It's the same shit in a different place. But that's the cost of success. Every successful person I've met has the same exact story.

ALEXANDRA: Is it worth it?

ALVIN: I ask myself that every day. I'm a simple dude. I could totally live off Spam and Top Ramen every day. If I want to save up for a trip, I'll eat $3 ham sandwiches. I'll tell Angela, "We don't need this." Maybe I could be a line cook at the Marriott in Hawaii and be happy. Once you find your way, your momentum starts to build and everything gets easier. That's the scariest part about this. I love what I do. Going to work isn't going to work, because I truly love what I do. You meet the best people. They share their secrets. It doesn't stop. But you lose a lot. There are certain things you have to lose. Hanging out all the time brought me and my homies together. And that was the first thing to go. New Year's Eve, I'm working. Your birthday, I'm working. Your firstborn kid arrives, I'm working. There are friends that I've had since I learned to walk. They've gotten married and had three kids and I haven't seen any of them. I don't know the kids' names. We're having family problems or there's a funeral? I can't be there.

I have employees. Some have four kids. What are they going to do if I screw up? It's so much pressure, but I take it on the chin. I love what I do. When I'm there in the kitchen, I can't fail. If I went back to Pico Rivera, I could still act like nothing happened. But my friends can't forgive me. I can forgive them, but they can't forgive me. If I lost everything, they would rejoice at my failure more than they would ever rejoice at my success. Losing Nicky has always been a problem. Ex-girlfriends, old business partners—none of that hurt me as much as not being able to call my boy. Nicky is what hurts most. I don't know what I did wrong. It's just what happens when you come from the hood. I don't know anyone else who has a different story.

The Slut

This dish changed my life. No one really knew who we were until Ruth Reichl came to the truck and had the Slut. For a while, it was our number-one-selling dish. Marisa Tomei had it. Colin Hanks had it. The girl who played Jean Grey in *X-Men* ate it every day off the truck. One of the dudes from ZZ Top loved it. In Aspen, we did a pop-up with Drew Barrymore. We paired the Slut with her wine, and it was chaos. It felt like all of Aspen was in front of our booth, eating Sluts and drinking her pinot grigio.

The Slut was what set us apart from everyone else. It was our flex, how you knew we were chefs. In culinary school, I remember making a coddled egg in a coffee mug. Back then, Joël Robuchon had made his famous mashed potatoes, topped them with an egg, and served them in a martini glass. I thought that was so rad, super classic but also new. I blurred the two and there was the Slut. The first time I made it at home, it blew my mind. It was so simple.

¼ **cup sea salt, plus more for garnish**

1 **pound russet potatoes, peeled and cut into large dice**

11 **tablespoons unsalted butter, cut into tablespoons**

Kosher salt

4 **large eggs**

2 **tablespoons thinly sliced fresh chives, for garnish**

Toasted bread, for serving

SPECIAL EQUIPMENT
Food mill

Pastry bag, fitted with a large tip

4 **(1-pint) mason jars**

Jar lifter (optional)

Fill a large stockpot with a couple gallons of water and bring it to a rolling boil over high heat. Add the sea salt and the potatoes and cook, stirring occasionally, until fork-tender, 15 to 20 minutes. Meanwhile, set your food mill over a large bowl. Using a spider or slotted spoon, transfer the potatoes to the food mill and leave the water in the pot. Run the potatoes through the food mill until smooth. Fold the butter into the potato puree and season with salt.

Bring the water in the pot to a simmer.

Transfer the potato puree to a pastry bag fitted with a large tip and pipe the puree into the mason jars. Each jar should be about one-third full. Crack 1 egg into each jar over the puree and close the lids tightly. Place the jars in the pot of water and simmer until the egg whites are solid but the yolks are still super soft, about 15 minutes.

Using a jar lifter or long tongs, carefully remove the jars from the water and dry them with a towel. Use the towel or oven mitts to open the lids. Garnish each egg with a sprinkle of chives and sea salt. Serve directly from the jars when cool enough to handle, about 10 minutes. Mix the egg and potato puree really well with the salt and chives and enjoy with toasted bread.

The Reality
of Success

When I was young, I had a strict timeline for my life. I would be married by 23, have a six-figure salary by 25, first child by 26, another kid two years after, and my first million by the time I was 30. LOL.

Here's my reality: I was out of college by 25, had a dead-end job at 26, lived on $30K—cook's wages—for the next two years, broke up with my longtime girl and nearly crashed out as a business owner at 30, dated everything that moved for the next year, parlayed Eggslut's fame into free trips to NYC and Las Vegas, and turned down $150 million for the business like it was no big deal. That progression is honestly the most dangerous thing that can ever happen to a person. The vapors were real. My ambitions and goals were shifting under me. Every day, I had to figure out exactly what I wanted out of life.

I still feel strongly that Eggslut was meant to be one or two locations—max. My dream was to create a classic Los Angeles eatery like Philippe's or Langer's, but we had so many offers. I remember talking to my partners. What was our plan? We started letting other people shape Eggslut's future. Lawyers, franchise advisors, and business consultants got involved. Dark times were ahead.

Don't get me wrong, I should've sold the fuck out of Eggslut for $150 million. It would have taken care of my family forever. I know now that kind of deal is a unicorn. But back then, I wouldn't take chump change in exchange for damaging the brand. I wanted to just keep it as is, growing our clout as one of the most iconic restaurants in Los Angeles.

I'll be the first to admit that I'm not Gordon Gekko—though I thought I wanted to be. I'm not a tycoon or a fierce business shark. I was a cook, so when Eggslut started to become a corporation, I looked for inspiration elsewhere—specifically, every ramen restaurant in Los Angeles. I went to my friend's ramen restaurant three times a week just to watch him do service. The party life died out, and the craft of making something brilliantly became my new infatuation.

I began to develop a ramen concept. I gave my Eggslut partners a chance to be a part of my new-found love, but they tried to shape the business into something I didn't agree with, so I pulled the plug. But I couldn't give up on ramen completely, so I began a separate idea—still ramen but with a new crew. We created Ramen Champ, and through it I met George Yu, the unofficial mayor of LA's Chinatown, where we were based on the second floor of Far East Plaza. Later, he became a mentor.

Ramen Champ was for tonkotsu ramen lovers, and we knew it was going to be the new hot spot for ramen addicts. It opened with three-hour lines out the door. Our broth required a three-day process to achieve rich and full umami. Japanese people would come in and rave about it. Other people preferred the salty shio/shoyu Chinese-style; they thought our broth was too rich.

Either way, we were killing it. It was a cool place to dine. We had Anthony Bourdain's graphic artist

Mike Houston animate a mural there, and it turned out amazing. We competed in local ramen cook-offs, and even brought the ramen shop to Coachella. But the crash was coming. I found myself in a legal battle. I would love to give more detail, but I can't. The lessons of it are: Get a lawyer early, and don't trust everyone to get along just cuz you were friends once. The lawsuit took me away from the restaurant, and Ramen Champ began to feel the effect of my absence. My new partners agreed to sell to a Japanese ramen chef to keep its integrity intact.

It makes me sad to think about what should've, could've, and would've happened if I'd been able to stay. Here's a recipe that makes me proud of my Ramen Champ days.

Bulalo Ramen

SERVES 4

In 2013, right at the end of my time at Eggslut, I lived with my cousin. I was fresh off a breakup, and my cousin and his girlfriend were always home together. I didn't want to watch them be lovey-dovey, so I hung out more and more with my buddie Nate at his ramen shop in Little Tokyo and staged till I'd absorbed everything I needed to know.

My broth in this recipe is simple. Its flavor comes from roasted beef bones (I like to use knuckles and femur). You simmer them in a pot with water and aromatics, letting all the collagen and flavor release. Then, you use that same broth to braise bone-in short ribs, oxtails, or beef shanks till they're super soft.

Then I hybridize, because while I love Tsujita-style Japanese ramen, I also love bulalo—Filipino beef shank stew—which is basically Filipino ramen if you swap in noodles for rice, which I do. They share the same deep, rich bone marrow–forward broth that almost makes your lips stick together. But bulalo has a few additions: a little bit of fish sauce and garlic, corn, and bok choy for crunch.

Because Ramen Champ was a love letter to Japanese ramen culture, I never wanted to put anything fusion on the menu. So only the staff, friends, and the people we loved enjoyed this recipe. And now you.

Warning: Ramen broth takes time. Just like lechon, you can't turn it on and forget about it. You have to sit with it. You have to play with the fire.

BROTH

- 1 tablespoon canola oil
- 2 pounds beef shank, sliced into 1-inch-thick rounds (ask your butcher to do this)
- 12 garlic cloves, peeled
- 4 quarts Homemade Beef Stock (page 45)
- 1 large ear yellow corn, sliced into 1-inch-thick medallions
- 2 bunches baby bok choy, quartered lengthwise with the stems kept intact, or ¼ head napa cabbage, thinly sliced
- Kosher salt and freshly ground black pepper

MAKE THE BROTH: Heat a large Dutch oven over medium-high heat until hot. Add the oil and heat until you see the oil ripple, about 30 seconds. Working in batches, add 3 beef shank rounds to the pan and sear them until caramelized and brown, 2 to 4 minutes on each side. This is important—it not only adds color to the broth, it gives the meat the perfect texture. Transfer each seared batch to a plate.

Add your garlic cloves and cook, stirring, for just 30 seconds to take off the raw edge. Add the beef stock and bring to a boil, scraping up all the browned bits from the bottom of the pan. Then cut the heat to super low and return the shanks to the pan, along with any accumulated juices. Simmer, stirring and skimming off the fat occasionally, until the beef shanks are fork-tender, 2 to 3 hours.

(ingredients and recipe continue)

Rufina patis (Filipino fish sauce; available at Asian markets and on Amazon), for serving

NOODLES
½ cup kosher salt

4 (100-gram) portions fresh ramen noodles

FOR SERVING
¼ cup Crispy Garlic Chips (page 40)

Add your corn and cook, stirring occasionally, for 20 minutes over super-low heat. Add the bok choy, submerging just the stems so they get a head start cooking, and cook for 3 minutes. Then, push the leaves into the broth and simmer until the bok choy is crisp-tender, about 2 minutes. Season the broth to your liking with salt, pepper, and fish sauce. I like my broth a little bit more fish sauce-y.

MEANWHILE, PREPARE THE NOODLES: Fill a large stockpot with water and bring to a rolling boil over high heat. Stir in the salt and boil your ramen noodles according to the package instructions. Drain the noodles and set aside.

FOR EACH SERVING: Transfer 1 portion of noodles to a nice deep ramen bowl. Ladle in enough broth to cover the noodles. Add 1 beef shank round, a couple pieces of bok choy or cabbage, and 1 corn medallion. Ladle in more broth to cover. Top your bulalo ramen with garlic chips and enjoy!

CHAPTER 12

Unit 120

I WOULD WAKE up at three o'clock in the afternoon. I had nowhere to go. I was spending more time at law offices than in kitchens. All my money was going to legal fees. At one point, I had no new money coming in. The thought of having to start from zero slowly became a reality. I had hit rock bottom, and I was alone.

I hadn't spoken to my parents for three years. The Eggslut truck ruined that part of my life. My parents didn't believe in me. They thought the food truck was another one of my harebrained schemes. They wanted no part of it. I don't think my mom ever went to the truck or had any of my food. One day, my parents sold the house I grew up in, the one they promised they would never sell. It broke my heart. I'm a Pico boy to the bone. Knowing I had no home there—and no need to be there anymore—fucked me up.

All my friends from my neighborhood stopped talking to me. I had neglected them for too long. My cousins heard that I had changed, and they started to treat me differently. Except for Lorie and Kevin—I love you guys! You knew I was just trying to make my dreams come true. You made time to see me at work, and I'll never forget it.

During the Ramen Champ days, I started going out with Angela Gomez. She was the cashier at Sticky Rice,

the Thai chicken rice counter at Grand Central Market. I pursued her for a year. I would eat at the counter every day just to flirt with her.

Angela and I eventually worked together at Eggslut when she started as the cashier. She needed more hours than she was getting at the Thai spot, and it was good timing because Eggslut had become extremely busy. Naturally, we added her to our team, and it was a perfect fit because she was already friends with all of us. As I got to see her more often, I shifted my lifestyle. I started to calm down and party less, hoping she would notice. I even quit smoking after fifteen years because I knew it bothered her. Months later, all the little things that I'd changed made the right impression on her, and we started dating.

When she took a chance on me, I fell in love hard. She became my heart. She was the one person I could rely on when I was going through a lawsuit, the sale of Ramen Champ, and Eggslut's transformation into a mini corporation.

Believe it or not, I still screwed that up. Angela left me twice before I got my shit together. Now, she's the only person I can ever see myself with. She's my rock, and because of her, my life has changed for the best.

This is the story of leaving Eggslut and Ramen Champ, and finding the love of my life.

Angela

ALEXANDRA: What was Angela like when you first met her?

ALVIN: Angela was super sweet and soft-spoken. She dressed like a little skater girl. She talked shit to the boys. She worked in the restaurant industry, but she was a sweetheart. She had no care in the world for fashion. She was a T-shirt, Vans, and jeans girl. She was a typical LA girl, but she had a nice heart. I was attracted to that right off the bat, especially coming off such a turbulent relationship.

Girls I dated before her were very scantily clad. Then I realized, dude, these girls are awful. I started looking at my life. I thought, "Why can't I find a girl who's very pretty, and who works hard?" I decided to go after something different.

Angela loved being out with her friends. She would go downtown to all of the young places, like Down and Out and the Lash. I loved how simple she was. I thought, "If I'm ever going to get with another girl, this would be the direction I would go, because I am not used to this."

When Angela and I got together, everything changed. I realized that this was the life I wanted.

The extravagant, hip-hop baller lifestyle was no longer me. I wanted to be a diligent businessman. I wanted to have a happy family and live a normal life. I wanted to slow down. I didn't want to lose everything due to stupid decisions. I wanted to hang out with people who made sound, thought-out choices. I saw that the people who invested their time properly were continually successful. I wanted that more than anything because I didn't want to lose what I had built. I didn't want to go back to Pico Rivera. It was time for me to grow up, business-wise. I had something special, and I had to take care of it.

Angela was step one. I changed my routine at night. I stopped getting drunk every day. I stopped sending stupid texts and direct messages to random women. The allure of being a playboy wasn't interesting anymore. All that mattered was the next ten years.

Now, my life is always about the future. How do we plan? How do we get there? Without goals, you have nothing to work toward. You don't know your progress.

The Grass Is Always Greener

Love conquers almost everything, even a disaster year like 2015, when I gave up control of Eggslut. Suddenly, Angela and I had all the time in the world. I would wake up and start cooking. I made her Filipino food, mostly adobo and bistek. We would explore LA's Filipino food scene, eating pinakbet in Eagle Rock, pancit Malabon in West Covina, crispy pata in Cerritos, and BBQ in Filipinotown. Most of it was comforting, but a lot of it was god-awful.

We thought we should look deeper into the avant-garde Filipino food world. There were murmurs of pop-up concepts in Chino Hills and Long Beach. Charles Olalia was doing his Pinoy pop-up at his apartment in downtown. He was making beautiful pillows of pan de sal and super crispy lechon. LASA was the hottest ticket in town. I tried and tried, but could not for the life of me get into their pop-up dinners.

Meanwhile, the legendary restaurant space that had housed Pho 79 became available. George Yu, the president of the Chinatown Business Improvement District, hit me up and said it was mine for the taking. I used to eat there as a kid, back when my dad had his shop on Beaudry; we'd go there for lunch. It was sentimental. I grabbed the opportunity and signed the lease.

At the same time, a media firm was relentlessly pitching me on speaking at their "food for thought" event. It was a Filipino food conference called Next Day Better, and they wanted me to give a 45-minute speech on who I was, what I've done, and what I aspire to do. I said no through email, via text, and in person, but their representatives didn't give up, so I finally gave in.

Next Day Better was my first public-speaking engagement. Angela was in charge of holding up my cue cards. I gave it a shot, and it was a hit. I vibed with the crowd. I told them that I spent my career screwing up all the time. In spite of that, I found a way to stick to my guns and make my dreams happen. The talk ended with a standing ovation. That moment I had chills. I knew I could count on the Filipino community to have my back if I ever decided to open a Filipino concept. Afterward, I got to meet the boys behind

LASA and finally found a way into their dinners.

Most important, that night I met Alexandra Cuerdo, my coauthor of this book. It truly was a magical event.

Afterward, it became clear to me that the new restaurant space in Chinatown would be an incubator. I had a ton of chef friends throwing pop-up dinners all over the city. I could be their home base. That's how Unit 120 was born. I built a classic French-style kitchen with an art gallery–white dining room. I envisioned it as a blank canvas for chefs to practice their craft. I signed up the best: Howlin' Ray's, Here's Looking at You, and 71Above. They all got their start at Unit 120. Some people could even argue that Unit 120 was ground zero for the renaissance of Filipino food in LA.

At the same time, Angela, God bless her, convinced me to end the beef with my parents. She encouraged me to reach out to them and take them out to lunch. It started with my mom; we shared some laughs and all was forgiven. My dad was a tough pill to swallow, but it had to be done. I spoke to him on the phone first, then we had dim sum as a family. We're civil now, but there's still something inside me that won't completely open up with him. It's a work in progress.

At Unit 120, Amboy came to life as a pop-up lunch window. We served food wrapped in banana leaves and butcher paper. We threw lechon parties. It was amazing.

Ultimately, the Filipino concept that truly soared was LASA. They were the resident weekend concept at Unit 120, and within a year, they were reviewed by most of the top food publications in the country. So when they were ready to open their new restaurant, I passed them the baton and they took over the space. A year later they were one of *Food & Wine*'s 10 Best New Restaurants of 2018. Unit 120 became tangible evidence that Filipino food was a cuisine that sparked mainstream attention.

The recipes that follow are the ones cooked up at Unit 120—the place that saved me and gave me purpose.

Amboy Chicken Inasal
(Grilled Chicken with Annatto)

SERVES 8 TO 12

Chicken inasal is my favorite street food. The first time I had it, I was eight years old, in the Philippines. Then, as an adult, I craved it. I've always had a love for roasted rotisserie chicken. One day, I was playing with chicken fat in the kitchen. I made an infused chicken fat with lemongrass, garlic, lemon, and annatto seeds. It was so good, and the flavor was so inasal. I started to examine how to make a restaurant-style chicken inasal and came up with this recipe.

First, we brined the chicken. Then, we air-dried it for three days, so the skin would become nice and crispy. I'm a huge fan of crisping the skin in the oven, because I hate when the chicken skin sticks to the grill. So I bake the chicken skin-side up in the oven. Then, I glaze it with the inasal chicken fat. It crisps up and gets this really cool amber color. I'll finish the chicken on the grill, skin-side up. This is a simplified version. It's a hybrid of perfect skin and charred, smoky meat—the best of both worlds.

BRINE

4 quarts water

1 cup kosher salt

1 cup packed light brown sugar

⅔ cup chopped garlic
(about 2 heads)

6 large lemongrass stalks, thinly
sliced crosswise (use a heavy
knife or cleaver)

¼ cup chopped fresh ginger

2 teaspoons coarsely ground
black pepper

¼ cup fresh calamansi juice
(see Note, page 68)

2 (3½- to 4-pound) chickens,
backbones removed,
opened up flat; or 4 bone-in
breast halves, 4 wings, and
4 whole legs

BASTING SAUCE

1 cup canola oil

½ cup annatto seeds
or 1½ tablespoons ground
annatto

Grated zest of 5 lemons

½ teaspoon kosher salt

¼ teaspoon freshly ground
black pepper

TOYOMANSI SAUCE

3 tablespoons Datu Puti or
Silver Swan soy sauce (see
page 60; available at Asian
markets and on Amazon)

3 tablespoons fresh calamansi
juice (see Note, page 68)

1 teaspoon Rufina patis
(Filipino fish sauce; available
at Asian markets and on
Amazon)

3 garlic cloves, minced

FOR SERVING

Steamed Jasmine Rice
(page 20), for serving

Crab Fat Sauce (page 321;
optional)

(recipe continues)

BRINE THE CHICKEN: In a large stockpot, combine the water, salt, brown sugar, garlic, lemongrass, ginger, and pepper and bring to a boil over high heat, stirring often. Fill the sink with ice water and set the pot in it to cool to room temperature. Stir in the calamansi juice, then add the chicken (or transfer to a large bowl if the pot is too small). Set a plate on top of the chicken to keep it completely submerged in the brine. Cover and refrigerate for 1 to 2 days.

MEANWHILE, MAKE THE BASTING SAUCE: Heat the oil with the annatto in a small saucepan over low heat, stirring often, until the oil is deep orange and flavorful, 3 to 5 minutes. Remove from the heat and stir in the lemon zest, salt, and pepper. Let cool, then cover and refrigerate until ready to use.

MAKE THE TOYOMANSI SAUCE: Combine all the ingredients in a squeeze bottle or small bowl. Cover and refrigerate until ready to use.

PREPARE THE GRILL: Prepare a grill for indirect medium heat (350°F to 450°F). For charcoal: Ignite a full chimney of briquets (about 90) on the fire grate. When the coals are dotted with ash, about 20 minutes, bank them evenly on opposite sides of the fire grate and, if needed, let burn to medium. Set a 9 x 13-inch foil drip pan in the center and set the cooking grate in place. For gas: Remove the cooking grates. Turn all the burners to high, close the lid, and heat for 10 minutes. Turn off the center burner(s) and reduce the heat for the others to medium. Set a 9 x 13-inch foil drip pan on the turned-off burner. Set the cooking grates in place. If the drip pan sticks up, push on the grates to flatten the pan a bit to create an even surface.

GRILL IT: Strain the basting sauce through a fine-mesh strainer. Remove the chicken from the brine and discard the brine. Place the chicken, skin-side up, on your grill over indirect heat. Brush the chicken all over with the basting sauce. Grill, covered, for 20 minutes. Baste the chicken, then flip and baste the other side. Grill, covered, basting one more time, until the chicken is no longer pink in the thickest part of any piece, 10 minutes more for separate wing pieces and 20 to 30 minutes more for everything else. Now, move the chicken to direct heat so you can brown it some more, for about 10 minutes, until the internal temperature reaches 155°F for the breasts and thighs.

Squeeze or brush the toyomansi sauce all over the chicken. Transfer the chicken to a cutting board. If using whole flattened chickens, cut off the legs and wings and quarter each whole breast through the bones. Transfer to a platter and serve hot with rice and crab fat sauce.

Liempo (Roast Pork Belly)

SERVES 4 TO 6

Growing up, liempo was a no-no at my house. My mom and dad were scared to death of cholesterol. One day, I had liempo in some West Covina Filipino restaurant. It blew me away. It was sweet, porky, fatty greatness, and so much more nuanced than lechon kawali, which is basically deep-fried pork belly. I decided to try a hybrid lechon kawali–liempo.

I got skin-on pork belly, exfoliated it with salt, and perforated the skin with a meat tenderizer. Then, I steamed the pork and braised it in the oven over a pan of water. Because the skin was exposed to the dry heat, it ended up being super crispy, almost like a Chinese-style pork belly. The fat would render out into the water, and that same water would keep the meat tender. But there was still something missing. I ended up slicing the belly in portions. I left the skin untouched and glazed just the meat part. Then, I put the strips on the grill so I could get the char marks on the meat. Again, it was the best of both worlds. I sometimes finish it with toyomansi, like Italians do with olive oil.

It was a perfect dish for Amboy, the restaurant. I'd preserved what I loved about Filipino food, applying restaurant techniques to make it perfect.

---

1 (2-pound) center-cut skin-on
   pork belly

1 cup kosher salt

Amboy Adobo Glaze
   (recipe follows)

Steamed Jasmine Rice
   (page 20), for serving

SPECIAL EQUIPMENT
Meat tenderizer

DAYS 1–3: PREP

Rinse your pork belly thoroughly with cold water. Pat dry with paper towels and place it on a rimmed baking sheet lined with a silicone mat. Rub ½ cup of the salt all over the pork skin and let it cure, uncovered, in the refrigerator for 2 hours. This process will pull out a lot of the moisture.

Brush off the salt and discard it. Using a meat tenderizer, perforate every inch of the pork belly skin. If you don't have a meat tenderizer, you can use a fork, but it'll take 10 times as long. You literally want the skin of the pork belly to look like a perforated piece of paper. Or, you know how crackers have holes in them? You want the skin to look like that.

Place the pork belly on a wire rack set over a rimmed baking sheet. Let it air-dry, uncovered, in your refrigerator for 3 days, or until the skin is completely dry to the touch. Something magical happens, and you will be rewarded with super-crispy skin—if you're patient.

(recipe continues)

DAY 4: COOK

Set up a large wok or pot with a steamer insert over medium-high heat. Pour 2 to 3 inches of water into the pot and bring to a rolling boil. Add the pork belly, cover, and steam for 1 hour over low heat, so you can render the fat out without the meat getting tough.

Pull the pork out of the steamer and let it cool on a wire rack to room temperature. Meanwhile, preheat your oven to 500°F, or the hottest your oven goes.

When the pork is cool enough to handle, rub the remaining ½ cup salt all over the skin and season the flesh with some of that salt. Place the pork belly, skin-side up, in a roasting pan. Add just enough water to submerge most of the pork belly, stopping about ¼ inch from the pork skin. You want the skin to be completely dry.

Pop that in the oven and roast the pork, rotating the pan carefully every 5 minutes, for 15 to 20 minutes, until the skin is evenly crisp. Remove from the oven and transfer the pork to a wire rack set over a rimmed baking sheet. Let it stand until cool enough to handle. Cut your oven temp down to 375°F, if you choose to bake the liempo pieces. Or heat your grill to 375°F, if you choose the grilling option.

Place the pork skin-side down on a cutting board. Using a serrated knife, slice the pork crosswise into 1-inch pieces. You want to cut through the meat first because it'll be easier to create even slices before you shatter through the crispy skin.

Using a barbecue brush, brush the adobo glaze over just the meat, taking care to avoid the skin.

To bake the liempo, place your glazed pork pieces, skin-side up, on a rimmed baking sheet lined with a silicone mat. Bake until the glaze is cooked through and beautifully caramelized, 8 to 12 minutes.

To grill the liempo, place your glazed pork pieces, skin-side up, over indirect heat—not right above the charcoal, where the fire will flare up and burn. Make sure it's slightly offset. Grill the pork, including the skin side, until the glaze is cooked through and beautifully caramelized, about 4 minutes on each side.

Transfer the pork to a platter and serve immediately with hot rice.

Amboy Adobo Glaze

MAKES ABOUT 1¼ CUPS

2 cups Homemade Chicken
  Stock (page 44)

¼ cup Datu Puti or Silver Swan
  soy sauce (see page 60;
  available at Asian markets and
  on Amazon)

2 tablespoons Datu Puti
  cane vinegar (see page 137;
  available at Asian markets and
  on Amazon)

8 garlic cloves, peeled and
  lightly smashed

Combine the chicken stock, soy sauce, vinegar, and garlic in a medium saucepan and stir to combine. Bring to a boil over medium-high heat, then cut the heat to a simmer and cook, stirring occasionally, until the sauce is reduced by half, 25 to 30 minutes. Use immediately or let cool to room temperature and refrigerate in an airtight container for up to 5 days. Strain out the garlic before using.

Grilled Pompano

SERVES 2

Pompano is a farmed fish from Vietnam. The first time I ever had it was at my old friend Mark Tagnipez's house. It was covered in garlic, and we ate it with vinegar. I grew up with tilapia, so, to me, pompano was baller.

Pompano is my favorite fish to grill: It has a perfect amount of fat, a perfect amount of meat, and not a lot of bones. It's full of great oily, fishy flavors. When the skin is crispy, it's so good.

For Amboy, I wanted to refine it a bit. I started with vinegar, calamansi juice, and garlic. I slowly blended butter into that puree. Then I salted the fish, set it on the grill, and basted it with the butter sauce. The reaction between the fire and the butter created this awesome garlicky, nutty flavor. The pompano was a perfect foil. Once we put it on the menu, it became the number-one-selling dish.

---

1 whole pompano, cleaned and scaled

2 teaspoons kosher salt

3 tablespoons Amboy Butter Base (recipe follows)

1 cup water

Kosher salt

Steamed Jasmine Rice (page 20), for serving

Score the skin on both sides of the pompano three times—like Adidas stripes—about 1 inch apart. Rub 1 teaspoon of the salt onto each side of the fish.

Heat a grill to 375°F. Place the pompano on the grill over indirect heat with the nose pointing at 10 o'clock. As it starts to cook, brush some of the butter base on the top of the fish. That butter will trickle down and slick up the skin, and help loosen it from the grates of the grill.

Grill for 4 minutes. Have a cup of water on standby. Using a spatula, test the fish to see if the skin releases easily from the grill. When the skin releases without tearing, flip the fish over carefully so the nose is still pointing at 10 o'clock. Don't flip until your fish is absolutely ready, or else the skin will tear and you'll have a mess on your hands.

Once the fish is flipped, the butter will hit the flame and, most likely, flare up a bit. You want this because it creates a great taste. The fire hitting the milk solids of the butter will make it nutty, adding another level of complexity to the flavor. If the fire flares too high, douse the flames with water and continue cooking.

(recipe continues)

Baste the cooked side of the fish with more butter base and grill the fish for another 4 minutes. Test the fish to see if the skin releases easily from the grill. When the skin releases without tearing, flip the fish over again carefully so the nose is still pointing at 10 o'clock. Grill until the skin is crisp and the fish is cooked through, 2 to 4 minutes. Keep your cup of water on standby to battle any big flare-ups.

Pull the fish off the grill, transfer to a platter, and season with salt. Serve immediately with hot rice.

Amboy Butter Base

MAKES ABOUT 2 CUPS

16 garlic cloves, peeled and lightly smashed

½ cup Datu Puti cane vinegar (see page 137; available at Asian markets and on Amazon)

½ cup fresh calamansi juice (see Note, page 68)

1 pound (4 sticks) unsalted butter, softened

In a blender, combine the garlic, vinegar, and calamansi juice. Blend on high until the garlic is a smooth paste. Add your butter and pulse until the butter is fully incorporated. Now you have a great butter base for fish or chicken!

Butter can be stored, refrigerated, for 2 weeks, wrapped in plastic or sealed in an airtight container.

Munggo (Mung Bean Stew)

SERVES 8

As a child, I hated the Filipino mung-bean dish called munggo. My parents used to make me sit at the dinner table, and I wouldn't be able to leave until I was done eating it. Munggo is supposed to be good for you, but when I was a kid, I thought it tasted like dirt. I never understood it. When I got older, I discovered the health benefits of eating munggo, and I tried to improve on the recipe. I read around, but every version I found was made with pork fat. It totally negates the goodness of eating mung beans. I needed to get the umami out of legumes without it.

With trial and error, I discovered that when you roast shiitakes, they exude a kind of pork flavor. So I started to make my own shiitake broth, and I used it to cook my munggo, adding tons of ginger, plus liquid aminos to amplify the flavor of the aromatics. That's how I learned to love this dish. And it gives contrast to my Amboy menu: If a customer orders liempo and mung beans, she isn't getting a double whammy of pork fat in both dishes.

---

2 cups dried whole green mung beans

1 tablespoon canola oil

1 medium onion, finely diced

3 garlic cloves, minced

4 cups Shiitake Mushroom Stock (recipe follows), plus more as necessary

1 tablespoon minced fresh ginger

½ tablespoon liquid aminos (preferably Bragg, available at Whole Foods or on Amazon), plus more if desired

Kosher salt (optional)

Crispy Garlic Chips (page 40), for garnish (optional)

Put your mung beans in a large bowl and cover with plenty of water. Let soak for at least 2 hours or up to overnight at room temp, then drain and set aside.

Heat a medium Dutch oven over medium-high heat until hot. Add the oil and heat until you see the oil ripple, about 30 seconds. Cut the heat to medium. Add the onion and garlic and cook, stirring constantly, until the onion is slightly translucent, 1 to 2 minutes.

Add your drained mung beans to the pot and cook, stirring constantly, for 5 minutes. Add the shiitake stock and cook, scraping up all the browned bits from the bottom of the pot. Add the ginger and bring to a simmer. Adjust the heat and continue to simmer, stirring occasionally, until the mung beans are soft, almost mushy, and the liquid is reduced by half, 35 to 50 minutes. If the mung beans are still too firm, add more stock and continue to simmer until the beans are soft.

Stir in the liquid aminos. Taste and add more liquid aminos or season with salt, if desired. Ladle into a bowl, garnish with garlic chips, and serve immediately as a great side dish to everything!

Shiitake Mushroom Stock

MAKES ABOUT 2 QUARTS

12 ounces dried shiitake mushrooms

2 gallons water

½ sheet kombu (available at Asian markets and on Amazon)

Combine all your ingredients in a large stockpot and bring to a boil over high heat. Cut the heat to a simmer and cook until the stock is intensely savory and mushroomy, about 2 hours. Strain and discard the solids. Use the stock immediately or let cool to room temperature and transfer to airtight containers, leaving behind any grit. Refrigerate for up to 1 week or freeze for up to 3 months.

Kalderetang Chickpeas (Stewed Chickpeas)

SERVES 4 TO 6

Like Munggo (page 310), this dish is the perfect pair with a grilled main. If you order bistek and kalderetang chickpeas, you're eating something like mechado. It's still Filipino, but minimizing the animal-fat usage.

1 cup dried chickpeas

6 cups Shiitake Mushroom Stock (page 311) or water

1 onion, quartered

1 carrot, cut crosswise into 4-inch lengths

1 celery stalk, cut crosswise into 4-inch lengths

4 cups Spicy Kaldereta Base (recipe follows)

Cayenne pepper (optional)

1 tablespoon liquid aminos (preferably Bragg, available at Whole Foods or on Amazon)

Kosher salt

Steamed Jasmine Rice (page 20), for serving

Put your chickpeas in a large bowl and cover with plenty of water. Cover and let soak overnight at room temperature. Drain the chickpeas, then transfer to a large stockpot. Add the mushroom stock, onion, carrot, and celery. Bring to a boil over medium-high heat, then reduce the heat and simmer for 30 minutes.

Drain the chickpeas and discard the liquid. Using tongs, pull out the onion, carrot, and celery and discard.

In a medium saucepan, bring the kaldereta base to a simmer. Add the chickpeas, then cook over medium-low heat, stirring occasionally, until the tartness of the tomatoes is gone, about 45 minutes. Season with cayenne, if desired. Add your liquid aminos and cook, stirring occasionally, for another 5 minutes. Season with salt, ladle into bowls, and serve immediately with rice.

(recipe continues)

Spicy Kaldereta Base

1 tablespoon canola oil

¼ cup diced onion

2 tablespoons chopped garlic

1 carrot, diced

1 (16-ounce) can whole peeled tomatoes, with their juices

1 red bell pepper, roasted (see page 129), seeded, and diced

1 russet potato, peeled and diced

2 cups Shiitake Mushroom Stock (page 311)

2 tablespoons smoked paprika

1 teaspoon cayenne pepper

Heat a medium saucepan over medium-high heat until hot. Add the oil and heat until you see the oil ripple, about 30 seconds. Cut the heat to medium. Add your onion and garlic and cook, stirring constantly, until the onion is translucent, about 2 minutes. Add the carrot and cook, stirring, until softened, about 5 minutes. Add the tomatoes and their juices and break up the tomatoes with a wooden spoon. Add the roasted bell pepper, potato, and mushroom stock.

Bring to a boil, then cut the heat to a simmer. Simmer, stirring occasionally, until the base has thickened and the flavors have married, about 1 hour. Stir in the smoked paprika and cayenne. Use right away or let cool to room temperature, then refrigerate in an airtight container for up to 3 days.

Kare-Kare Lentils
(Peanut Butter Curry Lentils)

SERVES 4

Kare-kare has an interesting history. Thai people brought curry to the Philippines, and we loved it. Unfortunately, the spices in curry were so expensive, we couldn't replicate the dishes. Instead, we replicated the color with peanuts. In that moment, kare-kare—or curry-curry—was born. Kare-kare was an example of our ingenuity!

As with Munggo (page 310) and Kalderetang Chickpeas (page 313), I've created a version of kare-kare to reduce the fat content, so you can eat it more often. Kare-kare is usually made with oxtail, but oxtail is just straight-up fat. It's collagen.

With this version, I get you the Filipino flavors without the bypass surgery. I didn't want to shake tradition; I just wanted to create a dish you could eat every day. Serve with grilled meats or rice, or as a savory accompaniment to any dish.

1 tablespoon canola oil

1 cup diced red onion

1 tablespoon minced garlic

1 cup red lentils

2½ cups Shiitake Mushroom Stock (page 311), plus more as necessary

1 teaspoon liquid aminos (preferably Bragg, available at Whole Foods or on Amazon)

2 tablespoons creamy peanut butter

Kosher salt

1 scallion, thinly sliced

Heat a medium saucepan over medium heat until hot. Add the oil and heat until you see the oil ripple, about 30 seconds. Add your onion and garlic and cook, stirring constantly, until the onion is translucent, 2 to 3 minutes. Add the lentils and toss to combine. This is vital: The aromatics will flavor the lentils. Cook, stirring occasionally, until the lentils darken slightly to a deep orangey-red, 4 to 5 minutes.

Pour in your mushroom stock and cook over medium-high heat, stirring constantly, for 5 minutes. The lentils should be bubbling the entire time. Then, cut the heat to medium and cook, stirring occasionally, until the lentils have softened, 5 to 7 minutes. Add the liquid aminos, stir to combine, and cook, stirring occasionally, until slightly thickened but still a little loose, 1 to 2 minutes. Add more stock if necessary.

Add your peanut butter and cook, stirring and scraping down the sides of the pan occasionally, until the peanut butter is heated through, about 1 minute. Season, if necessary, with salt. Ladle the kare-kare lentils into a bowl, top with the scallions, and serve immediately.

Cucumber and Tomato Side Salad

SERVES 4

When I was growing up, my dad would always make a side salad of tomatoes with patis, onions, and duck egg. I loved it. When I wanted to make my own atchara, I went the tomato route because it felt like home. I remember growing fresh tomatoes and cucumbers in my family's backyard. My version had a calamansi and patis vinaigrette, raw garlic, tomatoes, and cucumbers. That became our side salad at Amboy. Its zingy citrus flavor would cut through the fat and create a necessary balance within the meal. It's the perfect side for any heavy dish.

SALAD

3 medium plum tomatoes, cut into 1-inch chunks

2 cucumbers, halved lengthwise and sliced into ¼-inch-thick half-moons

1 small red onion, diced

2 garlic cloves, minced

DRESSING

1 cup extra-virgin olive oil

2 tablespoons Rufina patis (Filipino fish sauce; available at Asian markets and on Amazon)

1 tablespoon fresh calamansi juice (see Note, page 68)

MAKE THE SALAD: Toss your tomatoes, cucumbers, onion, and garlic in a medium bowl.

MAKE THE DRESSING: In a small bowl, whisk together the olive oil, fish sauce, and calamansi juice.

Pour the dressing over the veggies and toss to combine. The fish sauce will pull more moisture out of the veggies, adding to the vinaigrette. Plate and serve immediately.

Amboy Hot Sauce

I always wondered, "Why don't we have a hot sauce in the Philippines?" So I made my own by pureeing chiles, vinegar, roasted bell pepper, and garlic. It almost tasted like a Filipino sriracha, minus the fermentation.

Why not take something so classically Filipino—vinegar with chiles—and add complementary flavors? Could I have possibly made the first Filipino hot sauce? We'll see.

3 cups drained roasted red bell peppers from a jar

½ cup minced garlic (about 20 large cloves)

3 Fresno chiles, stemmed and coarsely chopped

3 Thai bird chiles, stemmed and coarsely chopped

¾ cups Datu Puti cane vinegar (see page 137; available at Asian markets and on Amazon)

¾ teaspoon kosher salt, plus more if desired

Combine the bell peppers, garlic, chiles, and vinegar in a food processor. Process until thoroughly blended and smooth. Season with the salt. Use immediately or refrigerate in an airtight container for up to 1 week.

Calamansi Vinaigrette

MAKES ABOUT 2½ CUPS

I started this dressing recipe with olive oil, a little bit of Dijon mustard, shallots, salt, and pepper. Then I added calamansi juice and it just took off. The acidity of calamansi is very specific. There's no sweetness whatsoever, and it's more tart than astringent. Calamansi vinaigrette became an Amboy house flavor, and I put it on everything.

1 shallot, chopped

1 tablespoon Dijon mustard

½ cup fresh calamansi juice (see Note, page 68)

2 cups extra-virgin olive oil

1 teaspoon kosher salt

½ teaspoon freshly ground black pepper

Combine all the ingredients in a blender and blend on high until fully incorporated. Toss immediately with arugula salad, or any kind of leafy greens. Or refrigerate in an airtight container for up to 5 days.

Crab Fat Sauce

MAKES ABOUT 1 CUP

If liver sauce is for pork, crab fat sauce is for chicken. In this recipe, you mix the crab fat (aka tomalley) with garlic, calamansi juice, and shallots. If it's too pungent, you can mellow it down with coconut milk. Crab fat sauce is my choice of condiment for Amboy Chicken Inasal (page 301). It's umami to the tenth degree, and when mixed with warm fluffy rice and juicy chicken, it's nirvana.

1½ teaspoons canola oil

1 tablespoon minced shallot

4 garlic cloves, minced

2 tablespoons fresh calamansi juice (see Note, page 68)

1 cup Crab Fat (recipe follows)

1 tablespoon Annatto Oil (recipe follows)

Roast chicken or Amboy Chicken Inasal (page 301), for serving

Heat a small saucepan over medium heat until hot. Add the oil and heat until you see the oil ripple, about 30 seconds. Add the shallot and garlic and cook, stirring constantly, until the shallot is slightly translucent, 1 to 2 minutes. Add your calamansi juice and scrape the browned bits from the sides and bottom of the pan.

Cut the heat to medium-low. Add the crab fat and cook, stirring, until firm and brown in color, 5 to 8 minutes. Add your annatto oil and cook, stirring, to let the flavors marry, about 1 minute. Remove from the heat and serve the crab fat sauce immediately with chicken.

(recipe continues)

AMBOY

Crab Fat (aka Tomalley)

MAKES ABOUT 1 CUP

1½ cups kosher salt
20 live blue crabs

Fill a very large stockpot with about 3 gallons of water and bring to a boil over high heat. Stir in 1 cup of the salt, then add your crabs and cook until the shells have gone from blue to red, 7 to 10 minutes.

Meanwhile, fill a very large bowl or pot with fresh cold water and ice, plus the remaining ½ cup salt. Stir to combine.

Once your crabs are cooked, drain them and immediately plunge them into your salted ice bath. Let soak until they're cool enough to handle, 10 to 15 minutes.

Using your hands, pull the legs off each crab. Then, remove the chest plate. Wedge your fingers into the crab and pull the top shell off. Flip over the top shell and use a small spoon to scrape the greenish-gray fat from the crab into a bowl. If there's roe, scrape that in, too. Use the crab fat right away or refrigerate in an airtight container for up to 1 day. Reserve the crabmeat for another use.

Annatto Oil

MAKES ABOUT 1 CUP

1 cup canola oil
½ cup annatto seeds

In a small saucepan, combine your oil and annatto seeds. Bring to a simmer over medium heat. Take the pan off the heat and let the oil steep for 45 minutes. Strain out the annatto seeds and use the oil right away or pour into a heatproof jar and store at room temperature for up to 1 week.

CHAPTER 13

Amboy

I WAS DRIVING to Las Vegas on my way to a promotional photo shoot for the Cosmopolitan Hotel. As we passed all the alien billboards and rest-area signs, I got a phone call from Dana Cowin. Dana was the former boss of *Food & Wine* magazine, and the new curator-of-cool for Chefs Club, a restaurant in NYC with a menu by major chefs from all over the world. Dana told me she wanted me to work on a new project for Chefs Club. Something casual. Something pop-up. Like Eggslut.

So, Angela and I packed our bags and headed east. We stayed for a week and scoped out the new project. I met the CEO of the company. He offered us the world to get Eggslut at his new Chefs Club. I told him I'd sleep on it, and we went back to LA.

We had just transformed Unit 120 into LASA. I was again kitchen-less. So I thought, why not try this? What's so bad about New York City for a couple months?

Off we went. The Standard in the East Village was my new home. At Chefs Club, I was as hands-on as I'd

first apprentice at the Eggslut truck, had already moved east to work at Momofuku Noodle Bar, so he just shuffled over to Chefs Club to be my right hand. In the middle of it all, I did a string of Amboy pop-up dinners.

When that year was up, I decided to stay in New York for good. I got rid of my LA apartment. I recruited my friend Kim Trac, one of the best dining room managers in LA. Together, we built The Usual in Nolita. The concept was American comfort food cooked by the children of immigrants. It was the best way to break out in New York. A year later, we forged the deal for Amboy. Now, we're living that dream. My ticket to heaven, if it even exists, is these two concepts and my journey to get here. It's saying to every Filipino, every kid, every minority, every person who's heard "no" their entire lives—you can make it.

For decades, Filipinos have felt like the doormat of Asia. Everyone has to drag their feet across the Philippines before they cross. In 2015, I met with a Chinese guy who had a failing sandwich restaurant that he wanted me to take over. I remember when he turned to me, and said, "You know what, dude, I hate Filipino food. It's not even a cuisine." I looked at him and said, "You want me to bail your bitch ass out, and you're insulting my culture?"

Now, it's different. Filipinos have stats that say we're a force. In the culinary world, we're a force. We're the real deal. Amboy is a thing. That's the soul of this book: We can do it.

The recipes that follow are the result of years of hard work. They're the ones I hope to serve at Amboy, my Filipino restaurant I'm planning to open in Los Angeles soon. See you at the dinner table!

ever been. The pop-up took off, and I was the talk of the town.

After the agreed-upon three-month timeline of the pop-up, I was offered a consulting position with Chefs Club, which meant I'd have to be in New York for the next year. I flew back and forth from New York to LA, like George Clooney in *Up in the Air*. My job was to rebuild the system at the restaurant. I asked my entire crew from LA to move to New York to help me. Christian, my

Slow-Cooked Crispy Pata
(Fried Pork Knuckle)

SERVES 6

There's a lot of meat in the pork knuckle—pata—and this is the best crispy pata you'll ever have. The only downside is that it costs a lot. Honestly, though, I feel like crispy pata should cost a lot, because it will straight-up kill you if you eat too much. No joke, this is a devil dish. There's so much fat and collagen involved. Worse, sometimes you get pata that's so tough, it seems like you have to be a legit butcher to cut it up.

Testing this dish took me forever. There could be no risk of shoe leather. I tried to cook it so many different ways, because the old-school way where you boil it and then fry it wasn't right. Then I figured it out: Cook it for so long that the meat surrenders. A 36-hour sous vide at constant temperature. When I removed the meat from the vacuum-sealed pack, it was super gelatinous. I put it in the refrigerator so it wouldn't fall apart in my hands. I air-dried it for another two to three days to wick out all the moisture. Then, I deep-fried the entire thing in a super-hot wok. The skin crisps up and creates a shell. Then, crack the skin and all the shredded meat comes out.

This recipe takes anywhere from four to eight days, depending on your patience level. Don't rush. It's a special dish, so you want to put some love into it—and don't eat it every day!

---

3 cups kosher salt, plus more for massaging

1 large pork knuckle

Canola oil, for frying

Sarsa (page 136), House Toyomansi (page 71), Chile-Vinegar Dipping Sauce (page 151), Lola's Pancit Bihon (page 93), or Danilo's Pancit Canton (page 177), for serving

SPECIAL EQUIPMENT
Sous vide bag and machine
Meat tenderizer

DAYS 1–3: BRINE

Pour a gallon of water into a large bowl and add 1 cup of the salt; stir to dissolve. Add your pork knuckle and let it soak in the brine in the refrigerator for at least 24 hours, or preferably 3 days. The longer the soak, the better, because you're essentially brining the meat while also purging the blood out of the bones. Discard the brine and soak the knuckle in a new batch of brine every 24 hours.

DAYS 4–6: SOUS VIDE

Transfer the pork knuckle to a sous vide bag. Vacuum-seal and submerge in a sous vide bath set at 155°F for no less than 24 hours, or preferably up to 3 days. The longer the sous vide, the more tender the meat will be. Fill a large bowl with ice and water. Remove the pork knuckle from the bag and plunge it into the ice bath for 10 minutes to stop the cooking. Drain and pat dry with paper towels.

(recipe continues)

DAYS 7–8:

Using a meat tenderizer (or a fork), perforate the skin all over. Massage the skin with salt, then place the pork knuckle on a wire rack set over a rimmed baking sheet. Let it air-dry, uncovered, in your refrigerator for at least 24 hours, preferably up to 48 hours.

Pour 4 inches of oil into a large, heavy-bottomed pot and heat to 350°F over medium-high heat. Add your pork knuckle and deep-fry, flipping as necessary, until the skin is super crispy all around, 7 to 12 minutes. Drain on paper towels to wick away the excess oil.

Plate and serve immediately with your choice of dipping sauce or noodles.

Fish Sarsiado Shakshuka-Style

SERVES 4

Growing up, I never understood this dish. My dad would make it with scrambled eggs, tomatoes, onions, and fish. Sarsiado is a salsa, but this dish just looked like throw-up.

It was so extremely Filipino, though, so I had to figure it out, and a big dinner I was preparing for the Filipino tourism attaché and some Filipino heavy hitters in 2016 forced me to hurry it up. I decided to play with it, incorporating techniques from shakshuka, which was having a moment.

I'll spare you the mad science details—the recipe that resulted is below—but I will say this: The first time I served this, I presented it with an entire side of salmon seared perfectly. Sunny-side-up eggs peeked up from the bed of sarsiado. It completely transformed the dish and the faces of those who ate it. To me, this is Amboy cuisine at its finest.

---

3 tablespoons canola oil

1 medium onion, diced

6 garlic cloves, minced

1 (28-ounce) can whole peeled San Marzano tomatoes, with their juices

1 red bell pepper, roasted (see page 129), seeded, and chopped

2 teaspoons Datu Puti or Silver Swan soy sauce (see page 60; available at Asian markets and on Amazon)

1 (1-pound) salmon fillet

Kosher salt

4 large eggs

2 scallions, sliced

Steamed Jasmine Rice (page 20), for serving

Heat a large ovenproof skillet over medium-high heat until hot. Add 1 tablespoon of the oil and heat until you see the oil ripple, 30 seconds. Cut the heat to medium. Add your onion and garlic and cook, stirring, for 5 minutes, or until the onion is slightly translucent.

Cut the heat to low. Add the tomatoes and their juices, roasted pepper, and soy sauce. Simmer, breaking up the tomatoes with a wooden spoon and stirring occasionally, for 30 to 45 minutes, until the sauce has thickened. Remove from the heat and keep the sauce warm.

Preheat the oven to 375°F.

Season the salmon with salt. Heat a large saucepan over medium-high heat until hot. Add the remaining 2 tablespoons oil and heat until you see the oil ripple, about 30 seconds. Cut the heat to medium. Add your salmon, skin-side down, and sear until the skin is crispy, 4 to 5 minutes. Do not flip the salmon; it will finish cooking in the sauce.

Carefully transfer the salmon to the tomato sauce, skin-side up. Make sure the skin doesn't touch the sauce.

Make four wells anywhere in the sauce where there's no fish. Crack 1 egg into each well. Bake until the egg whites cook all the way through but the yolks are still runny, 10 to 13 minutes. Remove from the oven, garnish with the scallions, and serve immediately with hot rice.

Bone Marrow Fried Rice

SERVES 7

This dish was inspired by my love of the oxtail fried rice from Blue Ribbon in New York and the bone marrow gnochetti from Bestia in Los Angeles. Finally, fried rice that doesn't have bad seafood in it or crab with a "k"—a marrow dish that's playful. (Ori Menashe at Bestia is a big inspiration to me, and whenever I feel like I'm in a rut, I eat at his restaurant and change my tune.)

In this recipe, you start with a Filipino garlic fried rice. Then, you wow that with a piece of bone marrow. Together, it's fatty, rich, and instantly badass.

---

9 tablespoons kosher salt, plus more for seasoning

7 (5-inch-long) pieces beef marrow bones, whole or split lengthwise

6 cups cold Steamed Jasmine Rice (page 20)

¼ cup Datu Puti or Silver Swan soy sauce (see page 60; available at Asian markets and on Amazon)

6 large eggs

Canola oil, for drizzling and frying

Freshly ground black pepper

10 garlic cloves, minced (see page 110)

30 fresh chives, sliced (see page 110)

For two days, you will have to treat the bone marrow like a fragile baby. You have to clean it and take care of it, but it's worth it. Fill a large container with about 3 gallons of water. Stir in 3 tablespoons of the salt until it dissolves. Add the bones to the brine, cover, and refrigerate overnight. This will do two things: purge the marrow of blood and season the marrow.

Now, you've got to do it all over again. Repeat this process twice the next day (when you get up in the morning and right before you go to bed): Strain the bones and discard the brine. Make a new batch of brine and soak the bones for 8 to 12 hours. Do not skip either of these brinings or your marrow will be boo-boo and will taste like a bloody ear lobe!

So now you've soaked the marrow and are hungry AF. Strain the bones, discard the brine, and pat the bones dry. Keep them in the refrigerator while you prepare the mise en place for the fried rice.

Preheat the oven to 375°F.

Put the cold rice in a large mixing bowl. Run the rice through your fingers to separate the grains from each other. You don't want clusters of rice in this dish—it's not a good look. Once you feel the rice is loose and separate, add the soy sauce and toss until the rice looks uniformly brown. This method is nontraditional, but it'll make your fried rice look baller and professional. Set that bowl aside.

(recipe continues)

Next, beat the eggs: I like using a Vitamix blender for this step so the eggs don't get runny. Add the eggs to a blender and blend until uniformly yellow. Pour into a bowl and set aside.

On a rimmed baking sheet, place the marrow bones marrow-side up so the fat doesn't melt away. If your bones are split lengthwise, drizzle a little oil on the surface of the marrow, and season with salt and pepper. Roast until the marrow is hot all the way through, 10 to 15 minutes. A good way to check is to poke a metal skewer into the marrow and touch it to your wrist to see if it's hot enough. Make sure to keep an eye out and check them every few minutes—roasting the marrow too long will just melt it and you'll be left with hollowed-out bones. Remove the bones from the oven and set aside.

Now start the fried rice: Heat a large wok over super-high heat until very hot. Add 1 tablespoon oil, and when it sizzles, add the garlic. Cook, stirring, until the garlic begins to brown evenly and the oil is fragrant, 2 to 3 minutes.

Cut the heat to medium-low. Add the rice and soy sauce mixture. Cook, stirring, until the rice and garlic are uniformly mixed and the rice is piping hot. There shouldn't be any large clumps of garlic. Also, make sure that the rice is super hot. If you add the eggs too soon, the rice will absorb the egg, it will take forever to cook, and your arm will fall off from stirring too much.

Make a well in the center of the rice, exposing the bottom of the wok. Add 1 teaspoon oil to the well, add the beaten eggs, and stir vigorously with a silicone spatula to begin incorporating them into the rice. Don't wait until all the eggs are cooked in the well—you want the wet eggs to work their way thoroughly into the hot rice. Continue stirring with your spatula until the eggs are cooked and the rice grains are separated from the eggs. At this point, taste the rice and season with salt and pepper to your liking. Cut the heat to low and stir in the chives until everything is harmonious.

Divvy up the fried rice into 7 bowls and garnish each bowl with 1 marrow bone. For your personal bowl of fried rice, scrape the bone marrow into the rice, mix well, and advise your guests to do the same. If this doesn't make you look like a badass, then you need to get new friends.

Bagoong (Fermented Shrimp Paste) Chimichurri

A lot of times my main question is: "How do I get my friends to try Filipino flavors?" They aren't necessarily picky eaters, but some of them won't eat straight-up shrimp paste. So I looked at bagoong and wondered how I could turn it into a "gateway drug." I loved the umami pungentness of it. Then I thought, "What does this taste good with? Steak." So I made a chimichurri and mixed it with bagoong and this sauce was born—a blur of traditions. Enjoy it on steak, salad, or raw young mangos.

1 cup extra-virgin olive oil

1 cup fresh parsley leaves

1 cup fresh cilantro leaves

2 garlic cloves, coarsely chopped

1 teaspoon crushed red pepper

1 teaspoon red wine vinegar

1 tablespoon pink or brown ginisang bagoong (Filipino fermented fish or shrimp paste; available at Asian markets or on Amazon—I like the Kamayan brand)

Kosher salt and freshly ground black pepper

Throw your oil, parsley, cilantro, garlic, crushed red pepper, vinegar, and ginisang bagoong into a blender and blend on high until fully incorporated. Taste the chimichurri, then season with salt and pepper. Serve immediately or refrigerate in an airtight container for up to 3 days.

Roasted Sweet Potatoes

WITH PATIS BUTTER

I love deep-fried sweet potato, aka camote cue, aka Filipino's version of funnel cones. I remember the super-sweet brown sugar almost getting stuck to my teeth. Since I loved those flavors, I wanted to make something similarly comforting and sweet. So I made a patis butter and put it on a sweet potato—delicious!

2 sweet potatoes, well scrubbed

Olive oil, for greasing

2 teaspoons kosher salt

Patis Butter (recipe follows)

2 scallions (green parts only), sliced

Preheat the oven to 375°F.

Rub your sweet potatoes all over with olive oil. Coat the entire outside of the sweet potatoes with the salt. Tightly wrap each potato in aluminum foil and place them on a rimmed baking sheet lined with a silicone mat.

Roast the potatoes until a paring knife glides all the way through the potatoes, about 45 minutes. Unwrap, halve the sweet potatoes lengthwise, and serve right away with patis butter and a sprinkle of scallions.

Patis Butter

MAKES ABOUT 2 CUPS

½ cup Rufina patis (Filipino
   fish sauce; available at Asian
   markets and on Amazon)

½ cup rice wine vinegar

1 cup sugar

1 pound (4 sticks) unsalted
   butter, cut into tablespoons,
   at room temp

Combine your fish sauce, vinegar, and sugar in a medium saucepan and bring to a boil over medium-high heat, stirring. Cut the heat to a simmer and cook until the mixture is reduced by half, syrupy, and like a really amber maple syrup in color, about 6 minutes. Remove from the heat and pour into the bowl of a stand mixer. Let the syrup cool to room temperature.

Fit the stand mixer with the whisk attachment. Whip the syrup at medium-high speed until it becomes aerated and the color of light, milky coffee, about 5 minutes. Drop the speed down to low and fold in the butter, 1 tablespoon at a time. Once all the butter is added, whip at medium speed until fully combined and the consistency of butter-cream, about 2 minutes.

Now you have this crazy amazing, salty, tangy, umami butter. Serve immediately with hot roasted sweet potatoes or on any vegetables. Or refrigerate in an airtight container for up to a month.

White Adobo Sauce

MAKES ABOUT 3 CUPS

White adobo sauce is prevalent in the southern regions of the Philippines because there's an abundance of coconut. My recipe is inspired by that white adobo and the sauce on the Halal Guys' chicken rice. It's so simple: reduced coconut milk steeped with garlic, pureed with vinegar, and thickened with mayonnaise. Serve with Patis Fried Chicken (page 81), roast chicken, pork chops, sautéed leeks, pizza, pan de sal, or anything at all!

---

1 (13.5-ounce) can coconut milk

8 garlic cloves, peeled and lightly smashed

½ cup Datu Puti cane vinegar (page 137; available at Asian markets and on Amazon)

1 cup Bring Out the Best Mayo (page 59)

In a medium saucepan, bring the coconut milk to a boil over medium-high heat. Cut the heat to a simmer, add your garlic, and cook, stirring occasionally, until the liquid has reduced a bit, about 20 minutes. Stir in the vinegar, then pour the mixture into a food processor. Let cool to room temp, then process until the garlic is completely incorporated. Add your mayo and process until fully blended. Serve immediately or refrigerate in an airtight container for up to 1 week.

Bicol Express Mazemen

SERVES 4

Bicol express is a pork dish, classically made with chiles, coconut cream, coconut milk, pork belly, bagoong, onions, and garlic. Sometimes, you use ground pork instead of pork belly.

One day, I saw Chef Miguel Trinidad at Jeepney in New York make a smothered pork chop with bicol express. It inspired me, so I thought, "What does spicy pork with coconut milk, hella chiles, and fish sauce sound like? Dan dan mien."

Instead of using Chinese noodles, we use ramen noodles. We put a beet-cured egg on it, along with crispy garlic and scallions. It ends up as this super-spicy bicol express, but in noodle form. Hence the "Mazemen" surname. Two years ago, we made this dish during the coldest point of winter, when I just wanted a bowl of spicy to warm my body up. This was perfect.

MAZEMEN TOPPING

1 pound ground pork

1 teaspoon kosher salt

1 teaspoon freshly ground black pepper

1 teaspoon canola oil

2 tablespoons minced shallot

3 Thai bird chiles, stemmed and chopped

1 tablespoon minced fresh ginger

½ cup Sofrito (recipe follows)

1 tablespoon tomato paste

1 tablespoon brown ginisang bagoong (Filipino fermented shrimp paste; available at Asian markets and on Amazon—I like the Kamayan brand)

½ cup Amboy Hot Sauce (page 319)

2 cups Homemade Chicken Stock (page 44)

1 cup canned coconut milk

Juice of 1 lemon

Rufina patis (Filipino fish sauce; available at Asian markets and on Amazon)

NOODLES

⅓ cup kosher salt

½ pound fresh ramen noodles, Chinese egg noodles, or spaghetti

FOR SERVING

1 Beet-Cured Hard-Cooked Egg (page 123), sliced, or crispy fried egg

Crispy Garlic Chips (page 40)

1 cup thinly sliced scallions (about 10 scallions)

MAKE THE MAZEMEN TOPPING: In a large bowl, combine the pork, salt, and pepper. Mix by hand until fully incorporated. Let the mixture come to room temperature.

Heat the oil in a large straight-sided sauté pan over medium-high heat until you see the oil ripple, about 1 minute. Add your seasoned pork

(recipe continues)

and sear, stirring and breaking up the meat, until browned, crusty, and caramelized, 5 to 8 minutes.

Using a slotted spoon, transfer the pork to a bowl and set aside. Reserve the fat in the pan. Cut the heat to medium-low. Add your shallot, chiles, and ginger and cook, stirring constantly, until fragrant, 3 to 5 minutes. Return the pork to the pan and stir to combine. Stir in the sofrito and cook, stirring constantly, until fragrant, 3 to 5 minutes.

Add the tomato paste and bagoong and cook, stirring constantly, until the tomato paste is toasted, 2 to 5 minutes. Stir in the hot sauce and chicken stock, scraping up all the browned bits from the bottom of the pan. Bring the mixture to a simmer. Cut the heat to low. Add the coconut milk and continue to simmer, stirring occasionally, until slightly thickened, 30 to 40 minutes. Season to your liking with lemon juice and fish sauce.

PREPARE THE NOODLES: Fill a large stockpot with water and bring to a rolling boil over high heat. Stir in the salt and noodles and boil the noodles according to the package instructions. Drain your noodles and set aside.

For each serving, transfer 1 portion of noodles to a nice deep ramen bowl. Ladle over some mazemen topping. Top with a few slices of beet-cured egg or a fried egg, some crispy garlic chips, and a shower of scallions and enjoy!

Sofrito

MAKES ABOUT 1½ CUPS

2 tablespoons canola oil

2 cups diced onions
(about 2 medium onions)

1 cup minced garlic
(about 40 large cloves)

Heat a medium pan over medium-high heat until hot. Add the oil and heat until you see the oil ripple, about 30 seconds. Cut the heat to low. Add your onions and garlic and cook, stirring occasionally, until the onions are completely caramelized and broken down, 45 minutes to 1 hour. Let cool to room temperature. Use immediately or refrigerate in an airtight container for up to 2 weeks.

Kare-Kare

WITH JAPANESE CURRY

SERVES 4 TO 6

This recipe was a no-brainer. I love Japanese curry. I love kare-kare, and kare-kare originated from curry. But also, I didn't want to lose the peanut butter element because it's so uniquely Filipino. When recipe-testing, I realized Japanese curry blocks are basically Japanese roux. You break off a little piece, throw it into the kare-kare, and it's flavor heaven. That's how this dish was born.

2 pounds bone-in oxtails (about 4 oxtails), cut crosswise into 1½-inch-thick coins (ask your butcher to do this for you)

8 teaspoons kosher salt, plus more for seasoning

2 tablespoons canola oil

1 medium onion, diced

2 tablespoons minced garlic

8 cups Shiitake Mushroom Stock (page 311) or Homemade Beef Stock (page 45)

2 medium russet potatoes, peeled and cut into large chunks

2 carrots, cut into 1-inch-thick chunks

1 cup creamy peanut butter

2 cubes S&B Golden Curry sauce mix, medium hot (available at Asian markets or on Amazon)

Steamed Jasmine Rice (page 20), for serving

Carefully trim some of the fat from the oxtails. (Use your judgment—there's a good level of fat and a gross level of fat. Cut off the gross.) Season each oxtail with about 1 teaspoon salt on each side.

Heat a Dutch oven over medium-high until hot. Add your oil and heat until you see the oil ripple, about 30 seconds. Working in batches, add the oxtails in a single layer and sear until both sides are an even brown, about 4 minutes on each side.

Transfer to a plate and set aside, reserving the fat in the pot. Cut the heat to medium. Add your onion and garlic and cook, stirring constantly, until the onion is translucent, 3 to 5 minutes. Add the stock and cook, scraping the bottom and sides of the pot to incorporate all that goodness, for 2 minutes.

Return your oxtails to the pot, bring the mixture to a boil over high heat, and then cut the heat to low. Simmer until the oxtails are fork-tender, 1 to 2 hours.

Crank the heat up to medium-high and add the potatoes and carrots. Cook, stirring occasionally, until the potatoes are tender, 10 to 15 minutes. Add the peanut butter and Japanese curry and cook, stirring, until thickened, 3 to 5 minutes. Season with salt and serve immediately over hot rice.

Kinilaw (Vinegar-Cured Fish)

SERVES 2

Last year I went to the Philippines and met a historian who told me the story of kinilaw. I was blown away. Turns out that ceviche, kinilaw's better-known cousin, came second by like two hundred years. The first kinilaw recipe—basically a raw ingredient mixed with something sour like vinegar or juice—was printed in the Philippines in 1503. The first ceviche recipe dates to the 1700s, he said. Further proof that when you don't win in history, history erases you. Till now!

1 cup canned coconut milk

2 tablespoons Datu Puti cane vinegar (see page 137; available at Asian markets and on Amazon)

1 tablespoon fresh calamansi juice (see Note, page 68)

¼ teaspoon minced fresh ginger

¼ teaspoon thinly sliced Thai bird chiles, plus more for garnish

1 teaspoon Rufina patis (Filipino fish sauce; available at Asian markets and on Amazon), plus more for serving

½ pound sushi-grade tuna or other fish, thinly sliced into ¼-inch pieces (see Note)

2 scallions (green parts only), sliced into super thin threads

In a medium bowl, whisk together the coconut milk, vinegar, calamansi juice, ginger, chiles, and fish sauce to make a dressing.

Place the fish in another bowl. Pour your dressing over the fish and toss with a spoon. Let that hang out, marinating for 15 to 20 minutes at room temperature.

Plate your fish, top with a drizzle of fish sauce and a sprinkle each of scallions and chiles to your liking, and serve immediately.

> **NOTE:**
>
> In this recipe, we use tuna, but you can use any kind of sushi-grade fish.

Index

Note: Page references in *italics* indicate photographs.